GUIDE TO
PUERTO RICO
AND THE
VIRGIN ISLANDS
including the DOMINICAN REPUBLIC

HARRY S. PARISER

mcon
PUBLICATIONS

Please send all comments, corrections, additions, amendments and critiques to:

HARRY PARISER
MOON PUBLICATIONS
P.O. Box 1696
Chico, CA 95927, USA

GUIDE TO PUERTO RICO AND THE VIRGIN ISLANDS
including the Dominican Republic

Published by
Moon Publications
P.O. Box 1696
Chico, California 95927, USA
tel. (916) 345-5473/5413

Printed by
Colorcraft Ltd., Hong Kong

All rights reserved Harry Pariser 1986

Library of Congress Cataloging in Publication Data

Pariser, Harry S., 1954-
    Guide to Puerto Rico and the Virgin Islands
including the Dominican Republic.

    Bibliography: p. 217
    Includes index.
    1. Puerto Rico—Description and travel—1981-   —
Guide-books. 2. Virgin Islands of the United States—
Description and travel—Guide-books. 3. British Virgin
Islands—Description and travel—Guide-books.
4. Dominican Republic—Description and travel—
1981-   —Guide books. I. Title.
F1959.P37 1986   917.29   85-31070
ISBN 0-918373-08-5

*For the people of the Americas—
may they yet learn to function
in mutual harmony, peace, and
creative interaction together
and with the whole world.*

ACKNOWLEDGEMENTS

Thanks go out to the following individuals who helped with the production of this book. **MOON STAFF:** Project editor Mark Morris for his editing, conversion (Scripsit to Wordstar), typesetting, and proofreading; Deke Castleman for his thorough editing; Asha for her painstakingly accurate typesetting of charts and special settings as well as her work on the mechanicals; Louise Foote, Kirk Tozer, and William Beach for their patient and painstaking work on the maps; publisher Bill Dalton for his advice; Dave Hurst for his finely crafted and diligent work on the dummy, layout, camera work, cover, etc.; and to Moon writers Dave Stanley, Carl Parkes, and Peter Harper for their advice. **OTHERS:** Hunter Mann, Dalitza Ramirez, champion of Puerto Rican crafts Walter Murray Chiesa, Mrs. Josephine Llera, Prof. Janet Scheff, Prof. Than Porter, Prof. Juan Rafael Palmer for his assistance on the Puerto Rican and DR chapters; BVI *Welcome* publisher Cyril Woodfield for his proofreading of my BVI chapter; the entire staff of *Que Pasa;* my mother Trudi for her advice and support; magazine publisher Ron Lippert for his companionship, encouragement, and example of diligence in the face of adversity; Sharan Doowa, Saif Shaikh, Nancy Kaufman, Mary Lou "Fluffy" Manning, "El Nino" Ramsey, and David Minor for putting up with living with me — to various extents and durations — during the hair-pulling period while this manuscript was being forged; the 21 Hayes and 5 Fulton buses who, along with San Francisco's Tenderloin district, served to remind me that America, too, is very much a Third World country; to the *San Francisco Comicle* whose humorous (albeit unintentionally) editorial pages energized my mornings; to San Francisco Mayor Diane Feinstein and President Ronaldo "Grenada" Reagan whose gaffes abroad and poor policy planning made it clear why more and better travel guides are necessary; and finally, to the Art Ensemble of Chicago, Don Cherry, Ed Blackwell, Ornette Coleman, Cecil Taylor, Sun Ra, Anthony Braxton, Joseph Jarman, Dave Holland, Sam Rivers, David Murray, and the World Saxophone Quartet, whose performances, live and on vinyl, helped keep this Urban Bushman safe, sound, and writing.

about the cover: The front cover photo is of Trunk Bay, St. John, USVI, while the back is of El Morro in San Juan, Puerto Rico. Both were shot by the author using a Konica FC camera with 55mm, f1.4 lens and Kodak KR-36 color transparency film.

black and white photo credits: Harry S. Pariser: p. 23, 29, 49, 52, 54, 58, 80, 97, 99, 110, 123, 131, 132, 142, 146, 147, 148, 149, 175, 201, 208; Institute of Puerto Rican Culture: p. 31, 32, 33; Puerto Rican Tourist Board: p. 50, 56, 57, 64, 77, 89, 109; Virgin Islands Tourist Board: p. 129, 135, 156; Cyril Woodfield, 179; Mrs. Anne Z. Louden, 181; Dominican Republic Tourist Office: p. 196, 204, 207. **line illustrations:** Harry S. Pariser: p. 100, 151, 164, 189, 210, 214; Hopie Windle: p. 15, 84, 103, 126; Mary Beth Brooker: p. 114, 163, 211; Jennifer Ewing: p. 14, 74, 76, 83; Diana Lasich: p.11, 71, 85, 95, 105, 113, 127, 138, 153, 167, 173, 187.

CONTENTS

PUERTO RICO

UNITED STATES VIRGIN ISLANDS

LIST OF MAPS

ABBREVIATIONS

a/c — air conditioned
B.V.I. — British Virgin Islands
C — centigrade
C — century
CP — Continental Plan (European breakfast
    served)
Carr. — Carretera (road)
d — double occupancy
E — east
ft. — foot
ha — hectare
in. — inch
I. — island
Is. — islands
km — kilometer
L — left
m — meter

min. — minute
N — north
no. — number
OW — one way
pd — per day
pp — per person
pn — per night
R — right
RT — round trip
Rte. — route
s — single occupancy
S — south
t — triple occupancy
tel. — telephone number
U.S.V.I. — United States Virgin Islands
W — west

PUERTO
RICO

INTRODUCTION

Despite the fact that Puerto Rico has been part of the territorial United States since 1898, most Americans know little or nothing about the island. Yet, Puerto Rico is perhaps the most exotic place in the country—a miniature Latin America set in the Caribbean. It's also one of the oldest locations in the territorial U.S.: San Juan was a thriving town while Jamestown was still an undeveloped plot of land. A very attractive island, Puerto Rico contains numerous forest reserves, beaches, ancient Indian sites, an abundance of historical atmosphere, and the only tropical national forest in the United States. Sadly, the vast majority of visitors get stuck in the tourist traps of Condado and never experience the island's charms.

THE LAND

the big picture: The islands of the Caribbean extend in a 2,800-mile (4,500-km) arc from the western tip of Cuba to the small Dutch island of Aruba. The region is sometimes extended to include the Central and S. American countries of Belize (the former colony of British Honduras), the Yucatan, Surinam, Guiana, and Guyana. The islands of Jamaica, Hispaniola, Puerto Rico, the U.S. and British Virgin Islands, along with Cuba, the Cayman, Turk and Caicos islands form the Greater Antilles. The name derives from the early geographers, who gave the name "Antilia" to hypothetical islands thought to lie beyond the no less imaginary "Antilades." In general, the land is steep and volcanic in origin: chains of mountains run across Jamaica, Cuba, Hispaniola, and Puerto Rico, and hills rise abruptly from the sea along most of the Virgin Islands.

geography: Smallest and most easterly of the Greater Antilles, Puerto Rico's 3,435 sq miles (8,768 sq km—roughly the size of Connecticut or Corsica) serve as one of the barriers between Caribbean and Atlantic waters: the N coast faces the Atlantic while the E and S coasts face the Caribbean. The Virgin

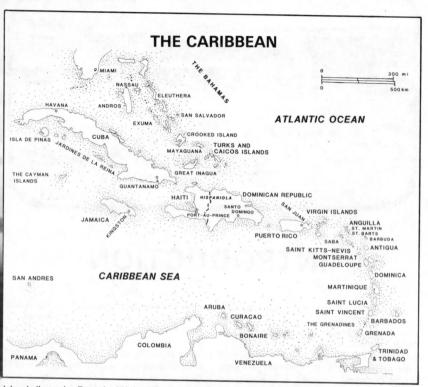

THE CARIBBEAN

Islands lie to the E; to the W the 75-mile-wide (121 km) Mona Passage separates the island from neighboring Hispaniola. The seas off the coast are peppered with numerous cays and some small islands. The small archipelago of Culebra and the island of Vieques lie off the E coast, while the even smaller Mona lies to the W. An irregular submarine shelf, seven miles at its widest, surrounds the island. Two miles off the N coast the sea floor plummets to 6,000 ft. (1,829 m); the Milwaukee Deep, which at 28,000 ft. (8,534 m) is one of the world's deepest underwater chasms, lies 45 miles (72 km) to the north. The nearly rectangular island runs 111 miles (179 km) from E to W and 36 miles (58 km) from N to south. Numerous headlands and indentations punctuate its coastline. Volcanic in origin, Puerto Rico is the tip of a huge volcanic mass. The coastal plain, an elevated area of land which

rings the island, encircles the mountainous center. Two mountain ranges, the Luquillo and the Cordillera Central, cross the island from E to west. The Sierra de Luquillo in the E contains El Yunque ("The Anvil"), which reaches 3,843 ft. (1,171 m). A smaller range, the Sierra de Cayey, is in the southeast. Cordillera Central, a broader *sierra* to the W, contains Cerro De Punta, which at 4,398 ft. (1,319 m) is the highest peak on the island. Spectacular shapes along the NW of the island are the result of karstification—a process whereby over a million-year period, heavy rains seeping through the primary structural lines and joints of the porous limestone terrain carved huge caves, deep sinkholes, and long underground passages. As a result, the island is honeycombed with caves, the most famous located near Aguas Buenas. There are a total of 57 rivers and 1,200 streams on the island. Commercially valuable minerals include iron, manganese, coal, marble, gypsum, clay, kaolin, phosphate, salt, and copper.

CLIMATE

With an average temperature of 73 degrees F during the coolest month and 79 F during the warmest, the island has a delightful climate. Located within the belt of the steady NE trade winds, its mild, subtropical climate varies little throughout the year. Winter temperatures average 19 degrees warmer than Cairo and Los Angeles, seven degrees warmer than Miami, and four degrees warmer than Honolulu. Temperatures in the mountain areas average eight to 10 degrees cooler than on the coast. Lowest recorded temperature (40 degrees F) was measured at Aibonito in March 1911. Only five days per year are entirely without sunshine. Rain, which usually consists of short showers, is most likely to occur between June and October. The N coast receives much more rain than the S, with San Juan receiving 60 in. per year as compared with Ponce's 30. Trade winds produce the greatest amount of rain in the mountain areas, with El Yunque averaging 183 in. (4,648 mm) per year, which falls in some 1,600 showers.

hurricanes: Cast in a starring role as the bane of the tropics, hurricanes represent the one outstanding negative in an otherwise impeccably hospitable climate. The Caribbean as a whole ranks third worldwide in the number of hurricanes per year. These low-pressure zones are serious business and should not be taken lightly. Where the majority of structures are held together only by nails and rope, a hurricane is no joke, and property damage from them may run into the hundreds of millions of dollars. A hurricane begins as a relatively small tropical storm, known as a cyclone, when its winds reach a velocity of 39 mph (62 kph). At 74 mph (118 kph) it is upgraded to hurricane status, with winds of up to 200 mph (320 kph) and ranging in size from 60-1,000 miles (100-1,600 km) in diameter. A small hurricane releases energy equivalent to the explosions of six atomic bombs per second. A hurricane

PUERTO RICO CLIMATE CHART	Daily Average Air Temp. °F	Rainfall Days	Rainfall Inches
January	80	20	4.3
February	80	15	2.7
March	81	15	2.9
April	82	14	4.1
May	84	16	5.9
June	85	17	5.4
July	85	19	5.7
August	85	20	6.3
September	86	18	6.2
October	85	18	5.6
November	84	19	6.3
December	81	21	5.4

may be compared to an enormous hovering engine that uses the moist air and water of the tropics as fuel, carried hither and thither by prevailing air currents—generally eastern trade winds which intensify as they move across warm ocean waters. When cooler, drier air infiltrates it as it heads N, the hurricane begins to die, cut off from the life-sustaining ocean currents that have nourished it from infancy. Routes and patterns are unpredictable. As for their frequency: "June—too soon; July—stand by; August—it must; September—remember." So goes the old rhyme. Unfortunately, hurricanes are not confined to July and August. Hurricanes forming in Aug. and Sept. typically last for two weeks while those that form in June, July, Oct., and Nov. (many of which originate in the Caribbean and the Gulf of Mexico) generally last only seven days. Approximately 70 percent of all hurricanes (known as Cabo Verde types) originate as embryonic storms coming from the W. coast of Africa. Fortunately though, they are comparatively scarce in the area around Puerto Rico. Since record-keeping began in 1508, 73 hurricanes have wreaked havoc on the island. The most serious of these have been San Felipe and San Ciprian, which hit in 1928 and 1932. The most recent hurricane to visit Puerto Rico was Santa Clara, on 12 Aug. 1956.

FLORA

Puerto Rico's central location in the northern Caribbean, together with its variations in elevation, rainfall, and soil, have served to stimulate the development of a varied plant life. These variations account for five differing areas of natural vegetation: humid sea forest or marshland, humid wood forest, the humid tropical forest found in the center of the island, the subhumid forest along the NW coast, and the thorny dry forest on the S coast. Although 75 percent of the island was covered by forest a century ago, today it's only 25 percent, with a bare one percent of the forest retaining its virginity. Natural ground cover can be found in El Yunque Park and the forest reserves of Puerto Rico. Although a considerable number of the 3,355 species of flora are indigenous, many have been introduced from neighboring islands. Native trees include the *ceiba,* or silk cotton tree; famous for its enormous size, it may live 300 years or more. Masks and eating utensils have traditionally been made from the gourd of the

higuero or calabash tree. The unopened leaves of the Puerto Rican hat palm are still put to use in weaving fine hats and baskets, but the *ausobo,* a type of ironwood used for ceiling beams during the colonial era, has virtually disappeared. Imported trees include the Australian casuarina, the cassia, the Mexican *papayuelo,* the Indo-Malayan coconut palm, the mango, and the tamarind. Altogether, there are 547 native species of trees, with an additional 203 naturalized species—an incredible variety for such a small area. Ornamental vines and shrubs include bougainvillea, *carallita,* jasmine, hibiscus, shower of orchids, gardenia, thunbergia, poinsettia, and croton.

FAUNA

Except for bats, dolphins, and sea cows, Puerto Rico has no indigenous mammals. One extinct species of Mammalia is the multicolored mute dog, which the Indians liked to fatten up and roast. Cows, pigs, mongooses, and horses were all imported by the Spanish. Although there was once a great demand in the Spanish Antilles for Puerto Rican horses and cattle, this industry has almost died out. *Paso fino* and *anadura* horses are still held in popular esteem; the former can walk at a pace which enables a rider to carry a full glass of water in his hand and not spill a drop. Mongooses, imported from India to combat

Considered to be the island's "national animal," the coqui *comes in 16 varieties. The sweet call of the male—which usually rings out in the evenings—has won it a special place in islanders' hearts.*

rats and now-extinct poisonous reptiles, have propagated to the point where they too have now become an agricultural pest.

birdlife: Approximately 200 species of birds include the Puerto Rican grackle, the kingbird, the petchary, several species of owls, and the Puerto Rican sharp-shinned and West Indian red-tailed hawks. Once a million strong, the colorful Puerto Rican parrot has dwindled to numbers bordering extinction and now resides only in the outback areas of El Yunque. Among the smaller birds are the onomatopoetically named *pitirre,* and the *reinita* ("little queen") which hangs out around kitchen windows and tables.

reptiles and amphibians: If Puerto Rico can be said to have a national animal, it must be the diminutive *coqui.* This one-and-a-half inch (36 mm) streamlined treefrog features bulging eyes, webbed fingers and toes with 10 highly efficient suction discs, and smooth, nearly transparent beige skin. Its cry is enchanting, so sweet that it's sometimes mistaken by newcomers for that of a bird. Once thought to be only a single species, it actually comes in 16 varieties. Its evening concert has won it a special place in the hearts of Puerto Ricans all across the island. A rather different type of animal is the protected gigantic tortoise which is closely related to its more famous cousins on the Galapagos. Culebra's population of giant leatherback turtles, which come ashore to lay their eggs, is on the verge of extinction.

insects and spiders: A full 15,000 species of insects include a vast variety ranging from the lowly cockroach to 216 species of butterflies and moths. *Mimes* are tiny, biting sand flies. The local tarantula, the *guaba,* is one of about 10 spiders on the island. Another is the *arana bobo* or "silly spider." The bite of the centipede, which grows up to 15 in. (38 cm) long, will prove traumatic if not fatal.

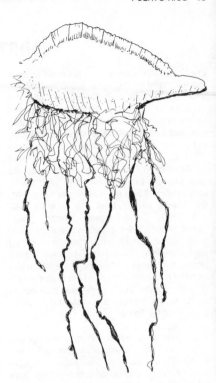

Jellyfish are known as agua viva *or "living water."*

fish and marinelife: Species of fish include the leather jacket, sawfish, parrotfish, weakfish, lionfish, big-eye fish, bananafish, ladyfish, puffer, sea-bat, sardine, mullet, grouper, Spanish and frigate mackerels, red snapper, eel, barracuda, and a variety of sharks. While swimming, beware of stings from jellyfish, called *agua viva* or "living water," and avoid trampling on that armed knight of the underwater sand dunes, the sea urchin. Hard- and soft-shelled crabs include the *cangrejo, buruquena, juey,* and *jaiba.*

HISTORY

pre-European habitation: Believed to have arrived anywhere between 5,000 and 20,000 years ago on rafts from Florida via Cuba, the Arcaicos or Archaics—food gatherers and fishermen—were the first settlers. Little evidence of their habitation survives. Believed to have reached the island perhaps as early as 200 B.C., the Igneri, a sub-group of northern S. America's Arawaks, were agriculturists who brought tobacco and corn with them. Last to appear and most culturally advanced, the Tainos arrived from the S from A.D. 1000-1500; these copper-skinned, dark-haired people were expert carvers (in shell, gold, stone, wood, and clay) and skilled agriculturalists, cultivating cassava, corn, beans, and squash. They gave the island the name of Boriquen—"Land of the Noble Lord," after the creator Yukiyu who was believed to reside in the heart of the present-day Caribbean National Forest.

European discovery: During his second voyage in 1493, Columbus stopped off at the island of Santa Maria de Guadalupe. There, he met 12 Taino women and two young boys who said that they wished to return to their home on the island of Boriquen (Puerto Rico). Columbus took the Indians along with him as guides. On 19 Nov., the Indians, spying their home island, leapt into the water and swam ashore. Columbus named the island San Juan Bautista ("Saint John the Baptist") after the Spanish Prince Don Juan. The island was colonized under the leadership of Juan Ponce de Leon in 1508, and he was appointed governor in 1509. Soon, Franciscan friars arrived with cattle and horses; a gold smelter was set up and production begun. On 8 Nov. 1511, this first settlement was renamed Puerto Rico ("Rich Port") and a coat of arms was granted. King Ferdinand distributed the island's land and the 30,000 Tainos among the soldiers. Under the system of *repartimiento* ("distribution"), Indians were accosted and set to work in construction and in the mines or fields. Under a similar system, termed *ecomienda* ("commandery"), they were forcibly extracted from villages and set to labor for a *patron* on his estate. Although in return the Indians were supposed to receive protection and learn about the wonders of Catholicism, this system was but a thinly disguised form of slavery which ultimately led to the extinction of the

Spaniard Diego Salcedo being drowned by Indians as a test of the Spaniards' alleged immortality.

native inhabitants as a distinct racial and cultural group. The Indians tragically assumed that these newcomers, owing to their remarkable appearance and superior technology, were immortal. A chieftain decided to put this theory to the test, and a young Spaniard, Diego Salcedo, was experimentally drowned while being carried across the Rio Grande de Anasco in the NW part of the island. When he did not revive after three days, the Indians realized their mistake, then killed nearly half the Spaniards on the island. The revolt was put down, however, and many Indians fled to the mountains or neighboring islands. Most of the Indians were freed by royal decree in 1521, but it was too late: they'd already been absorbed into the racial fabric. With the depletion of both Indians and gold, a new profit-making scheme had to be found. That proved to be the new "gold" of the Caribbean: sugar. The first sugar mill was built in 1523 near Anasco, and the entire economy changed from mining to sugar over the next few decades. The first Portuguese slavers, filled to the brim with captive Africans intended to provide agricultural labor, arrived in 1518. The city of Puerto Rico was moved to the site of present-day San Juan, which name it took, and the entire island, in turn, was renamed Puerto Rico. Puerto Rico became one of Spain's strategic outposts in the Caribbean; ignoring the economic potential of the island, hardnosed military commanders appointed by Madrid treated the island as if it were one huge military installation. An attack by Sir Francis Drake's fleet in 1595 was repelled; the English Count of Cumberland launched a successful invasion in 1598. Harsh natural elements, coupled with the effects of dysentery, caused him and his troops to exit shortly thereafter. The Dutch besieged San Juan in 1625; defeated, they did succeed in torching a great deal of the city. Forbidden to trade except within the Spanish Empire, a brisk interisland business in contraband goods (ginger, tobacco, and cattle hides) developed during the mid-16th century. In April 1797, the British, under the command of Abercrombie, led an unsuccessful attack against San Juan.

the nineteenth century: The Puerto Rican political scene was divided into loyalists, liberals, and separatists. In March 1812 a new constitution, more liberal than the previous one, was approved for Puerto Rico, and Puerto Ricans became Spanish citizens. With the arrival of Canary Islanders, Haitians, Louisiana French, Venezuelans, and black slaves, Puerto Rico became a lively potpourri of cultures. As the population exploded, a new nationalism—a distinct sense of being Puerto Rican—began to emerge. From 1825-67 the island was governed by a series of ruthless, despotic military commanders known as the "Little Caesars." During the 1850s, Ramon Emeterio Betances became the leader of the separatist movement and founded the Puerto

The garito or sentry box has come to stand as one of the island's symbols.

Rican Revolutionary Movement in Santo Domingo. At midnight on 23 Sept. 1868, several hundred rebels marched into and took over the town of Lares. Hearing news of the revolt, the government placed reinforcements at nearby San Sebastian, and the rebels took to the hills. A guerilla war ensued and lasted a month. This was the famous *Grito de Lares* ("The Cry of Lares"). Even though this first (and only) attempt at rebellion failed, it is cited by *independentistas* as a major event in Puerto Rican history. In 1869, Puerto Rico sent its first representatives to the Cortes, the Spanish House of Representatives. A law abolishing slavery became effective on 22 March 1873, though "freed" slaves had to continue toiling for their masters for another three years as indentured laborers; full civil rights were granted five years later. Led by Luis Munoz Rivera, the Autonomous Party was formed in

IMPORTANT DATES IN PUERTO RICAN HISTORY

1493: 19 November, Columbus "discovers" the island of Puerto Rico on his second voyage, naming it San Juan Bautista.

1508: Juan Ponce de Leon is appointed governor and founds Caparra, the first settlement.

1509: Government seat is moved and named Ciudad de Puerto Rico.

1521: The capital is renamed San Juan while the entire island takes the name Puerto Rico.

1530: Having exhausted the gold supply, many colonists migrate to Peru in search of new plunder while those remaining become farmers.

1595: Sir Francis Drake unsuccessfully attacks San Juan.

1598: The Count of Cumberland, capturing San Juan, holds it for seven months.

1625: 24 September, attack by a Dutch fleet is repelled but not before its troops sack the city.

1631: Construction begins on El Morro.

1680: Ponce is founded.

1760: Mayaguez is founded.

1775: Population reaches 70,000, including 6,467 slaves.

1778: Private ownership of land is granted by the Crown.

1790: British attack and pull out after a one-month siege.

1800: Island population estimated at 155,406.

1821: First of a series of 19th C. slave rebellions takes place in Bayamon.

1822-1837: Tyrannical rule of Governor Miguel de la Torre, Spanish Commander defeated by Bolivar in Venezuela in 1821.

1833: Blacks forbidden to serve in the military.

1859: Patriot and leader Luis Munoz Rivera born.

1860: Population reaches 583,308.

1868: The famous *Grito de Lares* revolt occurs.

1873: Abolition of slavery.

1891: *Independista* leader Pedro Albizu Campos is born.

1897: 25 November, autonomy granted by Spain.

1898: 25 July, American troops land at Guanica and establish control.

1899: 11 April, Spain cedes Puerto Rico to the U.S. under the Treaty of Paris.

1900: Under the Foraker Act, Puerto Rico becomes a U.S. territory; an American-led civil administration replaces the military.

1917: 2 March, the Jones Act makes Puerto Ricans U.S. citizens.

1937: 12 March, the "Ponce Massacre" occurs when police fire on an *Independista* parade, killing 19 and injuring 100.

1938: Attempted assassination of Gov. Winship.

1942: Tugwell, last U.S. governor, appointed.

1950: Public Law 600 permits Puerto Rico to draft constitution. *Independistas* attack La Fortaleza; riots result. Attempted assassination of Truman on 1 Nov.; wounding five Congressmen. Campos and other jailed.

1965: Abolishment of literacy tests under the Civil Rights Act.

1967: Commonwealth status wins approval by 60.5 percent in a referendum.

1972: Roberto Clemente, Pittsburgh Pirate and island hero, dies in a plane crash while on relief mission to earthquake-struck Managua, Nicaragua.

1973: Bishop of San Juan, Luis Aponte Martinez, appointed Cardinal by Pope Paul VI.

1882. On 28 Nov. 1897, Prime Minister Sagasta signed a royal decree establishing "autonomy" for Puerto Rico, though on paper only. Included in the package was voting representation in the two houses of the Spanish Cortes (legislature).

American annexation: Spurred by the blowing up (by American newspaper barons Hearst and Pulitzer) of the explosion of the battleship *Maine* on 15 February 1898, President McKinley declared war on Spain. In July, just as the new government had barely begun to function, Gen. Nelson A. Miles landed with 16,000 U.S. troops. The Puerto Rican campaign of the Spanish-American War lasted only 17 days and was described by one journalist as a "picnic." On 10 Dec. 1898, under the Treaty of Paris accords, signed by the U.S. and Spain, Puerto Rico was ceded to the United States. With no consultation whatsoever, the Puerto Ricans overnight found themselves under American rule after nearly 400 years of Spanish occupation. Intellectuals on the island had high expectations from the U.S. government; after all, Gen. Miles had promised "to give the people of your beautiful island the largest measure of liberty (and) to bestow upon you... the liberal institutions of our government." Naturally, this meant attempting to make the Puerto Ricans as "American" as possible, up to and including changing the name to "Porto" Rico—in order to make it easy to spell! Hopes for independence were dashed, however, as two years of military rule were followed by the Foraker Act. In effect from 1900-16, the act placed Puerto Rico in an ambiguous purgatory in which the government was a mix of autocracy and democracy. Americanization continued by importing teachers who taught classes entirely in English—an unsuccessful tactic. Requests by island leaders for a plebiscite to determine the island's status were ignored. In 1909, enraged by the provisions of the Foraker Act, the Puerto Rican House of Delegates refused to pass any legislation at all. This protest brought no change in status, and by the beginning of WW I, there was widespread talk of independence.

Members of Puerto Rico's short-lived autonomous government pose for an official portrait. Luis Munoz Rivera is seated at far left.

citizenship: In order to secure both a strategic defense bastion (Puerto Rico) and a ready supply of "raw materials" for the slaughter mills of Europe, Puerto Ricans were granted American citizenship by the Jones-Shafroth Act. Under this bill, which President Woodrow Wilson signed into law on 2 March 1917, Puerto Ricans automatically became U.S. citizens unless they signed a statement rejecting it. If they refused, they stood to lose a number of civil rights, including the right to hold office, and would have received alien status! Naturally, only a few refused. Another request two years later for a plebiscite also failed. In 1922, local politician Antonio Barcelo tried a new approach: he proposed an association which would be modeled after the Irish Free State; the bill died in committee. The same year marked the formation of the Nationalist Party.

the 1930's depression: High unemployment,

Actually the Cuban flag with the colors (red and white) reversed, the Commonwealth's flag was originally designed for use by the 19th C. autonomous government.

political anarchy, and near starvation reigned as the depression years of the 1930s hit Puerto Rico even harder than the mainland. Pedro Albizu Campos, a Harvard Law School Graduate and former U.S. Army officer, emerged as head of the new Nationalist Party. After members of the party turned to violence, followed in turn by police brutality and oppression, Campos and seven of his followers found themselves in jail in Atlanta, Georgia. On 21 March 1936, after a permit to hold a Palm Sunday parade was revoked by the government at the last moment, Nationalists went ahead with it anyway. As *La Bouriquena* played in the background, police opened fire on protestors, innocent bystanders, and fellow policemen. This event, known as *La Masacre de Ponce,* resulted in the deaths of 20 and the wounding of 100 persons.

commonwealth status: Luiz Munoz Marin, son of Luis Munoz Rivera, and his Popular Democratic Party came to power in 1940 with a 37 percent plurality. Perhaps the dominant figure in all of Puerto Rican history, Munoz presided over the governmental, economic, and educational transformation of the island. He served for eight years as Senate majority leader before becoming the island's first elected governor in 1948. After his election he changed from being pro-independence to pro-commonwealth. On 30 Oct. 1950, there were *independentista* uprisings on the island. That same week, *independentistas* opened fire outside Blair House, President Truman's temporary abode in Washington, D.C. Resistance leader Pedro Albizu-Campos was charged with inciting armed insurrection and imprisoned. On 4 June 1951, Puerto Ricans approved a referendum granting commonwealth status to

Puerto Rico. As the only other alternative was continued colonial status, many Puerto Ricans failed to show up at the ballot box. In a second referendum the new constitution was approved, and commonwealth status (*Estado Libre Asociado* or "free associated state") was inaugurated on 25 July 1952. While the new status superficially resembled that of a state of the Union, Puerto Ricans still paid no income tax and were forbidden to vote in national elections or elect voting representives to Congress. In l954, two Puerto Ricans (New York City residents) wounded five congressmen when they opened fire in the House of Representatives in Washington. In 1964, Munoz stepped down, and Roberto Sanchez Vilella became the island's second elected governor. A plebiscite sponsored by the *Populares* was held on 23 July 1967, although the statehooder Luis A. Ferre and *independentista* Hector Alvarez Silver bolted to form their own parties. The buoyant economy, coupled with strong support for commonwealth status by the ever-influential Munoz, caused a record turnout (with 65.9 of the eligible voters participating) in which 60 percent of the voters supported commonwealth status, 39 percent supported statehood, and .06 percent supported independence. In 1968, Luis A. Ferre, head of the newly created New Progressive Party, was elected governor, and he began to push actively for statehood. On 26 Sept. 1969, when an *independentista* was jailed for one year for draft evasion, college students set fire to the ROTC building at Rio Piedras. In the aftermath, seven students were suspended and marches and counter marches degenerated into riots. Polarization between the varous political elements continues to this day.

GOVERNMENT

There is possibly no other island of its size where politics is as hot an issue as it is in Puerto Rico. In spite of the fact that elections determine nothing save who will deliver what slice of the political patronage, Puerto Ricans eat, drink, sleep, and breathe politics. Some even consider politics to be Puerto Rico's national sport. In addition, Puerto Rico has one of the most curious political systems in the world. Although it's a colony of the U.S., the island has commonwealth rather than colonial status. Puerto Ricans have both U.S. citizenship and freedom of travel to and from the States. Yet, although Puerto Ricans may be drafted, they may not vote for president. Undoubtedly, the ambivalence of Puerto Rico's status is unequaled anywhere in the world.

administrative organization: Divided into executive, legislative, and judicial branches just as it is on the mainland, Governors are elected for a four-year term. The executive branch is extremely powerful, and governors appoint more than 500 executive and judicial branch officials. The bicameral legislature consists of a 27-member *Senado* (Senate) and a 51-member *Camara de Representantes* (House of Representatives). In order to prevent one party from dominating the legislature, both houses may be increased by additional minority party members when any one party gains more than two-thirds of the seats in an election. In this situation, the number of seats may be increased up to a maximum of nine in the *Senado* and 17 in the *Camara.* These "at large" seats are apportioned among party members according to the electoral strength of each minority party. Spanish is the language used in both houses, as well as throughout the courts. Puerto Rico's Supreme Court heads the unified judicial system. Contested decisions made by the Court may be reviewed by the U.S. Supreme Court. Puerto Rico is also part of the Federal District Court System. Instead of being divided into counties, Puerto Rico is sectioned into 78 municipalities, many of them mere villages. Each has a mayor and municipal assembly elected every four years. Technically a congressman, Puerto Rico's non-voting Resident Commissioner sits in the U.S. House of Representatives in Washington, D.C. Unlike his fellow voting, congressmen, he is elected every four years and represents a constituency seven times as large as the average congressman's.

the question of status: The single most important and hotly debated issue in Puerto Rico centers on the issue of political status. There are three distinct possibilities for Puerto Rico's political status: one would be the continua-

Former governors of Puerto Rico: Luis Munoz Marin, Roberto Sanchez-Viella, Luis A. Ferre, and Carlos Romero Barcelo.

tion of the present commonwealth status in its current or modified form. The second is statehood. The third and least likely would be independence. Modification of the commonwealth status would involve granting more autonomy to the island government while retaining colonial ties with the United States. Autonomy would be granted over trade tariffs, immigration, the minimum wage, and federal grants, and would be coupled with exemption from ICC and FCC regulations. Elevation to statehood, on the other hand, would require severe economic transition. Chase Manhattan and Citibank, which provide most of the island's financing, would find themselves in violation of interstate banking regulations and would have to close their operations there. Income tax, now paid only to the local government, would have to be turned over to the federal government. Statehood would also mean forfeiture of tax-exempt status for Puerto Rico's industries. Support for statehood is growing, not because the islanders have an explicit wish to enter the American mainstream, but because the politicians are selling the story that it will bring increased revenues and more money. The coconut palm is the symbol of the New Progressive Party, and its leaders assure followers that *los cocos* (dollars) will rain down on them after statehood is achieved. However, there is little incentive for the U.S. Congress to grant Puerto Rico statehood status. Statehood is also controversial not only because most Puerto Ricans cannot speak English fluently but also because Puerto Rico's large population and high birth rate would give it more congressional representatives than 20 other states. Independence is supported by only a small but vocal minority. There has long been serious talk of independence in Puerto Rico, but as things stand now popular support is lacking. One reason is that Puerto Ricans fear the political and economic chaos that independence might bring. The independence movement in Puerto Rico has a long tradition of using terrorist tactics, which has resulted in official government repression. Recent attacks include the Nov. 1979 ambush of a U.S. army bus on the island in which two were killed and three wounded.

The island is of such strategic military importance and is so economically tied to the U.S. that a meaningful change in status is unlikely under the prevailing political and economic conditions.

political parties: If Puerto Rico's political status seems confusing, so are the vast number and varied politics of its many *partidos* (parties), some of which hardly engender enough support to be worthy of the name. There is no dominant party in Puerto Rican politics; instead, there are a number of factions, none of which ever receives majority support. The two major political parties are the *Partido Popular Democratico* (Popular Democratic Party or PPD), headed by Governor Rafael Hernandez Colon, and the *Partido Nuevo Progresista* (New Progressive Party or PNP), led by Carlos Romero Barcelo. Each has half a million hardcore supporters, out of a total two million registered voters. The Popular Democratic Party supports continued maintenance of commonwealth status provided it is revised to allow for more autonomy. The PNP's Carlos Romero Barcelo, nicknamed

SOCIALIST—Juan Mari Bras, head of the Puerto Rican Socialist party, speaking at a rally. He says: "We believe we have the right to reject colonialism . . . violently."

from a 1972 New York Times *article*

El Caballo ("the horse") by his detractors because he is allegedly stubborn, ruthless, and unintelligent, served a governor from 1976-84. His party supports statehood for the island, but because Americanization is seen as a prerequisite, he and his party (whose members are dubbed *estadistas* ("statehooders") are frequently regarded as enemies of Puerto Rican culture. San Juan Mayor Hernan Padilla's Puerto Rican Renewal Party is a PNP splinter party with 300,000 supporters. There are also two independence parties; the larger is the socialistic Puerto Rican Independence Party, formed in 1946 and led by Ruben Berrios-Martinez. The Puerto Rican Socialist Party, founded in 1946 and led by Juan Mari-Bras, advocates independence by any means. Bubbling below the surface are the *Fuerzas Armadas de Liberacion Nacional* (FALN), and the *Macheteros*. While the FALN terrorizes targets on the mainland, the *Macheteros* confine themselves to such island targets as the San Juan Power Station and Fort Buchanan. They claim responsibility for the 12 Sept. 1983 robbery of the Wells Fargo terminal in West Hartford, Connecticut, which netted $7 million—the second largest heist in U.S. history.

recent political history: Carlos Romero Barcelo of the New Progressive Party won over the Popular Democratic Party's Hernandez Colon for the governorship by 43,000 votes in 1976 and by a 3,000-vote margin in 1980. After the polls closed in 1980, Commandant Enrique Sanchez, security chief in charge of polling and a Romero henchman, refused for hours to turn over the ballots to the counting authorities. What happened to the ballots in that time remains a mystery. On 25 July 1978 security forces shot and killed two *independentistas* atop Cerro Maravillo, one of Puerto Rico's highest peaks, which is topped with communications towers. Apparently, two youths, Arnaldo Dario Posado and Carlos Soto Arivi, were lured by undercover agent Gonzalez Malave to the mountaintop to plant explosives. It is believed that the youths, one mentally disturbed and the other a

The oldest executive mansion in use in the Western Hemisphere, La Fortaleza stands at the end of Calle Fortaleza in Old San Juan. Its name, "The Fortress," stems from its original use.

teenager, were enticed there and then shot in order to discredit the independence movement. Though no one will ever know the exact truth, the official government story has been thoroughly discredited. In addition, seven former police officers involved in the case have since been sentenced to 20-30 years each on charges of perjury and obstructing justice. Three officers remain to be tried for first-degree murder for their involvement in the slayings. And disclosure of possible involvement by members of his administration or by Romero himself in the entrapment at Cerro Maravilla was a major contributing factor to his 1984 defeat to the PDP's Rafael Hernandez Colon.

ECONOMY

Much is made of the economic "miracle" which is taking place in Puerto Rico. It's true that in 1983 Puerto Rico's GNP reached $13 billion; not only is this the Caribbean's highest, but it is almost $2 billion above Cuba's, though that country has a much larger area and three times the population. Per capita income for 1983 was $3,900, highest in the Caribbean after the U.S. Virgin Islands. Yet, Puerto Rico's economy is troubled. Now economically interdependent with the U.S. to the point of absurdity, the entire economic structure has undergone a thorough transformation since the U.S. invasion in 1898. At that time Puerto Rico was a subsistence-level agricultural society largely dependent upon crops like sugar, coffee, and tobacco. While these are still of some importance to the economy, the overriding emphasis today is on manufacturing, with tourism coming second.

American involvement: The history of the Puerto Rican economy is the story of the U.S. economic presence in Latin America rendered in microcosm. After cession by Spain, the U.S. financial barons deemed the coffee crop, once the major generator of income, unprofitable. Devastated by the 1899 hurricane, coffee farmers were refused a loan by the Executive Council, set up by the Americans to rule the island. As a consequence, the coffee economy was soon supplanted by sugar, and American companies were quick to establish themselves. By 1930, 60 percent of the banking and 80 percent of the tobacco industry were under the control of American interests, and by 1935, nearly 50 percent of all lands operated by sugar companies were under the control of four big American concerns. Although a law limited farms to 500 acres, these giants had an average of 40,000 acres each under their control! This trend has continued to the point where the small cane farmer has virtually disappeared, replaced by the large sugar corporations like those of the Serralles family empire. The 1930's depression period hit Puerto Rico extremely hard and

resulted in the decline of the sugar, needlework, and tobacco industries. At the end of WW II, less than 10 percent of Puerto Rico's workers held industrial jobs. In order to modernize the island and spur the sluggish economy, Fomento, the Economic Development Administration, was set up to attract industry — the island's 1950 hourly wage of $0.40 compared favorably with the $1.50 average wage Stateside. A high rate of unemployment reduced the prospects for potential strikes.

Operation Bootstrap: By offering 10-to 30-year tax exemptions and low wages, this program has managed to lure 2,000 manufacturing plants to the island. Nearly 400 of these are operated by "Fortune 1,000" corporations. Needless to say, these companies are not here for altruistic reasons: they are here because, despite high power and shipping costs, tax incentives make the island a paradise for profitable investment. Under Section 936 of the IRS Code, American companies pay no federal taxes on profits earned in Puerto Rico. Although Congress acted in 1982 to slightly modify this section, U.S. companies still earned $2.8 billion in tax-free profits during 1982. Under President Reagan's current tax proposal, Section 936 will be repealed. The Treasury Department charges that the law has become a boondoggle, because it allows firms to reap huge profits while creating only a minimal amount of employment. Through a system known as "transfer pricing," corporations pay an inflated price for products purchased from their Puerto Rican subsidiary, thus reducing their U.S.-gained profits on paper and their taxable income along with it. The Treasury estimates that 50 percent of the tax-exempt income in Puerto Rico in 1980 was generated by this and other such nefarious means — such as transferring ownership of patents and trademarks to the island. If 936 is repealed, Puerto Rico Industrial Development Co. head Antonio Colorado estimates that 25-50 percent of all industrial firms will leave the island. In addition, the 21 companies which have planned to build "twin plants," which would link Puerto Rican plants with those in other Caribbean nations, have threatened to abandon their plans should the section be repealed. At present, total hourly labor costs on the island in manufacturing are half as high as in the States as a whole. Puerto Rico was intended to serve as a model to show what the miracle drug of capitalist investment can do for an undeveloped economy under the right circumstances. In these terms, Operation Bootstrap must be seen as a failure. Although U.S. investments in Puerto Rico are now the largest in all of Latin America (excluding Venezuela), the economy is in terrible shape: the economy has kept expanding, but employment has not. The explanation for this is very simple: capital-intensive, rather than labor-intensive, industries have been transplanted to Puerto Rico. For example, pharmaceutical companies do pay their workers more, but use relatively less labor.

manufacturing: Tax exemptions and other advantages have lured 24 pharmaceutical companies to the island; Puerto Rico produces seven percent of the world's total supply of pharmaceuticals, and *all* of America's birth control pills. Figures for the year 1973 show that U.S. firms produced $500 million worth of drugs on the island. A Chase Manhattan study of the top seven firms showed that they saved more than $66 million because of their tax-exempt status; Lilly and Searle alone saved over $33 million that year. Besides saving on taxes, companies also avoid safety inspections: Puerto Rican men working in the birth control pill factories have begun to grow breasts after handling estrogen, some have even had radical mastectomies, and others have become impotent. In the States, this would cause an outrage, but in Puerto Rico it passes almost unnoticed. Manufacturing represents some 20 percent of total employment and generates $180 million in tax revenues, in addition to providing jobs in the construction, trade, and service industries. More than one-third of all manufacturing jobs are still in apparel and textiles.

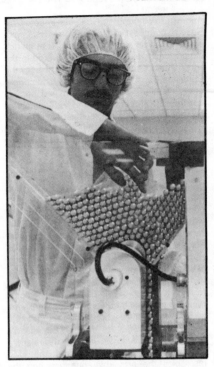

pharmaceutical plant employee

Many of these goods are destined for the States; the shoe industry ships 20 million pairs Stateside each year, and the island is the world's largest producer of rum. (Excise taxes on each case of rum sold in the U.S. are rebated to the Treasury. In 1982 this totaled $210 million, or 10 percent of the island's revenues.) However, more than half of the molasses used in its manufacture is imported from the Dominican Republic, and in order to keep down costs, most rum is exported in bulk and bottled on the mainland. To produce all of these goods, Puerto Rico uses incredible amounts of electricity, most of it generated by imported oil, making the island more dependent on foreign oil than any of the 50 states. The island's homes and industries use twice as much energy as Hawaii, three times as much as Alaska, and nearly as much as the entire continent of Africa.

mining: Although the original impetus for Spanish conquest of the island was gold, mining is no longer a major industry. Though rich copper deposits have been discovered in the Lares-Utuado-Adjuntas area in the heart of the Cordillera Central, a drop in the world copper price, coupled with the determined opposition of environmentalists and *independentistas,* has so far kept the multinationals at bay.

prospects for the future: It is unlikely that Puerto Rico's economy will improve in the near future. Sixth largest customer of U.S. goods, Puerto Rico purchases some $4.5 billion annually in manufactured products from the States. This represents $3.5 billion in gross income for American business and workers, and employment for 200,000 Americans. This does not include, however, the profits stemming from transport of goods and people, from financial and banking transactions, and from insurance and advertising. In 1982, $4.1 billion in federal funds was sent to Puerto Rico: $2.4 billion for personal transfers (such as food stamps and Medicare), and the rest for functions such as immigration, customs, and the military, the island's single largest employer. Indeed, the relationship between Puerto Rico and the U.S. resembles the proverbial one between the worker and the company store. Instead of company bills of promise, the Puerto Ricans shop with *cupones.* Some $100 million in food stamps reach 53 percent of the populace and comprise 10 percent of the total distributed nationwide. Although Puerto Ricans pay more for food and the cost of living in general is higher, federal subsidies make life comfortable. Rather than having the Puerto Ricans themselves pay for these subsidies or taxing the companies who reap immense profits, the American taxpayer is forced to foot the bill! Currently, unemployment continues to rise. While the official figure is 20 percent, unofficial estimates are 30 percent or higher. Teenage unemployment has soared to 60 percent.

Including the men who have given up looking for work, the *ociosos voluntarios* (voluntary idle), more than 300,000 are unemployed.

AGRICULTURE

Like the economy in general, the agricultural situation in Puerto Rico has been in constant flux since the U.S. occupation in 1898. Sugarcane, once the backbone of the economy and still a major crop, has become an economic drain. The government buys most of the crop and operates its own sugar mills, but even with subsidies, the $3.35 minimum wage dictates that the cost cannot compete with neighboring islands like the Dominican Republic, where labor is much cheaper. The government loses money on every pound of sugar, and this industry is little more than a costly, outmoded public employment program. Devastated by the 1899 and 1928 hurricanes, coffee production is now down to 26 million pounds per year. Once another flourishing crop, tobacco production continues to decline, and the largest processing plant shut its doors in 1977. The government neglect of agriculture in favor of industry since WW II has served to guarantee that local products are ignored in favor of expensive imports from the States. The percentage of farmers in the workforce has plummeted from 35 percent to five, and 80 percent of all food is imported. Imported canned vegetables are favored over local produce, and citrus fruit is flown in from California and Florida while local fruit rots on the trees. Other imports include such staples as frozen meat, butter, eggs, and pinto beans. To its credit, the government is trying to reverse this trend by offering tax and other incentives to spur production. Locally grown rice is now being marketed by the government under the name *Arroz D'Aqui* ("Rice from Here"). In spite of these measures, it will be decades before the island can feed itself.

Puerto Rico, U.S.A.
The ideal second home for American Business.

THE PEOPLE

Caribbean culture is truly creole culture. The word "creole" comes from *criar* (Spanish for "to bring up or rear"). In the New World, this term came to refer to children born in this hemisphere, implying that they were not quite authentic or pure. Later, creole came to connote "mixed blood," but not just blood has been mixed here—cultures have been jumbled as well. Because of this extreme mixture, the Caribbean is a cultural goldmine. Beliefs were merged in a new synthesis born of the interaction between different cultures— African and European. Today, many traces of influence remain in language, society, crafts, and religion.

native Indian influence: Although the Indians have long since vanished, their spirit lives on—in tradition, in the feeling of dramatic sunsets, and in the wafting of the cool breeze. Remaining cultural legacies include foods (*achiote*), place names (Mayaguez, Utuado, and Humacao—to name a few), and words (such as "hammock"—an Indian invention), and in native medicines still in use. Many Spanish towns were built on old Indian sites; the *bateyes* of the Indians became the plazas of the Spanish. There are numerous archaeological sites, most notably those at Utuado and Tibes.

African influence: Probably the strongest of all outside influences on those islands with large black populations. Arriving slaves had been torn away from both tribe and culture, and this is reflected in everything from the primitive agricultural system to the African influence on religious sects and cults, mirroring the dynamic diversity of W. African culture.

Spanish influence: The original intruder in the area. Although the Spaniards exited Puerto Rico in 1898 after 400 years of influence, the island's culture is still predominantly Spanish—as are neighboring Cuba and the Dominican Republic. Most Caribbean islands, whether the Spaniards ever settled there or not, still bear the names Columbus gave them 500 years ago. Major Spanish architectural sites remain in the old parts of San Juan and in Santo Domingo, Dominican Republic.

THE PUERTO RICANS

Like so many of the neighboring islands, Puerto Rico has forged a unique racial and cultural mix. The original inhabitants of the island, the Taino Indians, were forced into slavery. Some escaped into the mountains, where they intermarried with the local Spanish immigrant subsistence farmers. The offspring from those unions, the *jibaro,* the barefoot-but-proud peasant, have come to be regarded as a symbol of the island. The name itself comes from the Jivaro, a fiercely independent tribe of Amazonian Indians; they lived a highly individualistic and rugged existence. Residing in *bohios* (thatch huts), they were virtually self-sufficient and skilled in the production of crafts. With the urbanization and industrialization which have marked the 20th C., the *jibaros* have dwindled in numbers to emerge as a prototypical folk hero much like the American cowboy. Black slaves, although never arriving in the numbers that they did on surrounding islands, added another important ingredient to the racial-cultural stew. But Puerto Rico's complex cultural blend doesn't stop there. French families arrived from Haiti and Louisiana in the late 18th and 19th centuries. Loyalist Spaniards and Venezuelans sought refuge here from newly independent Latin American republics. A flourishing sugar economy attracted Scottish and Irish farmers. After abolition, farmers and laborers emigrated from Galacia and the Canary Islands. Chinese coolies were imported in the 1840s to help build roads, and numbers of Italians, Corsicans, Germans, and Lebanese also arrived. American expatriates founded an Episcopal church in Ponce in 1873, and many more arrived after the American annexation in 1898. Cubans fleeing Castro arrived in the 1960s, as did Dominicans following the 1965 upheavals. All of the diverse ethnic groups, intermarrying and multiplying, have helped forge modern Puerto Rican culture.

population: With 3.4 million people, Puerto Rico is one of the most crowded islands in the world. Its population density of over 1,000 persons per sq mile is higher than any of the 50 states. And still, another two million Puerto Ricans live within the continental United States. In fact, more Puerto Ricans reside in New York City than in San Juan. Most have been compelled to migrate by economic necessity; in recent years, however, declining economic opportunities in the States have reversed the trend, and many Puerto Ricans are returning to the island.

social values: Of course, no single description fits all Puerto Ricans; there are too many kinds of people for one mold to apply. Generally speaking, however, Puerto Ricans live in a tightly knit, class-structured society. Very conscious of their roles within that society, they submit passively to it. This attitude, which some have termed fatalistic, has deep historic roots. The centuries-old feudal system of social relationships under which the island has been governed continues to this day. Hacienda owners traditionally held immense power over the *agregados,* the landless peons on his property, and the Puerto Rican version of Catholicism has also worked to keep the peasants' aspirations in check. The world was seen as being ruled by supernatural forces, basically benevolent but beyond man's control. *"Acepto lo que Dios me mande,"* ("I accept whatever God will offer me") has been a common espression for generations, as is *"Ay Bendido!",* an utterance which is short for "Blessed is the Lord," but whose actual meaning is closer to "Ah, woe is me." This sense of resignation seems to pervade social interactions: Puerto Ricans are reluctant to say no, and direct confrontations are avoided. One tries to do things *a la buena,* the nice way." Resistance is undertaken via the *pelea monga* (literally "the relaxed fight") or passive non-cooperation. Puerto Ricans are very gregarious, but they are also highly independent. Their sensitivity to criticism, and their awareness that individual aims may best be achieved through collective efforts, helps keep them in line. One's expectations in life and one's behavior are formed and controlled by the ever-watchful eyes of one's peers. Social mobility is limited; behavior expected of persons at each class level is clearly defined and taught from birth. All of these factors combine to help the society run smoothly. Puerto Ricans in general accept their situation; the sense of being small and anonymous and not in direct control of their lives alleviates frustration and works to reinforce traditional customs and conventions.

compadrazgo: Literally "co-parentage," this important practice of social bonding resembles the system of godparents found in the States, but is much more solemn. Selected when a child is baptized, *compadres* and *comadres* can be counted on to help out financially in a pinch. A poor farmer may seek out a rich employer to be his child's *compadre.* The employer will assent because he knows that this will tighten the bonds between himself and his employee. Or such a relationship may be sought merely to cement a close friendship between males.

males in the society: Although Puerto Rico is indisputably a male-dominated society (as are all Latin cultures), men tend to be very immature. Women are instructed to search for a mate who is *serio* (serious), but such men are rare because they are raised to be insecure and unstable. Much effort is made to form *de confianza* ("confidential") relationships with other men, and exhibitionism is one way to do this. Fighting, heavy drinking, betting, and sexual prowess are all viewed positively by this male society. Sexual experience, both premarital and extramarital, is mandatory for establishing and maintaining one's *macho* status. In Puerto Rico's highly structured pecking order, women are at the bottom.

females in the society: Women are carefully groomed for their role from an early age. Soon after birth their ears are pierced and they begin wearing clothes, whereas their brothers may run around naked for some years. They are carefully separated from contact with the opposite sex; this guarding intensifies as the girls reach puberty. Traditionally, women

relaxing in Old San Juan

virginity, he owes her support and fair treatment. On the other hand, the wife is forbidden to associate with any other man, even on a casual basis. Women are simply not trusted around men. However, these days attitudes are changing rapidly. Among younger couples there is much better communication between husband and wife, and her status has improved tremendously. The problems of sexual discrimination, however, still remain.

attitudes toward Americans: Puerto Ricans may be numbered among the most hospitable people on Earth. A foreigner will not be long in a bar before someone is buying him a drink and conversing with him. However, a *gringo* may rest assured that he will always be regarded as a *gringo*. Although Puerto Ricans are American citizens and one-third of all Puerto Ricans live in the U.S., the visiting North American will be called *Americano*. Puerto Ricans are clearly doubtful and confused about their identity, as soon becomes evident in conversation. Puerto Ricans returning from the States are termed *Neoricans*, and are never completely readmitted into the society.

racial attitudes: As in all of the Caribbean islands, racial prejudice is part of a lingering colonial legacy. Although most Puerto Ricans have at least a pinch of *negrito* blood running through their veins, it is not socially desirable to admit it; the undesirability of being black stems from the fact that the blacks were once slaves. While the apartheid system of the American South never took root here, and Puerto Ricans do not believe in a biological inferiority of blacks, blacks are nevertheless stereotyped as being lower class, and it is difficult for them to rise within the society. Traditionally, upper- and middle-class islanders have been the most concerned about *limpieza de sangre* (purity of blood), and in the past, trials to prove purity of blood were conducted before an upper-class couple could marry. Today, although prejudice remains, it has been moderated over time: an upper-class man, for example, may marry a mulatto woman without much censure, but she may never be accepted by the wives of his associates. Factors such as economic position and social standing

were considered eligible for marriage at 15 or 16. All chances for girls and boys to meet were carefully controlled. Before *noviazgo* (engagement) there was little chance for them to talk to each other. *Noviazgo* differed from its English equivalent in that it implied a very serious commitment to marry and, accordingly, was very difficult to break. During the period of *noviazgo* the couple were never left alone; the assumption was that they were not to be trusted. Rather than spending the time trying to get to know each other better, the woman was expected only to learn how to accommodate herself to the will of her future husband. Even today, Puerto Rican society fosters a cult of virginity: the woman must be a virgin at marriage. The husband's authority is paramount in the home; the wife controls little money and has no right to make decisions. Husbands dictate; wives submit. Obedience rather than communication is of paramount importance. Because the man has taken her now tend to override racial considerations. Still, the darker child in a family may win less praise from his parents and be more likely to be teased by his brothers and sisters. Interestingly enough, the term *negrito,* as used in society, is a term of endearment, implying a sense of community or communal belonging, while *blanquito* ("little white") usually implies the opposite. (The latter term has historical roots: *peninsulares,* islanders born in Spain, held a higher rank than *criollos,* Spaniards born on the island. Today, this term is still used in reference to the elite). The vast majority of Puerto Ricans today are neither black nor white, but *trigueno,* tan or swarthy in color.

LANGUAGE

Spanish is the norm throughout the island. Although many Puerto Ricans can speak English, the more Spanish the visitor can speak the better — outsiders who can speak

Shortly after the American invasion in 1898, the island was renamed "Porto Rico" — thus coining the first "Spanglish" word. ("Porto" is a word in neither language, but easier for Americans to spell.)

Spanish are more readily accepted by locals. The Spanish here (often termed "Spanglish") is laden with borrowed English (*el coat* for example), local idioms, and numerous Indian and African words. When speaking with Puerto Ricans, keep in mind that the *"tu"* form of address connotes a high degree of familiarity; don't jump from the more formal *"usted"* until the relationship warrants it.

RELIGION

Catholicism: Although Puerto Rico is predominantly Catholic, its brand is a far cry from the dogmatic religion practiced in Italy. Distance, combined with the elitist attitudes of the all-Spanish clergy who chose to support slavery and exclude locals from the priesthood, have altered the religion here. Puerto Ricans have selected the rules and regulations they wish to follow while conveniently ignoring the rest. To them, being a good Catholic does not mean being dogmatic. Many strict Catholic couples, for example, have civil or consentual marriages and practice birth control.

Protestantism: Many other sects have proliferated here as well. Chief among these is Protestantism. Although the religion had reached the island prior to 1898, the U.S. invasion spurred a rapid increase in its popularity. Facilitated by the separation of church and state decreed in the U.S. Constitution, its emphasis on the importance of the individual, so much more in keeping with present-day society than the Catholic emphasis upon dogmatic ritual, won it many new converts. Also,

because it provides the rural and urban poor a sense of emotional security in the face of a rapidly changing world, evangelical fundamentalism has also gained in popularity.

SPIRITUALISM

As in other Latin areas, Catholicism has been lightly seasoned with a mixture of African and native Indian traditions. For example, the African influence on the costumes and statues in Loiza Aldea's patron saint festival is unmistakable, as is the dark-colored flesh of the Virgin of Monserrate. Some go so far as to claim that spiritualism (*espiritismo*) is the *real* religion of Puerto Rico. Illegal under Spanish rule, spiritualism surfaced only in this century. Many middle-class Catholics, while remaining formally within the confines of Catholicism, practice spiritualism at home. Few Protestants, on the other hand, are spiritualists, because the stress on application of ethical choices in day-to-day existence inherent in Protestantism runs counter to the spiritualist belief that one's fate is affected by outside influences or by acts committed in a past existence. Spiritualism is steeped in native Indian religion and folklore. The Tainos believed that *jipia* (spirits of the dead), slept by day and roamed the island by night, eating wild fruit and visiting relatives. Food was always left on the table because easily insulted *jipia* might haunt one's dreams at night if left unfed. Although many no longer know where the belief comes from, plastic fruit is still left atop refrigerators to appease hungry *jipia*. Folk beliefs continue to predominate among country folk. Many still believe in the *mal de ojo* or "evil eye." Although its possessor may be unaware of its power, one covetous glance upon a child, adult, or animal is believed to cause sickness or even death. Children have been traditionally protected by a bead-charm bracelet. Spiritualism is also closely connected with folk medicine and healing. One should not mix "cold" things with "hot," or touch "cold" things when one is "hot," or he risks suffering *empache* or *espasmo* — stomach cramps or muscular disturbances. "Cold" food, banana or pork for example, must never be mixed with hot food like meat or manioc. One should never wash clothes in a "cold" area while one is "hot," and one should avoid taking a cold bath after getting heated up through physical exercise. *Botanica,* the supermarkets of spiritualism, sell plants, herbs, oils, rubbing water, and spiritualist literature.

santos cults: Another complement to Catholicism is the half-magical cult of the saints or *santos.* Most households have an im-

An artist's portrayal of Loiza Aldea's patron saint festival.

age of one or two of these (see "Arts and Crafts"), usually St. Anthony and one of the Virgins. These are grouped together with the family crucifix and designated as the "Holy Family." Saints are selected in accordance with one's needs, and reciprocation is mandatory if devotions are to continue. The relation between saint and worshipper is one of *promesa* (promise or obligation); promises are made by the devotee and carried out if wishes are granted by the saint. Certain goods are offered to the saint, who is expected to reciprocate by providing prosperity and good fortune. Gamblers and drinkers offer up dice, cards, pennies, small glasses of rum, lottery numbers, and pictures of beautiful women to their patron San Expedito. If the saint does not respond, the icon may be beaten and kicked out of the house. Rituals of devotion, termed *rosarios,* are held to obtain relief from sickness or give thanks for recovery after an illness. Traditional events involving mass participation, such as the *Rosario de la Cruz* (see "events and festivals" under "Bayamon") and the *rogativa* or candlelight procession, are on the wane, as are *valadas,* or pre-funeral wakes in which neighbors gather at the home of a dying community member to render assistance in case of need.

carved santos

ARTS AND CRAFTS

Puerto Rico's art reflects its cultural diversity. With a growing coterie of young, dynamic artists, the island also has an indigenous crafts tradition with its roots in European, African, and Taino tradition. The best places to see art (and antiques) are in the numerous art galleries around San Juan. Find a good assortment of crafts at the Folk Arts Center inside the Dominican Convent at Plaza San Jose in Old San Juan. Other shops are located inside Sixto Escobar Stadium near the Caribe Hilton and inside Plazoleta de la Puerta across from Terminal Turismo in Old San Juan. Crafts are sold every weekend along Callejon de la Capilla in Old San Juan as well as in El Centro market inside Condado Convention Center. Annual crafts fairs are held on the grounds of the Bacardi Rum Plant, Catano, San Juan, and in Barranquitas. By far the best way to see local crafts, however, is by checking out the island craftspeople in their workshops. Try to obtain a copy from the tourist bureau of Fomento's Crafts Map *(Mapes Artesenal de Puerto Rico)* if one is available in print. Hammock-making is centered in and around San Sebastian. Hats are made in Agua and Moca. Other Puerto Rican crafts include ceramics, masks, musical instruments, wooden replicas of birds and flowers, and macrame. Two of the most important crafts, *santos* and *mundillo,* are described below.

santos: Among the oldest and certainly the most impressive of Puerto Rican traditional crafts are *santos,* eight- to 20-in.-tall figurines representing saints, carved of *capa* or cedar wood, stone, clay, or gold. While the oldest date back to the 16th C., the *santero's* craft is a continuation of the indigenous Indian tradition in which small statues *(zemi)* were placed in every home and village as objects of veneration. Thus, the carving of *santos* seems to be linked to the pre-Columbian era. Just as every town had its patron saint, so every home had its *santos* who would offer protection. And just as some people substitute a TV service for a visit to church, so Puerto Ricans substitute *santos* worship for the traditional Mass. *Santeros,* skilled carpenters using handmade tools, carved the statues out of wood, using natural dyes and sometimes even human hair to decorate them. Natural dyes were subsequently replaced by oils; the initial full-figure design was later joined by carvings of busts and group figures. Saints most commonly represented include the various Virgins (Pilar, Monserrate, Carmen, etc.) and the male saints (Jose, Rafael, Peter the Apostle, etc.). Accompanying symbols render them easily identifiable — just as Rafael carries his spear and fish trademark, so the Virgin of Monserrate holds the baby Jesus on her lap and St. Anthony is always shown with the infant Jesus and a book. Most popularly represented of the group figures are the Three Kings; others include the Nativity, the Trinity, and other biblical scenes. Most remarkable of all the *santos* is the carving of the *mano pederosa* ("powerful hand"), a hand with five fingers terminating in intricately carved miniature images of various saints. Although *santos*-making reached its artistic peak around the turn of the 20th C., *santeros* still practice their art at various locations all over the island. The best collection of antique *santos* may be seen at the Museo de Santos in Old San Juan. Despite their antiquity, the *santos* possess a singularly attractive and simple solemnity which remain as freshly inspiring today as the day they were carved. Unfortunately, it's difficult to find *santos* of similar quality being carved today, and new or antique, they are prohibitive in price.

mundillo: A Spanish import, this type of lacemaking derives its name from the *mundillo* frame on which it is worked. Today, this technique of bobbin lacemaking, which has a 500-year tradition, can be found only in Spain and in Puerto Rico. *Torchon,* or beggar's lace, was the technique first introduced and the one which still predominates today. Originally poorly made and of low quality, it has evolved into a highly intricate and delicate art form. The two traditional styles of lace bands are *entredos,* which have two straight borders, and *puntilla* with a straight and scalloped border. Although the craft once seemed destined to disappear from the island, today it is undergoing a revival. Probably the foremost instructor in San Juan is Maria A. Capella Ricci. One place to see *mundillo* is at the Puerto Rico Weaving Festival held annually at the end of April in Isabela. Otherwise, check the Folk Arts Center at the Dominican Convent (tel. 724-6250) for information on shops which make and sell *mundillo*.

art and artists: Expanding quickly after a belated start, Puerto Rican art has grown to include a wide range of artistic media including mural art, innovative ceramics, and poster art. The story of Puerto Rican art begins with painter Jose Campeche (1751-1809); indeed, painting on the island can hardly be said to have existed before him. His works, which

mask carver in Loiza Aldea

deal exclusively with religious themes, are easily identified through their characteristic style. A self-trained artist who mixed his own pigments, Campeche is today recognized as one of the great artists of the Americas. The next painter to hit the big time was Francisco Oller (1833-1917). Studying art in France and Spain, he returned to the island to create many masterpieces. Known as the first Latin American impressionist, this contemporary of Pissarro and Cezanne was commissioned by King Alfonso of Spain to be Court Painter for six years. An artistic renaissance took place during the 1950s when many artists returned to the island after studying in the States. During this period, poster art emerged as an important medium of artistic expression. Another art form which has gained popularity in recent years is the mural. Mural art, which draws on everything from complex Taino symbology to religious themes, decorates the sides of buildings of all sizes and shapes. Modern Puerto Rican artists of note include Carlos Irizarry, Carlos Osorio, Julio Rosado del Valle, Rafael Turfino, Lorenzo Homar, Carlos Raquel Rivera, and Julio Rosado del Valle.

MUSIC AND DANCE

Although many legacies of European, African, and Taino traditions survive in Puerto Rico, none are as expressive of cultural feeling or as illustrative of intercultural blending as music and dance. The story of Puerto Rican music begins with the Taino. At least one instrument, the *guiro* or *guicharo*, a hollow, notched, bottle-shaped gourd played with a wire fork, has been handed down by the Indians, and musicologists speculate that the *areytos* (Indian dance tunes) have also influenced the development of Puerto Rican music. Besides the Indians, Spanish influence is also evident in the design of musical instruments. Puerto Ricans have transformed the six-string Spanish guitar into four different instruments: the *tiple, cuatro, bordonua,* and *requinto,* which differ in shape, pitch, and number of strings. The 10-string *cuatro,* developed from the original four-string instrument which gave it its name, is the most popular instrument today. Other instruments

include the *maracas,* round gourds filled with small beans or pebbles, and the *tambor,* a hollowed tree trunk with an animal skin stretched on top. Bands of troubadours once traveled from town to town like European wandering minstrels.

folk music: Varied and multifarious. Sorrowful-sounding *cadenas* are danced to with surprisingly lively movements. *Caballos* resemble fast-moving waltzes. The *seis* is probably the liveliest and most popular of all Puerto Rican music. Originally limited to six couples, its more than 40 versions, composed of eight-syllable lines, range from contemporary to century-old standards. While some are representative of particular areas *(seis Bayamones* from Bayamon, for example), others are representative of the way the music is danced to. Their names may derive from the area or region from which the dance originated, the style of dance, or after their composers or most famous performers. A story set to song, the *decima* may carry a deep message. *Decimas* are strictly metered into 10-line stanzas controlled by eight-syllable lines and alternating rhyme structure. Another of the more popular forms of Puerto Rican music is the *danza*. Created in the 1850s, its refined, classical score resembles a minuet; the *danza* is a uniquely Puerto Rican musical interpretation which has no equivalent in Latin America. Juan-Morel Campos, know as the father of the *danza*, is the best-known early composer. Most famous composer of popular music is Rafael Hernandez who died in 1966. Known for such hits as "El Cumbanchero" and "Lamento Borincano," Hernandez is idolized on the island.

bomba y plena: The most famous type of music coupled with dance, the *bomba y plena* combines the elegance and coquetry of the Spanish tradition *(plena)* with the beat of Africa *(bomba)*. Though the origin of the *bomba y plena* is uncertain, some maintain that their arrangements were influenced by the Taino *areytos* (epic songs danced to by the Indians); certainly both are a mixture of European and African influences. Some say that the *plena* was brought to the island by a couple from St. Kitts. Historians do agree,

bomba *drum*

however, that the *plena* first emerged in Ponce. Once an important social event, the *bomba* provided the working people the only available relief from the monotonous drudgery of everyday life. Usually on Saturday or Sunday nights or on special occasions and festivities, the dance was performed in a circle. The soloist stood next to the drums, and the chorus stood behind the singer. While the soloist sang, the chorus provided the harmonies. The dancer, entering in front of the drums, performed the *piquete* (coquettish dance) before saluting the drums and exiting. The *bomba* is really a dialogue between drummer and dancer. The first drummer *(repicador)* challenges the dancer to a duel while the second drummer maintains the basic rhythmic pattern. The dance lasts as long as the dancer

can successfully challenge the drummer. (Unlike similar dances found elsewhere, the drummer follows the dancer rather than vice-versa.) The different rhythms of the *bomba* (the *Cunya, Yuba, Cuende, Sica, Cocobale, Danua, Holande,* etc.) represent the diverse ethnic roots of the dance. While the first five are African names, the latter two represent adaptations of Danish and Dutch styles learned from arriving immigrants. Another style, *Lero,* is an adaption of the French circle dance, *le rose.*

symphonic music: Interest in classical music has grown over the years in Puerto Rico, and the island has its own symphony orchestra and conservatory. A great inspiration was cellist and conductor Pablo Casals who retired at age 81 to the island, his mother's birthplace, to spend his last years there. Each year the month-long Casals Festival draws artists from all over the world to perform his music. The most notable native classical musician was master pianist Jesus Maria Sanroma (1902-1984) who toured and recorded internationally. A friend and collaborator of Casals', he promoted both symphonic music on the island and the *danza* — recording, editing, and performing the latter. Puerto Rico is also the birthplace of famed operatic tenor Antonio Paoli (1872-1946) who performed for Czar Nicholas II of Russia, Kaiser Wilhelm of Germany, and the Emperor Franz Joseph of Austria. The latter bestowed upon him the title of Court Singer. After earning and spending an estimated $2 million, Paoli returned home to the island in 1922 where he taught music to the island's youth.

FESTIVALS AND EVENTS

The Latin nature of the island really comes to the fore in its celebration of festivals and holidays. Puerto Ricans really know how to relax and have a good time. Although the centuries-old custom of midday siesta is in danger of extinction, *Viernes social* or "social Friday" is still popular. Every Friday men gather and eat *lechon asado* (roast pig) and gossip and gamble at local roadside stands. Most other celebrations, however, are in a religious vein. Many of these are famous, including those at Hormigueros and Loiza; the 24 of June Festival of St. John the Baptist in San Juan is one *long* night of partying. Every town on the island has its *fiesta patronales* or patron saint festival. They always begin on a Friday, approximately 10 days before the date prescribed. Although services are held twice a day, the atmosphere is anything but religious. Music, gambling, and dancing take place on the town plaza, and food stalls sell local specialties. On the Sunday nearest the main date, *imagenes* or wooden images of the patron saint are carried around the town by four men or (sometimes) women. Flowers conceal supporting wires, and the base is tied to the platform to prevent it from falling. A generally somber atmosphere prevails during Holy Week *(Semana Santa),* the week surrounding Easter, when processions and pageants are held island-wide. *Las Navidades* or the Christmas season, which stretches from 15 Dec. to 6 Jan., is the liveliest time of the year. Marked by parties and prayers, it's a time to get together with friends. Everyone heads for *el campo* ("the country") to join in celebrating the occasion with friends and loved ones. Out in the countryside, groups of local musicians known as *trulla* roam from house to house singing *aguinaldos* or Christmas carols. *Nacimento* (nativity scenes) are set up in homes and public places, the most famous being the one near San Cristobal fortress in Old San Juan. On *Noche Bueno* (Christmas Eve) most people attend midnight Mass *(Misa de Gallo)* before returning home to feast on the traditional large supper known as

cena. On 6 Jan. Epiphany or Three Kings Day is celebrated. The night before, children traditionally place boxes of grass under their beds to await the arrival of the Three Kings, Gaspar, Melchior, and Balthazar. After the camels eat all the grass, the kings leave presents in the now empty boxes. On the day itself, the Three Kings are put up in front of the Capitol building, and candy and toys are given away at El Morro fortress in Old San Juan.

PUERTO RICO FESTIVALS AND EVENTS

1 Jan.:   New Year's Day

6 Jan.:   Ephiphany or Three Kings Day; traditional day of gift-giving

11 Jan.:   Birthday of Eugenio De Hostos, Puerto Rican educator, writer, and patriot (half-day)

15 Jan.:   Martin Luther King Birthday (half-day)

18-20 Jan.:   San Sebastian Street Fiesta in Old San Juan. Crafts, shows, arts, games, processions, dancing, and *paso fino* horses on display.

Feb.:   Washington's Birthday (half-day, movable)

22 March: Emancipation Day

April: Good Friday (movable)

16 April: Jose de Diego's Birthday

May: Memorial Day (movable)

24 June: St. John the Baptist Day

4 July: Independence Day

17 July: Luiz Munoz Rivera's Birthday

25 July: Commonwealth Constitution Day

27 July: Dr. Jose Celso Barbosa's Birthday (half-day)

Sept.:   Labor Day (movable)

Oct.:   Columbus Day (movable)

11 Nov.:   Veterans' Day

19 Nov.:   Puerto Rico Discovery Day

Nov.:   Thanksgiving (movable)

25 Dec.:   Christmas Day

PRACTICALITIES

TRANSPORT

by air: Although the days of bargain basement flights are over, it's still possible to visit Puerto Rico relatively cheaply. And though the only really cheap way to get there is to swim, you can still save money by shopping around. A good travel agent should call around for you to find the lowest fare; if he or she doesn't, find another agent, or try doing it yourself. If there are no representative offices in your area, check the phone book—most airlines have toll-free numbers. In these days of airline deregulation, fares change quicker than you can say *"Menudo,"* so it's best to check the prices well before departure—and then again before you go to buy the ticket. Seven-day APEX (advance purchase excursion) fares, weekday and night flights, and one-way fares are among the options that may save you money. The more flexible you can be about when you wish to depart and return, the easier it will be to find a bargain. Whether dealing with a travel agent or with the airlines themselves make sure that you let them know clearly what it is you want. Don't assume that because you live in Los Angeles, for example, it's cheapest to fly from there. It may be better to find an ultrasaver flight to gateway cities like New York or Miami and then change planes. Fares tend to be cheaper on weekdays and during low season (mid-April to mid-December). The lowest fare you can hope to get out of New York City is in the range of $129 OW, $219 RT; from Miami, about $129 OW, $258 RT; and from Atlanta, $173 OW, $281 RT. Delta flies directly from Atlanta (3½ hours). Arrow Air (tel. 800-872-8000) flies directly from New York City (3½ hours), Philadelphia and Miami (both 2¼ hours), Orlando, Boston, Baltimore, Washington, D.C., and from Montreal and Toronto. Arrow also flies from New York to Aguadilla ($219 RT). Eastern Airlines flies direct from New York, Newark, Atlanta, and Miami. They offer a bewildering variety of APEX fares, so check to find the most conve-

nient. Puerto Rico may also be reached by air from everywhere in the Caribbean but Cuba.

by sea: Sadly, with the exception of cruise ships, the only passenger service between Puerto Rico and other Caribbean islands is a ferry between Charlotte Amalie, St. Thomas, and Fajardo on weekends. Unless you are willing to take a cruise ship—which not only costs more than flying but often isolates you from locals—there is no regularly scheduled alternative. One potentially rewarding opportunity if you can afford it is to sail your own yacht to Caribbean waters and travel about on your own. Or fly to St. Thomas or Tortola and rent a yacht to sail to Puerto Rico. (A ferry does leave from Charlotte Amalie, St. Thomas, for Fajardo on weekends). It's possible to crew on a boat coming over from Europe; most, however, head for the southern Caribbean, so you'd have to find a way (expensive) N from there.

getting around: You'll need to have patience! Always allow plenty of time to get to any island destination. City bus service in San Juan is cheap but painfully inefficient and slow. Around the island, the only regular passenger bus service runs from San Juan along the N coast to Mayaguez. Unscheduled but cheap rural services run all over the island, including along the mountain road from Arecibo down to Ponce. *Publicos* are Ford vans with seats which serve as shared taxis. A cheap and convenient form of transportation, they can be picked up or left at any point. Identifiable by the letter "P" on the license plate, their route is listed on the windshield. Unfortunately, except for the San Juan-Ponce

TRAVEL DISTANCES IN PUERTO RICO

(top number — km; bottom number — miles)

	Aguadilla	Arecibo	Caguas	Cayey	Coamo	Fajardo	Guayama	Humacao	Manati	Mayaguez	Ponce	San German	San Juan	San Sebastian	Yauco
Aguadilla		53 33	149 93	161 101	138 86	180 112	162 101	177 110	79 49	28 17	104 65	47 29	136 85	25 16	74 46
Arecibo	53 33		96 60	108 67	91 57	127 79	133 83	124 77	26 16	72 45	82 51	93 58	83 52	41 25	82 51
Caguas	149 93	96 60		26 16	61 38	54 34	53 33	28 17	70 43	172 107	95 59	152 94	35 22	137 85	126 78
Cayey	161 100	108 67	26 16		35 22	80 50	27 17	54 34	82 51	146 91	69 43	126 78	52 32	148 92	100 62
Coamo	138 86	91 57	61 38	35 22		115 71	42 26	89 55	65 40	111 69	34 21	91 57	80 50	113 70	65 40
Fajardo	180 112	127 79	54 34	80 50	115 71		92 57	33 21	101 63	199 124	149 93	206 128	59 37	168 104	180 112
Guayama	162 101	133 83	53 33	27 17	42 26	92 57		59 37	107 66	135 84	58 36	116 72	79 49	137 85	89 55
Humacao	177 110	124 77	28 17	54 34	89 55	33 21	59 37		98 61	194 121	117 73	174 108	60 37	165 103	148 92
Manati	79 49	26 16	70 43	82 51	65 40	101 63	107 66	98 61		98 61	82 51	119 74	57 35	67 42	108 67
Mayaguez	28 17	72 45	172 107	146 91	111 69	199 124	135 84	194 121	98 61		77 48	19 12	155 96	31 19	46 29
Ponce	104 65	82 51	95 59	69 43	34 21	149 93	58 36	117 73	82 51	77 48		57 35	114 71	79 49	31 19
San German	47 29	93 58	152 94	126 78	91 57	206 128	116 72	174 108	119 74	19 12	57 35		171 106	52 32	26 16
San Juan	136 85	83 52	35 22	52 32	80 50	59 37	79 49	60 37	57 35	155 96	114 71	171 106		124 77	145 90
San Sebastian	25 16	41 25	137 85	148 92	113 70	168 104	137 85	165 103	67 42	31 19	79 49	52 32	124 77		64 40
Yauco	74 46	82 51	126 78	100 62	65 40	180 112	89 55	148 92	108 67	46 29	31 19	26 16	145 90	64 40	

run, they cover only short hops between towns, which means changing vehicles innumerable times before reaching your final destination. Hitchhiking is slow but very possible and a good way to pass the time while waiting for buses. Cars may be rented at the airport; a valid U.S. driver's license is required. Expect to pay at least $25 per day, but weekend specials may be available. Smaller roads on the island are called *carretecas*. *Ruta Panoramica* is the name for the scenic roads (Carr. 182, 143, and 105) which transect the island from Maunabo to Mayaguez. It is highly recommended that you use a detailed road map while exploring Puerto Rico. A number of small airlines fly to the outlying islands of Vieques and Culebra; Dorado Wings flies to the plush tourist traps of Dorado and Palmas del Mar. Passenger ferries leave daily from Fajardo to Culebra and Vieques. Other ferries of note are the Catano Ferry in Old San Juan and the hand-pulled ferry at Loiza Aldea. Passenger boat service (free) is available on Dos Bocas Lake. An alternative to taking local transport or renting a car is the Fondo de Mejoramiento, a local travel organization that conducts tours to various spots of scenic, historical, and cultural interest (tel. 759-8366).

ACCOMMODATIONS

Breeze by the tourist traps and explore other areas of the island where things can be much cheaper. *Centros vacacionales* are clusters of rental cottages situated at Boqueron, Cabo Rojo, Humacao, Maricao, and Arroyo. These are available to "bona fide family groups" for $20 per night with a minimum stay of two and a maximum stay of seven nights. From 1 Sept. through 31 May there's a special weekly rate of $100. For more information and a reservation form (apply 120 days in advance) write to Oficina de Reservaciones, Compania de Fomento Recreativo, Apartado Postal No. 3207, San Juan, PR 00904 (tel. 722-1771/1551, 721-2800 ext. 225, 275). Attractive buildings set in lush surroundings, the government-run *paradores* have become pretty pricey hotels instead of inexpensive inns as planned

PUERTO RICAN TOURISM COMPANY OFFICES

PUERTO RICO
Calle San Justo 301
Old San Juan, PR 00903
(809) 721-2400

NEW YORK
1290 Avenue of the Americas
New York, NY 10104
(212) 541-6630

ORLANDO
201 East Pine Street, Ste. 422
Orlando, FL 32801
(305) 422-9900

LOS ANGELES
10100 Santa Monica Blvd.
Los Angeles, CA 90067

CHICAGO
11 East Adams Street
Chicago, IL 60603
(312) 992-9701

CANADA
10 King Street East
Toronto, Ontario, Canada
(416) 367-0190

WEST GERMANY
Zurichhaus AM Opernplatz, 6
Frankfurt/M1, Germany
(001) 49-611-726118

SPAIN
Oficina de Turismo de Gobierno de Puerto Rico
Avenida Jose Antonio, 57 1 AyB
Madrid, Spain 13

VENEZUELA
Edificio Las Vegas Penthouse
Ave. Liberator con Avenido las Acasias
Caracas, Venezuela

originally (see "Accommodations" charts for list). There are many campgrounds, but take good care to make sure your gear is safe.

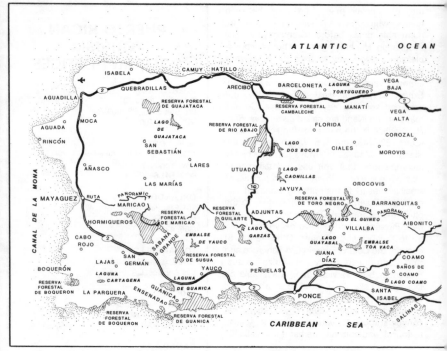

FOOD AND DRINK

You'll find plenty of places to eat. There are cafeterias which serve everything from grilled cheese sandwiches to rice and beans, simple local restaurants, and their more expensive cousins which serve the most elaborate combinations of Spanish and other cuisines imaginable. In addition, there are the ubiquitous fast-food joints and a proliferation of pizzerias. Combining African, Indian, and Spanish cuisine into something new and refreshingly different, food on the island provides a unique culinary experience. Although similar to Dominican, Cuban, and other Caribbean cuisines, it has its own distinct flavor. Seasonings used include pepper, cinnamon, fresh ginger, cilantro, lime rind, *naranja agria* (sour orange), and cloves. *Sofrito,* a sauce used to flavor many dishes, combines *achiote* (annato seeds fried in lard and strained) with ham and other seasonings. Many dishes are cooked in a *caldero,* a cast-iron kettle with a rounded bottom.

snacks: Street vendors and cafeterias sell a wide variety of tasty, deep-fried snacks. *Alcapurrias* contain ground plantain and pork, or (less commonly) fish or crab fried in batter. *Bacalitos fritos* are fried codfish fritters made with the dried, salted cod imported from New England. *Amarillos en dulce* are yellow plantains fried in a sauce of cinnamon, sugar, and red wine. *Empanadas* are made with *yuca* or plantain dough stuffed with meat and wrapped in plantain leaves. *Pastelillos* are fried dough containing meat and cheese. They are sometimes made using fruit and jam; *empanadillas* ("little pies") are larger versions available on some parts of the island. *Pasteles* are made from plantain or *yautia* dough which has been stuffed with ground pork, garbanzo beans, and raisins and wrapped in plantain leaves. *Pinonos* are a mixture of ground beef

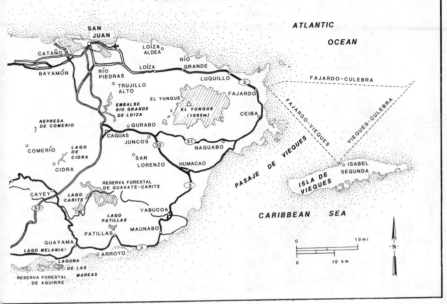

PUERTO RICO

and ripe plantains dipped in a beaten egg batter and then fried. *Surullitos* or *sorullos* are deep-fried corn meal fritters. *Rellenos de papa* are meat-stuffed potato balls fried in egg batter. *Mofongo* are mashed and roasted plantain balls made with spices and *chicharron* (crisp pork cracklings).

soups and specialties: Not particularly a vegetable-producing island, Puerto Rico nevertheless has its own unique *verduras* (vegetables), including *chayote* and *calabaza* (varieties of West Indian squash), *yuca* (cassava), *yautia* (tanier), *batata* (a type of sweet potato), and *name* (African yam). All are frequently served in local stews. *Asopao* is a soup made with rice and meat or seafood. *Lechon asado* or roast pig is an island specialty. Served in local *lechonera,* it's tastiest when the pig's skin is truly crisp and golden. *Chicharron,* chunks of crispy skin, are sold right by them. Other pork dishes include

cuchifrito, pork innards stew, *mondongo* (an African stew of chopped tripe), and *gandinga,* liver, heart, and kidneys cooked with spices. *Carne mechada* is a beef roast garnished with ham, onion, and spices. Goat is also quite popular and *cabro* (young or kid goat) is considered a delicacy. *Fricase,* a dish made with stewed chicken, rabbit, or goat, is usually accompained by *tostones,* plantains that have been fried twice. *Sopa de habichuelas negros* (black bean soup), is a popular dish, as are the standards *arroz con habichuelas* (rice and beans), and *arroz con pollo* (rice and chicken).

seafood: One of the most popular seafood items is actually imported from New England. *Bacalao* (dried, salted codfish) is cooked in several ways. *Bacalao a la Viscaino* is codfish stewed in rich tomato sauce. *Serenata* is flaked *bacalao* served cold with an oil and vinegar dresing and toppings like raw onions, avocados, and tomatoes. Although some

ham, chicken, and cheese inside a long, crusty white bread. A *medianoche* ("midnight") contains pork, ham, and cheese. **desserts:** Puerto Rican desserts are simple but tasty. They include *arroz con dulce* (sweet rice pudding), *cazuela* (rich pumpkin and coconut pudding), and *bien-me-sabe* (sponge cake with coconut sauce), *tembleque* (coconut pudding), and *flan* (caramel custard).

fruit: Although many fruits are imported from the U.S., Puerto Rico also grows a large variety of its own. Brought by the Spaniards in the 16th C., the sweet orange is known as *china* because the first seeds came from there. Vendors will peel off the skin with a knife to make a *chupon* which you can pop into your mouth piece by piece. *Naranja* is the sour orange. *Guineo* or bananas, imported by the Spanish from Africa, come in all sizes, from the five-inch *ninos* on up. Brought from southern Asia, the *platano* or plantain is inedible until cooked. Puerto Rican *pinas* are much sweeter than their exported counterpart because they are left on the stem to ripen. The white interior of the *panapen* or breadfruit is roasted or boiled as a vegetable. Some bear small brown seeds, *panas de pepita,* that are boiled or roasted. Another fruit indigenous to the West Indies, *lechosa* or papaya is available much of the year. The oval *parcha* (passion fruit) with its bright orange pulp was given its name by arriving Spaniards who saw it's white-and-purple flowers as a representation of the Crucifixion in botanical form. Coconut palms arrived in 1549 from Cape Verde, Africa, via Dutch Guiana. Other island fruits include the *mamey* (mammee apple), *guanabana* (custard apple), guava, *nispero* (sapodilla), *caimito* (star apple), *jobo* (hogplum), and the *jagua* (genipap). The *quenepa* or "Spanish lime" is a Portuguese delicacy about the size of a large walnut; its brittle green skin cracks open to reveal a white pit surrounded by pinkish pulp. Island avocados are renowned for their thick pulp and small seeds. *Acerola,* the wild W. Indian cherry, has from 20-50 times the vitamin C of orange juice.

other seafood like shrimp must be imported, many others like *chillo* (red snapper), *mero* (sea bass), *pulpo* (octopus), and *chapin* (trunkfish) are available locally. Fish dishes served *en escabeche* have been pickled Spanish-style. *Mojo isleno* is an elaborate sauce which includes olives, onions, tomatoes, capers, vinegar, garlic, and pimentos. The most famous dishes are *langosta* (local lobster), *jueyes* (land crabs), and *ostiones* (miniature oysters which cling to the roots of mangrove trees). The damming of the island's rivers has brought about a decline of another indigenous delicacy, *camarones de rio* (river shrimp).

cheese and sandwiches: *Queso de hoja* is the very milky, mild-flavored, local soft cheese. It must be eaten fresh. It is often combined with the local marmalade, *pasta de guayava* (guava paste). Many types of sandwiches are also available. A *cubano* contains

drinks: Delicious fruit drinks are made from passion fruit and others. These are usually found at roadside stands in the countryside areas. *Limber* (or *piragua*) is shaved ice covered with tamarind or guava syrup served in a paper cup; it's named after Charles Lindbergh, the famous pilot. Cool *cocos frios* or green drinking coconuts are available just about anywhere for around fifty cents. *Malta* is a unique-tasting, non-alcoholic malt beverage made with barley, malt, cane sugar, corn grits, and hops. *Mavi* is a local root beer made from tree bark. **alcohol:** Locally brewed Corona, India, and Medalla beers are available in seven- and 12-oz. ($0.75) bottles and cans in every *colmado* or bar. Blue laws are nonexistent in Puerto Rico; alcohol may be purchased anytime, anywhere. Puerto Rico is the world's largest rum producer and accounts for 83 percent of U.S. sales. Rum production began in the 16th C. with production of *pitrinche* or *canita* (bootleg rum), a spirit that is still popular today. Under the Mature Spirits Act, white rum must be distilled for at least one year at a minimum of 180 proof and gold label (amber-colored rum) for three years at 175 proof. Anejo, a special blend, requires six years. Although all brands are roughly equivalent, Bacardi is the largest distiller on the island. (See "San Juan Bay and Catano" under "Old San Juan" for tour information). Locals usually drink their rum with ice and water. Drinks such as *pina coladas* and banana daiquiris were developed especially for the tourist trade. *Pina coladas* are made by combining cream of coconut with pineapple juice, rum, and crushed ice. Aside from alcohol, the most popular drink in Puerto Rico must be coffee. It is served either as *cafe* or *cafe con leche* (coffee essence with steamed milk) along with generous quantities of sugar. *Pocillo* or *cafe negro* is a demitasse cup of strong coffee served after dinner.

OTHER PRACTICALITIES

money and measurements: Monetary unit is the U.S. dollar (called *"dolar"* or *"peso"*) which is divided into 100 cents (referred to as *"centavos"* or *"chavitos"*). Nickels (five cents) are referred to as *"vellons"* or *"ficha."* Quarters (25 cents) are called *"pesetas."* If coming from abroad, it's better to change your money in a major U.S. city or carry traveler's cheques. Deak Pererra, with branches at San Juan International Airport and Terminal Turismo in Old San Juan, issues traveler's cheques commission-free. Measurements are a confusing mixture of American and metric. Gasoline and milk are both sold by the liter *(litro)*. While road distances are given in kilometers, road speed signs and car speedometers use miles per hour. Land elevations are expressed in meters, but land is sold in units called *cuerda,* equal to 97/100 of an acre. Weights are measured in pounds *(libras)* and ounces *(onzas)* : a *tonelda* is a ton. *Pulgadas* are inches, and *pies* are feet.

broadcasting and media: TV serves up a combination of the worst of American programming rendered into Spanish and bad local imitations of the worst of American programming. As is the case with radio and the press, it dishes up AP and UPI stories as news. There are three daily papers: The English tabloid the *San Juan Star,* owned by the conservative Cowles chain, is the least partisan. Superficial and bland, its magazine format provides no investigative reporting. The Knight Chain has engulfed *El Mundo; El Nueva Dia* is the personal property of Luis A. Ferre Enterprises, and *El Ropertero* accents local politics. Almost comically grotesque, *El Vocero,* the newspaper of the masses, is full of really gory, bloody murders, many of which are featured on the cover.

visas: All visitors from abroad (except Canadians) require a U.S. visa. It's better to obtain a multiple entry visa and, if possible, to do so in your own country. Fill out forms perfectly; consular officials tend to be aggravatingly picayune.

health: Medical care is usually on a first-come, first-served basis. Although the quality of medical and dental services is reasonably high, it's not quite up to mainland standards. Most physicians are centered in San Juan, Ponce, and Mayaguez. Hospital costs are slightly lower than in the States, and Medicare and all other Stateside hospitalization policies are honored. Equipped with 24-hour emergency service, the Ashford Memorial Hospital, 1451 Ashford Ave. in Santurce, has many English-speaking staff members. For help in obtaining a physician, call the Medical Association at 725-6969 or check the Yellow Pages of the telephone directory under *Medicos Especilistas.* Either arrive with an adequate supply of any medications you may require, or bring your doctor's *legible* prescription with you. Although diseases like malaria which had been a problem in the past have been eliminated, bilharzia, a disease spread by

METRIC CONVERSIONS

Since this book is used by people from all around the world, the metric system (with feet and miles in parentheses) is employed throughout. Here are the equivalents:

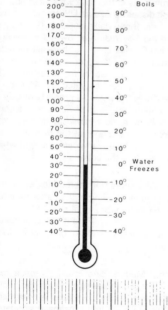

1 inch = 2.54 centimeters (cm)
1 foot = .3048 meters (m)
I mile = 1.6093 kilometers (km)
1 km = .6214 miles
1 nautical mile = 1.852 km
1 fathom = 1.8288 m
1 chain = 20.1168 m
1 furlong = 201.168 m
1 acre = .4047 hectares (ha)
1 sq km = 100 ha
1 sq mile = 2.59 sq km
1 ounce = 28.35 grams
1 pound = .4536 kilograms (kg)
1 short ton = .90718 metric ton
1 short ton = 2000 pounds
1 long ton = 1.016 metric tons
1 long ton = 2240 pounds
1 metric ton = 1000 kg
1 quart = .94635 liters
1 U.S. gallon = 3.7854 liters
1 Imperial gallon = 4.5459 liters

to compute centigrade: *Subtract 32 from Fahrenheit and divide by 1.8. To go the other way, multiply Centigrade by 1.8 and add 32.*
time: *To avoid confusion, all clock times appear according to the 24-hour airline timetable system, i.e., 0100 is 1:00 a.m., 1300 is 1:00 p.m., 2330 is 11:30 p.m., etc. From noon to midnight, merely add 12 to regular time to derive airline time.*

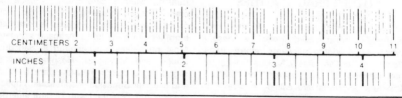

snails carrying the larvae of the parasite schistosoma, is still present. Although the chances of infection are remote, it's best to be circumspect when bathing in freshwater pools proximate to human habitation.

conduct: The more Spanish you speak the better. Keep in mind that while Puerto Rico is part of the United States, Latin cultural mores prevail here. Men and women alike tend to dress conservatively. If you want to be ac-

WHAT TO TAKE

CHECKLIST

CLOTHING

socks and shoes
underwear
sandals or thongs
T-shirts, shirts (or blouses)
skirts/pants, shorts
swimsuit
hat
light jacket/sweater

TOILETRIES

soap
shampoo
towel, washcloth
toothpaste/toothbrush
comb/brush
prescription medicines
Chapstick/other essential toiletries
insect repellent
suntan lotion/sunscreen
shaving kit
toilet paper
nail clippers
hand lotion
small mirror

OTHER ITEMS

passport
driver's license
travelers cheques
moneybelt
address book
notebook

pens/pencils
books, maps
watch
camera/film
flashlight/batteries
snorkeling equipment
extra glasses
umbrella/poncho
laundry bag
laundry soap/detergent
matches/lighter
frisbee/sports equipment

HIKING & CAMPING

internal frame pack
daypack/shoulder bag
foam sleeping pad
ripstop tape
tent/tent pegs
canteen
first-aid kit
binoculars
compass
hiking shorts/pants
candles/candle lantern
pocket knife
nylon cord
utensils
camping stove
can opener
food containers
spices, condiments
scrubbing pads
pots, pans
plastic wrap/aluminum foil

cepted and respected, dress respectably. Bathing attire is unsuitable on main streets, as is revealing female attire. Ninety years of American colonialism have had their effect here and you can expect some acrimony along with the hospitality, though once people come to know you, they will accept you.

theft: Should not be a problem if you're careful. By all means avoid the slum areas of San Juan, don't flash money or possessions around, and in general, keep a low profile.

services and information: Although the pay phone is still 10 cents, service is deplorable and it can cost as much to call from one side of the island to the other as it does to call the States. To use a pay phone, wait for a dial tone before inserting money. The number for local information is 123. For intra-island calls, dial 129; to call outside Puerto Rico, dial 128; for credit card or third-party calls, dial 130. WATS lines (800 numbers) may be reached by dialing 137 first. For informa-

tion in English, see the Blue Pages in the center of the telephone directory. Postal service is reliable. Have mail sent c/o General Delivery, Old San Juan, PR 00902. Tourist information centers are in San Juan. Be sure to pick up a copy of *Que Pasa,* the free monthly guide to Puerto Rico.

shopping: Opening hours vary but stores are generally open from Mon. through Sat. with some stores closing for an hour in the afternoon. Aside from local handicrafts, there isn't much to buy that can't be found cheaper somewhere else. There's an import tax on photographic equipment and accessories so bring your own. T-shirts make good souvenirs. Rum is cheap, and no import duties are charged if bringing it to the States. Poultry and mangoes are among the agricultural products prohibited from export to the States. For details, call the quarantine division of the U.S. Department of Agriculture in San Juan at 791-0356 or 753-4363.

SAN JUAN AND ENVIRONS

Second oldest city in the Americas (after Santo Domingo) and oldest city in the territorial
United States, San Juan presents two distinct
faces to the world: one is a vast, sprawling
collection of towering concrete monoliths,
freeways with crazy drivers, and bleak but
functional housing projects with attractive
murals painted on their sides. If it appears to
have grown too fast, it has. The other face is
that of Old San Juan, which retains the
original flavor of the city—like what the rest of
the city must have been like before the svelte
skyscrapers arrived. San Juan is divided and
subdivided into a number of districts, many of
which overlap, and it's nearly impossible to
say where one stops and another begins.
Metropolitan San Juan (pop. 1,086,370)
sprawls to includes the municipalities of
Bayamon, Canovanas, Carolina, Catano,
Guayanobo, Loiza, Toa Baja, and Trujillo Alto.
More than one-third of all Puerto Ricans live in
this concentrated 300-sq-mile area, the
economic, political, social, and cultural capital
of the island.

arriving by air: All international flights arrive
at Isla Verde Airport which is inconveniently
located on the easternmost side of town.
Moneychangers, banks, coin lockers, a rum-
tasting bar (open 1200-1600) and a taciturn
tourist information service (0900-1730) are at
the airport. If you don't have too much luggage, catch the free shuttle service out front
to the T1 bus ($0.25) which goes along Ave.
Fernandez Juncos to Old San Juan.
Limousine service, also out front, costs $1.75.
In order to shield the taxi drivers from competition, the service is one-way only.

getting around: San Juan was originally
served by streetcar lines. Although these have
disappeared, streetcar stops are still used to
identify destinations. Watch for yellow obelisk
posts or the upright metal signs (reading
Parada or *Parada de Guaguas)* which identify
bus stops. City buses are $0.25 (no transfers)
to any location. Service is irregular and ends
early in the evening. Bus terminals in Old San
Juan are at Ochoa (in the dock area) and at
Plaza de Colon. Other terminals are at Rio
Piedras, Country Club, Catano, and Bayamon.
For specific information phone the
Metropolitan Bus Authority at 767-7979.
Another alternative is to ask around about

MAJOR SAN JUAN BUS ROUTES

BUS	ROUTE	POINTS OF INTEREST
1. **Rio-Piedras** **San Juan**	Old San Juan Puerto de Tierra. Ave. Ponce de Leon Hato Rey Rio Piedras	The Capitol Munoz Rivera Park Fine Arts Center University of Puerto Rico
2. **Rio Piedras** **Calle Loiza** **San Juan**	Old San Juan Puerto de Tierra Condado Ave. Munoz Rivera Rio Piedras	The Capitol Munoz Rivera Park University of Puerto Rico
8. **Puerto Nuevo** **San Juan**	Old San Juan Ave. Ponce de Leon Puerto de Tierra Ave. Kennedy Ave. Roosevelt Rio Piedras	Fine Arts Center Puerto de Tierra The Capitol Roberto Clemente Stadium Hiram Bithorn Stadium Plaza Las Americas University of Puerto Rico
14. **Roosevelt** **Baldrich** **San Juan**	Old San Juan Puerto de Tierra Ave. Ponce de Leon Rio Piedras	The Capitol Fine Arts Center University of Puerto Rico
46. **Bayamon** **F.D.Roosevelt** **San Juan**	Old San Juan Puerto ed Tierra Ave. Ponce de Leon Ave. Roosevelt Bayamon	The Capitol Munoz Rivera Park Fine Arts Center Plaza Las Americas Caparra Bayamon Central Park
A7. **San Juan** **Condado** **Pinones**	Old San Juan Puerto de Tierra Ave. Ashford Ave. Fernandez Juncos Isla Verde Carr. 37 Boca de Cangrejos	The Capitol Munoz Rivera Park
T1. **Country Club** **Loiza** **San Juan**	Old San Juan Puerto de Tierra Ave Fernandez Juncos Carr. 37 Isla Verde Country Club	The Capitol Munoz Rivera Park Fine Arts Center
T2. **Country Club** **Rio Piedras** **Stop 18**	Ave. Ponce de Leon Hato Rey Ave. 65th de Infanteria Country Club	Fine Arts Center University of Puerto Rico

publicos which run from Old San Juan through several metropolitan area destinations, including Rio Piedras and Bayamon. Metered taxis charge $0.80 intitially with 10 cents for each additional 1/8 mile. Or better yet, use your feet. Assuming you are in halfway decent physical condition, no place in Old San Juan is too far to walk to. Although you'll occasionally see tourists being shuttled around in minivans, walking is definitely the best way to savor the atmosphere of the place. Indeed, you'd miss many things by getting around any other way. The section on sights which follows is arranged sequentially from El Morro to San Cristobal, allowing the entire old town to be as systematically and thoroughly explored as possible.

OLD SAN JUAN

For the amount of history, culture, and atmosphere that is packed into its seven-square-block area, no place in the territorial U.S. can begin to touch Old San Juan. Perched on the western end of an islet bordered on the N by the Atlantic and on the S and W by a vast bay, the town is connected to the mainland by the historic San Antonio Bridge. When seen from the harbor, the town takes on the appearance of a gigantic amphitheater with the ramparts and castles forming the outer walls. Colonial Spain is alive and well here. Brilliantly restored architecture complements what was well preserved to begin with. Old San Juan is not a place to hurry through — it cannot be seen in a day and can barely be appreciated in a week. Like a cup of the finest Puerto Rican coffee, it must be savored and sipped slowly. Stroll through the streets and take in the local color. See men playing dominoes, girls hanging out on the street corners waiting for marriage, groceries being hauled up to a second floor balcony with basket and rope. Get acquainted with the local characters: watch the crippled man on crutches who suddenly begins to move at top speed as soon as he is out of the sight of tourists. Note the man wearing a policeman's uniform who carries a billy club, wears badges, and shouts through a megaphone. Feed the pigeons in Parque de las Palomas or take in the view from the top of El Morro or San Cristobal. With the exception of the obnoxious police, nobody hassles anybody in Old San Juan. Enjoy.

history: Founded as a military stronghold in 1510, San Juan Bautista became a flourishing and attractive settlement by the end of the 19th century. Although the town lacks an historic hospital, university, or any of the other significant architectural structures found in Santo Domingo, its buildings nonetheless have a distinctive charm and appeal of their own. After the American invasion in 1898, Old San Juan deteriorated. Most of it became a red light district until 1949, when the seven-block downtown was declared a historical zone. Beginning in 1955, the Institute of Puer-

unofficial policeman

to Rican Culture, under the highly imaginative leadership of Ricardo Alegria, began the tremendous task of restoring the old buildings and homes in this historical area. Restoration on private residences was encouraged by legislation exempting owners from taxes for five to ten years on buildings that have been partially or fully restored, and offering bank loans for restorative work on liberal terms. Rather than becoming a pretentious museum piece, Old San Juan is a living historical monument where the past and present intermingle freely. As nothing within the historic zone may be changed without permission from the Institute, it is unlikely that Old San Juan will be subjected to the "modernization" that mars the rest of the metropolitan area.

SIGHTS

El Morro: A road bordered by wind-blown pines leads up to this dramatic structure, the most impressive legacy of the Spanish empire in Puerto Rico. Along with its sister structure in Havana, Brimstone Hill on St. Kitts (British), and Haiti's La Citadelle, El Morro is one of the premier forts in the Caribbean. Invincible from attack by sea during its time, it's now under the administration of the National Park Service. Open daily from 0800-1700, free admission; free guided tours at 0930, 1100, 1400, 1530, tel. 724-1974. Enter the small but cool and carpeted museum and see the exhibits. The rooms on the terrace level were used as living quarters. The doors were made of ultrahard *ausobo* wood, which is now a protected species. See the carefully labeled spots where The Forge, The Kitchen, and The Latrine (unlabeled) were. Stand in the *garito* (pillbox) and peer 140 ft. straight down to the sea below. This pillbox was once used as a lookout station for German subs. The triangular staircase, once an emergency passage, leads to the gun emplacement. The cannon on the Santa Barbara Bastion, also on the upper level, were found in the sea. A sum-

An impressive fortification, El Morro still attests to the power of Spanish rule.

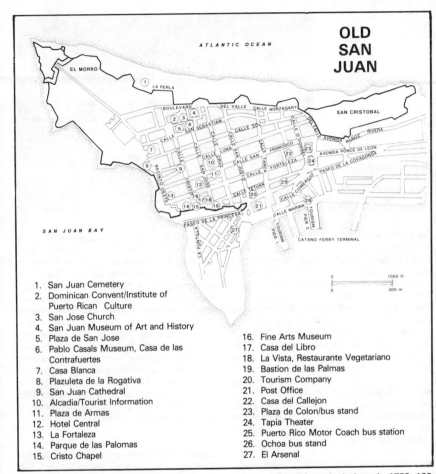

OLD SAN JUAN

ATLANTIC OCEAN

EL MORRO

① LA PERLA

BOULEVARD DEL VALLE CALLE NORZAGARY

SAN CRISTOBAL

AVENIDA MUÑOZ RIVERA

AVENIDA PONCE DE LEON

PASEO DE LA COVADONGA

SAN JUAN BAY

CATANO FERRY TERMINAL

TOURISM PIER 3

TOURISM PIER 1

0   1000 ft
0   300 m

1. San Juan Cemetery
2. Dominican Convent/Institute of Puerto Rican Culture
3. San Jose Church
4. San Juan Museum of Art and History
5. Plaza de San Jose
6. Pablo Casals Museum, Casa de las Contrafuertes
7. Casa Blanca
8. Plazuleta de la Rogativa
9. San Juan Cathedral
10. Alcadia/Tourist Information
11. Plaza de Armas
12. Hotel Central
13. La Fortaleza
14. Parque de las Palomas
15. Cristo Chapel
16. Fine Arts Museum
17. Casa del Libro
18. La Vista, Restaurante Vegetariano
19. Bastion de las Palmas
20. Tourism Company
21. Post Office
22. Casa del Callejon
23. Plaza de Colon/bus stand
24. Tapia Theater
25. Puerto Rico Motor Coach bus station
26. Ochoa bus stand
27. El Arsenal

mer arts festival, including crafts shows, dance groups, and other events, is held yearly from mid-Aug. through the end of Oct. on the fortress grounds.

fort's history: Built to protect San Juan Harbor, gateway for supply ships headed to Spain's many colonies to the W and S, construction (in 1539) was spurred after recurring attacks by royally commissioned pirates and Carib Indian raids. The site of the fort was moved several times before the present outer fortification was completed in 1584. It was only completed in today's form in 1783, 199 years later, through the efforts of two Irishmen (O'Reilly and O'Daly), by which time about 40,000 man-years had been spent building the fortifications and city walls. Sir Francis Drake, pursuing a cargo of gold pesos being temporarily stored in the fortress' vaults, struck on 22 Nov. 1584, and was repulsed. In 1598 the Earl of Cumberland attacked the Santurce area of San Juan with his 18 ships. Fighting tooth and nail, the Spanish, weakened by dysentery, held out for two weeks before surrendering. Cumberland and

The beautiful arcaded galleries lined with carved wooden railings above the paved courtyard make a fitting setting for the headquarters of the Institute of Puerto Rican Culture.

his forces were delirious with pleasure until they too succumbed to dysentery, followed by an epidemic of yellow fever. After just four months of control, the English sailed away, leaving 400 of their comrades buried. In 1625, the fortress was attacked by the Dutch, but this time the Spanish survived the attack and began work on San Cristobal on the other side of town, to provide further defense. An attack by British Lt. General Abercromby in 1797 failed (see "La Rogativa" below), and the last attack came during the Spanish-American War, when El Morro's batteries returned fire on U.S. Admiral Sampson's fleet. El Canuelo, which can be seen across the bay, was constructed to ward off hostile landings on the W side. The present structure was rebuilt in stone in the 1660s.

Cemeterio de San Juan: Dramatically situated below towering El Morro, this cemetery contains the graves of such prominent Puerto Ricans as Pedro Albizu Campos and Jose de Diego. The circular neoclassic chapel, dedicated in 1863, is a most unusual architectural edifice. Note its eerie stained-glass reflection. Full-size weeping widows, realistically cut from marble, stand and kneel over graves. Long rows of tombs are set into the wall Etruscan-style, while faded and frayed Puerto Rican flags fly over graves. Worth a visit, but stay clear at night or risk finding a knife at your throat.

La Perla: Elegant by comparison to the slums which line the banks of the Martin Pena Channel, this slum, situated along the Atlantic to one side of Cemeterio de San Juan, is a crowded group of houses which stretch from just below the remains of the colonial wall down a steep slope to the filthy beach below. Most houses have TVs and other conveniences, and the better part of the slum is served by electricity, water, and sanitation. The area is a center for drug trade and other activities; it is recommended that you not come here unless it's with a local you trust. Bring nothing of value. La Perla is the place where Oscar Lewis penned his study of prostitution and poverty, *La Vida.*

Casa Blanca: One of the gems of Old San Juan. Entering through the gates at 1 San Sebastian, a cool courtyard with a garden and beautiful chain of fountains is off to the left. Straight ahead is a house which has been restored to resemble a 17th C. nobleman's home, with simple but beautifully designed antique furniture and attractive white rooms. Even older than La Fortaleza, this house was designed to be given to Ponce de Leon as a reward for his services. Ponce, however, went off to search for the fountain of youth in Florida and, meeting his end from an Indian's poisoned arrow, never returned. A hurricane destroyed the original structure, which was replaced by another in 1523 that still stands today. In 1779, after more than 250 years' residence, Ponce de Leon's ancestors sold it to the government, which expanded it for use in housing military engineers and troops. Taken over by the U.S. military in 1898, it was vacated in 1967. Casa Blanca was declared a National Historical Monument the following year. A library (open Mon. to Fri. 0900-1800) has a superb collection of Caribbean literature in Spanish and English. The complex is open Tues. to Sun. 0900-1200, 1300-1630. Guided tours are available Tues. to Sat.; tel. 724-4102.

El Convento Dominicano: At Calle Norzagaray 98, dominating Plaza San Jose, is the former Dominican Convent, now headquarters for the Instituto de Cultura Puertorriquena, the organization responsible for the restoration of Old San Juan. Built in 1523 on land donated by Ponce de Leon, it's one of the major historical buildings in the city. After the closure of all convents in 1838, it was converted to a barracks. After the American occupation, it was the center of the U.S. Antilles Command until its termination in 1966. Carefully restored, the Convent is now a showcase for many fine exhibits of art and antiques, and cultural events. The restored chapel has old music sheets complemented by piped-in music, old medals, and the altarpiece of St. Thomas Aquinas. Concerts are held on occasion in the huge paved courtyard which lies below the beautiful arcaded galleries, lined with carved wooden railings. Centro de Artes Populares is a crafts shop on the ground floor (open daily 0800-1630; tel. 724-0700).

Museo de Arte y Historia: This former marketplace, located on Calle Norzagaray (corner Mac Arthur), was restored by the City of San Juan in 1979; it now serves as a cultural center which holds periodic exhibitions, audio-visual displays, and occasional concerts. Open Mon. to Fri. 0800-1200, 1300-1600; audio-visual shows: Mon. to Fri. 0900, 1000, 1100, 1315, 1415, 1515, $1 suggested donation, tel. 724-1875.

Iglesia de San Jose: Oldest church still in use in the Americas, San Jose Church was built by Dominican friars as a monastery chapel. Originally dedicated to St. Thomas Aquinas, it was renamed by Jesuits who took it over in 1865. The Gothic ceilings are unequaled in this hemisphere. Inside, a statue of Jesus Christ, bleeding and bound with ropes, stands in one corner. This church is most famous for what is missing or moved; most of the items currently on display have been donated. Ponce de Leon's tomb, after a three-and-a-half-century rest here, was moved to the cathedral. His coat of arms can still be seen to the L of the main altar. The famous Flemish masterpiece, "The Virgin of Bethlehem," brought to the island in 1511, was stolen (and presumably deflowered) in 1972. During the 1898 U.S. Navy bombardment, a cannonball crashed into one window and mysteriously disappeared; the chapel, crypt, and convent remained untouched. Open Mon. to Sat. 0930-1600.

Museo de Casals: This collection of memorabilia includes cellist Pablo Casals' medals, sweater, cello, domino set, a yellow plaster of Paris cast of his hands, and even his pipes — including one carved in the shape of Wagner! It also holds manuscripts, photographs, and an extensive videotape library (played on request). Open Mon. to Sat. 0900-1700; Sun. 1300-1700; tel. 723-9185.

Casa de los Contrafuertes; Museo del Grabado Latinamericano: Directly on Plaza San Jose at Calle San Sebastian, next-door to the Museo de Casals, this may be the oldest private residence remaining in Old San Juan. The Casa was constructed in the early 18th C.; the name means "heavily buttressed." Inside, a pharmacy museum is on the first floor. A reconstructed 19th C. shop is filled with antique crystal and porcelain jars and bottles, mysterious vials, antique medicine ads, as well as other furnishings and objects characteristic of Puerto Rican pharmacies of the time. The Latin American Graphic Arts Museum, which occupies the second floor, contains a superb representative collection of Puerto Rican artists past and present. Particularly notable are the collection of works by

Latin American engravers, along with a group of prized works from the San Juan Biennial. Open Wed. to Sun. 0900-1200, 1300-1630.

Plaza de San Jose: Restored to its original condition by the Institute for Puerto Rican Culture, the Plaza is quiet and peaceful during the day and the liveliest place in town at night. The statue of Ponce de Leon, first governor of Puerto Rico, was cast using melted bronze cannon captured in the 1797 British attack.

Plazuleta de la Rogativa: Designed and built by an Australian residing in Puerto Rico, this remarkable statue, which has a touching spiritual character to it, is located in a small plaza next to the sea wall near Caleta Las Monjas. It was donated by a citizens' group to mark San Juan's 450th birthday in 1971. The statue commemorates a legend concerning the seige of San Juan in 1797. After taking Trinidad on 17 Feb. of that year, Lt. General Abercromby proceeded to San Juan with 60 ships containing nearly 8,000 troops. With the

Pontificating from the center of San Jose Plaza, Ponce de Leon, done up in cast bronze, reminds us of the time when he conquered the island and served as governor (1509) before venturing off to find the fountain of youth in Florida, only to die from an Indian's poisoned arrow.

British apparently preparing to close in for the kill, the governor, weakened by dysentery, asked the head bishop to arrange a *rogativa* (procession) through the streets. The bishop, in turn, asked that it be held in honor of Santa Catalina (St. Catherine) and Ursula. The evening candle and torch procession moved from Catedral de San Juan Bautista through the streets. Abercromby became alarmed when he saw the huge masses of torchlights and heard the frenzied continual ring of church bells that increased in tempo until midnight, despite the steady barrage from his ships. Concluding that the town was being supplied by troops from the countryside, he ordered the fleet to sail immediately, which gave rise to the legend that the city had been saved by Ursula and her cohorts.

La Fortaleza: At the end of Calle Fortaleza stands the oldest executive mansion in the Western Hemisphere; it was in operation three centuries before the Washington White House had even been designed. Its name, "The Fortress," derives from its original use. Though replaced by El Morro, it continued to serve as part of the city's defense system. The $2 million in gold and silver which Sir Francis Drake sought during his 1595 attack was kept here. Occupied twice (by the Dutch in 1625 and the British in 1898), it had to be rebuilt in 1640 after the Dutch left. Usage as a governor's mansion dates from 1639, and continues today. It was completely remodeled in 1846. Pass by the brusque, rude security guards to join a guided tour (in English) of the downstairs area, 0900, 1000, 1130, 1400, 1530. (Tours in Spanish are given alternate half hours.) Open Mon. to Fri. (except holidays) 0900, 1000, 1130, 1400, 1530; tel. 721-7000, ext. 2211/2358. Inside, visit Santa Catalina's chapel, descend into the dungeon, and note the Moorish garden with its 19th C. parish tiles. If you stick your hand in the water, you will be granted any wish you request.

San Juan Gate: First of the three city gates built and the sole one remaining. Once the main gate for dignitaries and cargo entering the city, it now serves only to ornament the roadway which passes through it. During the

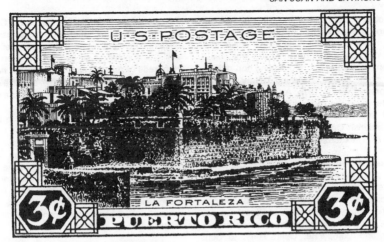

17th C. sloops anchored in the small cove just N of La Fortaleza. New bishops and governors, entering the city through this gate, would be escorted under a canopy to the cathedral where a Te Deum Mass would be offered in thanksgiving for the safely completed voyage.

Catedral de San Juan Bautista: On Calle Cristo across from Plazuleta de las Monjas and El Convento Hotel. Once a small, thatched-roof structure when constructed in 1521, the cathedral was completed in its present state in 1852. The only holdovers from the earlier structure are the partially restored Gothic ceiling and the circular staircase. See the remains of that ardent Catholic Ponce de Leon, who rests in a marble tomb. The wax-covered mummy of St. Pio, a Roman martyr who was persecuted and killed for his belief in Christianity, is encased in a glass box. He has been here since 1862. To his R is a wooden replica of Mary with four swords stuck in her bosom. Many, many beautiful stained glass windows. Open Mon. to Fri. 0630-1700; Sat., 0830-1600, 1800-2000; Sun., 0830-1300.

Provincial Deputation Building: Recently restored and once occupied by the island's first insular parliament, its cloister-like design is done up in late neoclassical style. Puerto Rico's first representative body, the Provin-

cial Deputation, was housed here. That body began doing business on 17 July 1898, after Puerto Rico was granted autonomy by Spain. The U.S. invaded only two weeks later. It seems only appropriate that the building's current occupant is the U.S. Department of State. Open Mon. to Fri. 0800-1630; tel. 722-2121.

Plaza de Armas: Relaxed square with pay telephones, supermarkets, small cafeterias, a fruit vendor, and a shaved ice cart. The four statues presiding over the plaza, representing the four seasons, are over a century old. This oblong square has an interesting history. Originally a marketplace (Plaza de las Verduras or Plaza of the Vegetables), it was designed to be the main plaza before Ponce de Leon moved the capital from Caparra. Used in the 16th C. for military drills by local militia, it was also the center of local nightlife. Bands played and singles walked around the square or sat in rented chairs. When the locals were replaced by Spanish garrisons, their cry of "Present arms!" resulted in a name change to Plaza de Armas. It went through several name changes before the name reverted to the present one a few decades ago.

Alcaldia: Right on Plaza de Armas. Work on this building, designed along the lines of its counterpart in Madrid, began in 1602. Constructed in stages, it was completed in 1799. During the years when it functioned as a city hall, many important events took place here, including the inauguration of the first Puerto Rican legislature, and the signing and ratification of the decree abolishing slavery. The last restoration was in 1975. A tourist information center is on the ground floor (formerly a jail) next to a small gallery which holds frequent exhibitions. Open Mon-Fri. 0900-1600; tel. 724-7171, ext. 2391.

Museo de Bellas Artes: At 253 Cristo St., this small but rich collection of Puerto Rican art is housed in a tastefully restored 18th C. building donated by local citizens. In addition to temporary exhibitions by local artists, there's a permanent collection of artists like Oller and Campeche. Open Tues. to Sun. 0900-1200, 1300-1630; tel. 723-2320.

La Casa del Libro: This museum of rare books and illuminated manuscripts, housed in a beautifully restored 18th C. townhouse, opened in 1958. Its 5,000-book collection, said to be the best of its kind in Latin America, includes over 200 books that date back to the 16th C., and manuscripts 2,000 years old. Other books are reference works on the graphic arts. Conveniently located at 255 Calle Cristo. Open Mon. to Fri. (except holidays) 1100-1630.

La Capilla del Cristo: At the foot of Cristo St. stands what must be the smallest chapel in the Caribbean. Dedicated to the Christ of Miracles, there are at least two stories explaining its origin. One claims that it was originally just an altar which prevented people from accidentally falling over the wall into the sea. The other story is more involved. On 24 June 1753, a rider, participating in the annual patron saint festival, missed the turn at the end of Calle Cristo and plunged into the sea. Miraculously, he was not injured, and the chapel was constructed to commemorate the event. In 1925 the city government planned to demolish the chapel, but after vehement public protest, the idea was abandoned. On 6 Aug. every year, the chapel's feast day, the Cardinal of Puerto Rico officiates at a High Mass. Open Tues. 1000-1600.

Parque de las Palomas: At the end of Cristo St., next to Cristo Chapel, is this small gem of a park, perched at the top of the city wall—nice place to sit early in the morning. Hundreds of pigeons circulate between nook, tree, and fountain. Feathers fly about everywhere; a man sells birdseed at the entrance.

Bastion de las Palmas: Constructed in 1678 as a gun emplacement, it once served as an integral part of the city's defense system. Now it's a small park overlooking San Juan Bay. Grab some morning caffeine at the coffee shop on San Jose and come here for the view. The statue off to the side is of Venezuelan patriot Gen. Miranda, comrade-in-arms of Bolivar against the Spanish. His liberal views led to his internment here.

Cristo Chapel nestles at the end of Cristo Street. The entrance to Parque de las Palomas is at the end on the right.

El Arsenal: Built in 1800, this former naval station was the last place in Puerto Rico to be handed over after the 1898 U.S. takeover. Here, the Spanish general waited for the ship which would return him and his men to Spain. The chapel houses the Museo de Imagineria Popular Santos, containing a rich variety of works by the island's most outstanding *santeros*. Exhibitions are held inside this building from time to time; tel. 725-5584.

Casa del Callejon: This 18th C. home, opened after restoration in 1965, houses the Museo de Arquitectura Colonial, along with the Museo de la Familia Puertorriquena. Downstairs are tiles, blueprints, fittings, and scale models of buildings restored under the auspices of the Institute of Puerto Rican Culture. A good introduction to Old San Juan. Exhibits upstairs show how the rich lived in Puerto Rico during the 19th century. Open Tues. to Sun. 0900-1200, 1300-1630. Guided tours Mon. to Sat.; tel. 725-5250. Check out the artisans' market along the same street (Callejon de la Capilla) on Sat. mornings.

Plaza de Colon: Once much larger and named Plaza de Santiago after the gate of the same name, in 1893, to mark the 400th anniversary of Columbus' discovery of Puerto Rico, the plaza was renamed and a statue of the explorer was unveiled. Ponce de Leon's statue was then moved to Plaza San Jose. Nowadays, it's chiefly of interest for the nearby Tapia Theater, Burger King, Old San Juan's bus terminal, and its largest liquor store.

Teatro Tapia: Funds for the construction of this theatre—third oldest (1832) in the Third World—were raised by an 1825 tax levied on bread and imported alcohol. After suffering damages in a series of earthquakes (1867-68), it was nearly demolished and rebuilt. Instead, it was renovated in 1878, renamed after the island's most prominent playwright in 1937, renovated again in 1939, and finally restored in 1976. Now it's the center of traditional Puerto Rican theater, and a festival is held here each May.

Tapia Theater, a cutural center, was constructed through funds raised by an 1825 tax levied on bread and imported alcohol.

San Cristobal: A strategic masterpiece, this imposing fortress, which in its prime covered 27 acres and contained seven independent but interlocking units, still dominates the E side of town. Though much smaller now than its more famous cousin El Morro, it has a less touristy atmosphere. It's nice to spend the morning sitting and relaxing on the upper-level fortifications, taking in the view and getting some sun. Enter the fortress and find the visitor center, a former guardhouse, on the left. The small museum, located across from the administrative offices on the ground floor, has illustrations detailing how the fort was constructed, a scale model of the original fortification, and a collection of life-sized dolls. On the second floor is a series of low, concave arches and barren rooms. Downstairs, the bronze cannon on an artillery mount was brought down from Delaware while the iron cannons, which deteriorate faster in the salt breeze, were taken from the ocean. Five 150,000-gallon cisterns are on the lower level, and another is on the uppermost level. Water was obtained by rope and bucket, and animals were prohibited inside the fort to prevent contamination. Now, the water is emptied into the sea. The statue of Santa Barbara, patron saint of the fort, also on the ground level, was venerated by the soldiers. The red-and-white flag flying from the upper level is the red cross of St. Andrew. In use from the 16th to 18th C., it symbolizes 400 years of Spanish culture in Puerto Rico. The outer walls are caving in due to erosion caused by waves. It will require an estimated $26 million to repair them, but President Ronald Reagan has slashed the National Park Service's budget by $5 million. Check out the Devil's Sentry Box. Built during the 17th C. at ocean level, a sentry posted here disappeared one night, leaving no trace save his armor, weapons, and clothes. He was thought to have been possessed by the devil. In actuality, he had run off with his girlfriend from La Perla, and they were found to be happily settled on a farm near Caguas years later. It's also possible to see whales migrating from this viewpoint from Nov. to January.

fort's history: After El Morro proved unable to defend the city, construction began on San Cristobal in 1634 and continued for the next 150 years. The basic structure, however, had been completed and joined to the city walls by 1678, and like El Morro, it was built entirely with materials gathered from the shoreline. Irishmen O'Reilly and O'Day enlisted in the Spanish army and developed ideas for its construction. Incorporating the most advanced defensive principles of the time, the complex contained six small forts supporting a central core. These were interconnected via an amazingly complex arrangement of passageways, moats, tunnels, bridges, roads, ramps, and dungeons. To storm the central fortress, the enemy would have to take over the six outer forts under continuous fire. Explosives placed under the moats could be ignited if the enemy gained control. In 1898, San Cristobal aimed its guns at an American Naval force, firing the first round in the Spanish-American War. After the American occupation, the U.S. Army moved into the fort. In 1949 it was placed under the National Park Service and opened to the public in 1961. Open daily 0800-1700; guided tours at 0930, 1100, 1400, 1530; tel. 724-1974.

Terminal Turismo: See tour boats come in at Old San Juan's Terminal Turismo. Take a stroll at night while the ships are in and see the tourists. The taxis outside whisk them off to Condado, depriving them of the opportunity to sample San Juan's wonderful nightlife.

Cruise ships dock regularly at the base of town.

Across the street is Plazoleta el Puerto, a commercialized and expensive municipal crafts center. Inside the Tourism Pier is the small Museo del Mar (Museum of the Seas) which, in addition to its displays of maritime equipment and models, has wall murals detailing the lifestyle of the Taino Indians. Open daily from 0900-2100. The Intendancy Building, located on the corner of San Jose and San Francisco, was once the offices of the royal Spanish Exchequer. It now houses Puerto Rico's State Department. Open Mon. to Fri. 0800-1630; tel. 722-2121.

San Juan Bay and Catano: A cruiseboat ($1.50) offers trips through San Juan bay on Sun. and holidays at 1430 and 1630. A more relaxed, leisurely experience is to take the Catano ferry across San Juan Bay to the suburb of Catano. Great views of El Morro and other historic buildings. Board at Pier 2 next to Terminal Turismo in Old San Juan. Ferries leave every half-hour from 0515-2400. The fare is 20 cents, and the trip is a delight. Bacardi Rum Factory, on the outskirts of Catano, offers free daily tours of its facilities and drinks on the house served under a huge yellow, bat-shaped canopy. It's a long walk to the entrance so take the Levitown bus or a minibus. A guard will open the gate; walk straight and then turn right. Orange-and-yellow train-buses carry visitors around the grounds. Although there are regular times posted, tours leave whenever there are sufficient passengers. The guide speaks in a high-pitched, hysterical voice. She may be tipsy or just bored. Visit the distillery, the ersatz museum, and other sites. It'll seem more interesting if you take advantage of the free drinks to get pissed *beforehand.* Bacardi, largest distiller on the island and largest single source of government tax revenue ($200 million yearly), is also the largest polluter; this plant discharges 634,000 gallons of residue daily into San Juan Bay. A crafts fair here, held on the first and second Sun. in Dec., features exhibits and sales by over 200 craftsmen on the grounds. Also in the vicinity of Catano is Cabras Island. Formerly two separate islands, Cabras and Canuelo, they have been connected by a causeway. Here are the ruins of 17th C. Fort Canuelo and

the remains of a leper colony. Great place for a picnic. Seafood restaurants at Palo Seco nearby. Punta Salinas Public Beach is alongside Boca Vieja Bay near Levitown.

PRACTICALITIES

accommodations: Although Old San Juan is the best place to base yourself for exploring the metropolitan area, there's a lack of reasonably priced accommodations. If staying for an extended period, ask around about renting a room. Rates given may be higher during peak season (Dec. to April). La Vista, 151 Tetuan, charges $10-15 s and $10-25 d; tel. 722-2514. Pleasant, airy rooms, some with balconies. Bring mosquito coils. There's also an attached bar and restaurant with a great view of San Juan Bay. Hotel Central, 202 San Jose, is $10-15 s and $18-22 d; tel. 722-2751. San Francisco Inn, 263 San Francisco, has rooms for $15 s and $30 d. La Fortaleza, 252 Fortaleza, goes from $18 s, $30 d, $45 t. The authentically restored 300-year-old El Convento, 100 Cristo (tel. 723-9020), has rooms from $55 s, $63 d off-season. (Also see "Accommodations" chart pages 60-62.)

food: The streets are lined with various eating houses and restaurants ranging from comparatively plush ones lining Cristo to budget eateries on the other side of the town. Highly recommended and reasonable is Govinda's, a *restaurante vegetariano* run by a Hare Krishna-ized Puerto Rican family. Natural food dishes like *sopa de vegetales, tortillas,* spinach and broccoli, lasagna, and a variety of fresh fruit drinks are lovingly dished out by Jayapatni and her family. Open Mon. to Fri. 1130-1430; Hare Krishna-sponsored free feed Sat. 1100-1300. Acropolis Greek Restaurant, 204 Tanca (open 0700-1700), has a $1.25 breakfast special. Maria's, 204 Calle Cristo, is famous for its delicious but pricey (around $2.50) fresh frozen fruit drinks. For honest Puerto Rican home cooking try El Jibarito. Mr. and Mrs. Ruiz's place, at 276 Sol. Tasa de Oro, corner of Tanca and San Justo, serves up rice and beans ($1.25) and other traditional foods. Fast-food freaks can find relief at an unusually aesthetic Burger King, right on Plaza Salvador Brau, and a spacious Taco Maker at 255 San Justo. La Vista, on Calle Tetuan, has good hamburgers. Just around the corner on Calle San Jose a cafeteria has the cheapest morning coffee in town along with sandwiches. For dinner, Charlie's Place on Cristo offers the best value, with set meals going for $6.95.

SAN JUAN ACCOMMODATIONS

All rates listed are off season (mid-April through mid-December). Room tax is 6% additional.
Key: CP = Continental Plan applies. CP★ = full breakfast served. F = free airport pickup. K = kitchenette.

NAME	ADDRESS	TELEPHONE	S	D	
OLD SAN JUAN					
El Convento	100 Christo Old San Juan	723-9020	55	60	
La Fortaleza	252 Fortaleza Old San Juan	722-5012	18	30	
MIRAMAR					
Excelsior	801 Ponce De Leon Miramar	721-7400	51	60	
Olimpo Court	603 Miramar Miramar	724-0600	26	27	
Toro	605 Miramar Miramar	725-5150	18	20	
CONDADO					
Atlantic Beach	1 Vendig Condado	721-6900	22	33	
Casa Cervantes	10 Cervantes Condado	723-8346	25	30	K
Condado Beach	Ashford Condado Beach	721-6090	70	80	
Condado Lagoon	6 Clemenceau Condado	721-0170	50	60	
Dutch Inn and Towers	55 Condado Condado	721-0810	55	60	
El Canario	1317 Ashford Condado	724-2793	32	42	
El Portal	76 Condado Condado	721-9010	30	40	
El Prado Inn	1350 Luchetti Condado	728-5925	30	40	CP
Hosteria del Mar	5 Cervantes Condado	724-8203	20	25	

SAN JUAN ACCOMMODATIONS (CONT.)

Jewel's by the Sea	1125 Seaview Condado	725-5313	25	35	
La Concha	Ashford Condado	721-6090	65	75	
Lindomar	4 Condado Condado	722-8640	28	33	CP
Sands	6 Earle Condado	724-7272	30	35	
Tamana	1 Joffre Condado	724-4160	21	32	
The Regency	1005 Ashford Condado	721-0505	50	55	
SANTURCE					
Bolivar	609 Bolivar Santurce	727-3823	18	22	
Pierre	105 De Diego Santurce	721-1200	56	61	
Simar	166 Villamil Santurce	723-9111	26	29	
OCEAN PARK					
Arcade Inn	8 Taft Ocean Park	725-0668	18	26	
Beach Buoy Inn	1853 McLeary Ocean Park	728-8119	25	25	CP
La Condesa	2071 Cacique Ocean Park	727-3968	28	34	
Numero 1 on the Beach	1 Santa Anita Ocean Park	727-9687	25	35	
San Antonio	1 Tapia Ocean Park	727-3302	29	39	
The Beach House	1957 Italia Ocean Park	727-4495	25	30	CP
Wind Chimes	53 Taft Ocean Park	727-4153	30	40	CP
PUNTA LAS MARIAS					
Buena Vista by the Beach	2218 General del Valle Punta las Marias	726-2796	22	28	
Safari on the Beach	2 Almendro Punta las Marias	726-0445	45	50	CP
Tres Palmas	2212 Park Punta las Marias	727-4617	35	35	CP ★

SAN JUAN ACCOMMODATIONS (CONT.)

ISLA VERDE

Carib-Inn	Carr. 187 Isla Verde	791-3535	36	41	
Casa Mathiesen	14 Uno Este Villamar, Isla Verde	726-8662	23	26	K
Don Pedro	4 Rosa Isla Verde	791-2838	26	30	
El Patio	7 Tres Oeste Villamar, Isla Verde	727-9640	30	33	
Green Isle	36 Uno Villamar, Isla Verde	726-4330	22	25	F
International Airport	3rd F, Airport Terminal Bldg. Isla Verde	791-1700	40	40	
La Playa	6 Amapola Isla Verde	791-1115	20	25	
Mario's	2 Rosa Isla Verde	791-3748	25	25	
Travel Lodge	Carr. 37 Isla Verde	728-1300	50	53	

entertainment: For its size, Old San Juan has a greater concentration and more variety of nightlife than anyplace else in the United States. Cobblestone-lined streets are packed wall to wall with nightspots ranging from sleaze to gay bars to elite discos. Its dynamic and unmistakably Latin environment gets wild at night — especially on weekends when cars pour in. Everyone is desperate to see and be seen in this modern version of the *paseo,* the traditional evening stroll along the plaza. Well-heeled couples promenade up and down Calle Cristo. Fashionable clothes and tons of makeup are everywhere in evidence — everyone heading up to the bar-lined streets surrounding the Plaza San Jose. On the Plaza, in addition to the young middle-class bar scene, there are often jams with congo bands or folk musicians. It has gotten so wild up here at times that the police have come by and fired shots into the air. One balcony overhanging the plaza still has bullet holes. Plenty of action and atmosphere in the sur-rounding streets as well. Innumerable bars, scattered throughout the town, have pool tables, TVs, and pinball machines. Here you can drink a beer for as little as 55 cents. Las Balconies, a plush bar across from Plaza San Jose, has balconies overlooking the harbor. Expatriates hang out at PJ's on San Jose; meet vivacious, graceful, and hospitable Effie from Germany and Chicago — she'll tell you her story of being highjacked to Cuba. Farther up San Jose is El Batey, another *Americano* hangout. Besides the great jams inside the local bars, The Place along La Fortaleza has excellent jazz and rock bands in an attractive setting. Museo de Jazz, 107 Calle San Jose, hosts rare jazz films and jam sessions most Fri. nights for $2 (0930-0100). Discos include Hollywood, Camelot and Neon's — mostly young crowd. Good value for films is The Royal, Calle San Justo 154. Double features are just $2.50. Sleazy prostitute bars are just across from Terminal Turismo down the street. Gay hangouts are on and around Calle Luna.

events and festivals: Most of the island-wide festivities find their fullest expression here. A Puppet Theater Festival is held in Jan., as is an international folklore festival and the San Sebastian Street Fiesta; this popular street fair has everything from processions and dancing in the plaza to displays of *paso fino* horses. The Festival de Claridad (Festival of Clarity) takes place in September. The Festival de Teatro Puertorriqueno (Festival of the Puerto Rican Theater) is held at the Tapia Theater each March. The Fiesta de la Musical Puertorriquena is held inside the Dominican Convent each May; the Festival de Verano (Summer Festival) and the Casals Festival (which attracts the top names in classical music) are in June. Centering on 26 June, San Juan's most famous fiesta, dedicated to San Juan Bautista, is celebrated as inhabitants (including the mayor) flock to the sea for the traditional midnight dip which is believed to wash away sin. A ceramics fair takes place each August. Events are subject to change so see the latest issue of *Que Pasa* to find out what, indeed, is happening.

crafts and shopping: Don't expect to find any great bargains here. Except at the so-called duty-free shops, most of the goods are imported from the mainland and, therefore, more expensive. Most of the shops here depend upon cruise ship passengers for their survival. Unfortunately, the tour companies are being paid off to show a film which indoctrinates the passengers so that they head directly for certain shops. Tour guides, often in cahoots with shopowners, frequently arrange to end their tours in front of their shops. It is, nevertheless, a great place for browsing and window shopping. The Museo de Jazz, 107 Calle San Jose, has T-shirts and a collection of books on jazz in Spanish. Check out the Bass Shoe Factory Outlet, 206 Calle Botello, for buys. The Gentle Swing, 156 Cristo, has imported and native hammocks from $20 and up. Barrachina, Calle San Francisco, gives out free rum samples. The Folk Art Center, inside the Dominican Convent on Plaza San Jose, has an excellent selection of island handicrafts — buy here and help support

The spirit of the great Spanish cellist Pablo Casals lives on in the Casals classical music festival, held each June.

a worthy cause. Jose E. Alegria's handsome shop at 154 Cristo houses a fascinating collection of *santos* and pre-Columbian artifacts. See men hand-rolling cigars at a shop inside the Ochoa bus depot. **art galleries:** Puerto Rican artists are well represented in Old San Juan's many galleries. Galeria Coabey is at 101 San Sebastian. Galeria Palomas is at 207 Cristo, while Galeria Botello, which displays the works of the Spanish expatriate, is next door at 208. Galeria Liga de Arte is on Calle San Jose, Galeria W. Labiosa is at 312 San Francisco, and Cafe Galeria is at 319 La Fortaleza.

information and services: Minimal tourist information is provided in offices in the Alcaldia (City Hall) on Plaza de Armas (tel. 724-7171), and at 301 San Justo (tel. 721-2400). Offices are open from Mon. to Fri. 0800-1200, 1300-1630. For changing money, the Bank of Nova Scotia, 251 Tetuan, and the Royal Bank of Canada, 204 Tetuan, are open Mon. to Fri. 0900-1430. An excellent bookstore is located on the corner of San Jose and Tetuan. An a/c library is located inside Casa Blanca. A post office is located at the corner of Recinto Sur and San Justo; pick up mail addressed c/o General Delivery, Old San Juan 00905 (most convenient location in the city). Have passport photos taken at Fortaleza 65. There's a laundromat at the corner of Cruz and Sol. Kodokdan Okinawan Karate, Fortaleza 56, gives morning yoga lessons.

METROPOLITAN SAN JUAN

PUERTO DE TIERRA

Literally named "Land at the Door," this compact area, once right outside the old city walls, was originally settled by freed black slaves. Nowadays, Puerto de Tierra contains numerous U.S. Naval Reserves, the Capitol, and other governmental buildings. Avenida Ponce de Leon runs right through its center.

sights: Seat of the Puerto Rican bicameral legislature, the Capitol was constructed during the 1920s. Its magnificent dome, with its coat of arms, looms over an urn displaying the 1952 constitution. Open Mon. to Fri. 0830-1700. For guided tours, call 721-6040, ext. 253. The once exclusive Casino de San Juan, constructed in 1917, has since been renamed the Manuel David Fernandez Government Center and converted to use by the State Department. Recently restored with marble floors and walls and a 12-foot chandelier (open Mon. to Fri. 0800-1630; tel. 722-2121). A statue of patron saint San Juan Bautista, across from the Capitol and overlooking the small beach below, bears an uncanny resemblance to Mr. Natural, of underground comic book fame. Gracefully landscaped Munoz Rivera Park contains a statue of its namesake which stands near El Polvorin, an ammunition depot and small museum. Eighteenth-century Fort San Geronimo, entered from the rear of the Caribe Hilton, houses a museum featuring dummies wearing military uniforms of different eras, ship models, and other war materiel. Open daily 0900-1630; tel. 724-0700.

practicalities: Stay at Ocean Side, 54 Munoz Rivera, which charges from $23 s, from $28 d; tel. 722-2410. Buy handicrafts at Mercado de Artesania Puertorriquena (open Sun. only) inside Munoz Rivera Park and at Mercado Artesania Carabali, Sixto Escobar Park. The Archives and General Library has been closed

girl, San Jose de Ocoa, Dominican Republic (Roger LaBrucherie)

above, clockwise: Usabon Falls, Puerto Rico (H. Pariser); Watermelon Bay with Watermelon Cay in background, St. John, USVI (H. Pariser); mountains near Bonao, Dominican Republic (Roger LaBrucherie); St. Thomas beach scene, USVI (USVI Division of Tourism)

down for several years now because the air conditioner has broken down, and no one can agree from which fund the sum for repairs should come. Try the small library inside the ornate Biblioteca Ateneo Puertorriqueno, Ave. Ponce de Leon Pda. (Stop) –2. The Volunteer Library, across the street and up on the third floor, is a musty old place run by an engaging old man. Open Mon. to Sat. 1300-1800, used books are for sale at very reasonable prices.

MIRAMAR

A high-class residential area just across the bridge from Puerto de Tierra. The many beautiful homes in this area include several by architect Antonin Nechodoma, whose work shows the marked influence of Frank Lloyd Wright. Isla Grande, just beside Miramar to the W, was formerly a U.S. Naval base. Now the site of Isla Grande Airport (domestic), a large number of birds can be seen in this area. Yachts shelter at Club Nautico on the bay side of the bridge. Many airline offices are based here: Air Jamaica, Iberia, Arrow, Capitol, Viasa, Mexicana, Lufthansa, Dominicana. The French Consulate is in Edificio Centro de Seguros, Suite 412, Ave. Ponce de Leon 701. Miramar Guest House, Calle Olimpo 609 (tel. 723-0100), is on a quiet, shady street. Rates, including use of the kitchen, are $6 per night

The island's coat of arms looms over an urn displaying the island's 1952 constitution.

or $35 per week s; $8 per night and $45 per week d. Excellent value. Just around the corner at 605 Miramar is the much pricier Hotel Toro (tel. 725-5150) with restaurant, bar, and sundeck, from $18 s, $20 d. More expensive rooms ($22-25) are a/c and have kitchenettes. Farther up the price scale, Olimpo Court, 603 Miramar (tel. 724-0600), charges from $26 s, $27 d. Black Angus is a sleazy strip bar; the Little Place is gay.

SANTURCE-CONDADO

Once the most exclusive area in the city, Santurce is now deteriorating rapidly as businesses move over to the neighboring financial district of Hato Rey. Condado, the tourist strip on the main bus route between Old San Juan and the rest of the city, is as near to a perfect replica of Miami Beach as you'll find in the Caribbean. Check out the scene if you must. If you want to escape from Puerto Rico, this is the place to do it. Avenida Ashford, once famous for its hookers, now hosts male prostitutes and drug pushers. Whatever you do, keep off the beaches at night, or risk a mugging.

accommodations and food: Simar, 166 Villamil (tel. 723-9111), charges $24 s, $33 d (tel. 723-9111, 722-4048). Bolivar has rooms for $18.05 s, $22.25 d, and $29.25 and up t (tel. 727-3823). Tanama, 1 Joffre, charges $16 s, $30 d, $35 t (tel. 724-4160). Seaview, 1123 Seaview, has rooms from $20 s or d; tel. 723-8262. (Also see "Accommodations" chart pages 60-62.) A Chinese buffet—all you can eat for $5.95—is laid out daily from 1900-2200 at 6 Earle St., Condado. Salud, a natural health food restaurant and store, serves great food Mon. to Sat. 0900-2000 (tel. 722-0911). For a splurge, Vegetarian Restaurant and Guest House, Calle Cervantes No. 5, has good food in a romantic setting (tel. 724-3203). The Taj Mahal, 102 Magdalena Ave., has gourmet Indian fare.

entertainment: The Centro des Bellas Artes (Fine Arts Center, tel. 724-4751), largest and best of its kind in the Caribbean, is also the most attractive building in the entire area.

Since it opened in 1981, the Center has featured internationally acclaimed musicians, ballet stars, opera and experimental dance performances, lectures, drama festivals, jazz concerts, and musical comedies. Tickets cost up to $25; student discounts available. Be sure to get there early or buy tickets in advance if you want the cheaper seats. Nuestro Teatro presents plays dealing with Puerto Rican life and social realities. Gay bars include Bachelor and Topaz.

services and information: Located across from the Dupont Plaza on Ave. Ashford are information service centers for the Dominican Republic and the Virgin Islands. Bell, Book, and Candle, the city's leading bookstore, is at 102 De Diego. Alianza Francesa (Alliance Francais) is at 206 Rosario, Santurce. They have a library and present films and other cultural events. The Dutch Consulate is at First Federal Savings, Pda. (Stop) –23, Ave. Ponce de Leon.

HATO REY

Sometimes called "the Golden Mile" or "the Wall Street of the Caribbean," Hato Rey is notable only for its skyscrapers, those lyrical concrete-and-steel paeans to the wonders of capitalist endeavor. The huge federal complex, the offices of Fomento, and the Western Hemisphere overseas operations headquarters of the Chase Manhattan Bank are all located here. Without these, Hato Rey would be only a desolate, land-filled marsh.

Rio Piedras: This student area of the city has the University of Puerto Rico, the attractive Paseo de Diego (cheaper than the shopping malls), and a great market near the bus terminal. At the center of the campus stands the Roosevelt Belltower. Done up in a gaudy pink, it is Spanish influenced but bears a passing

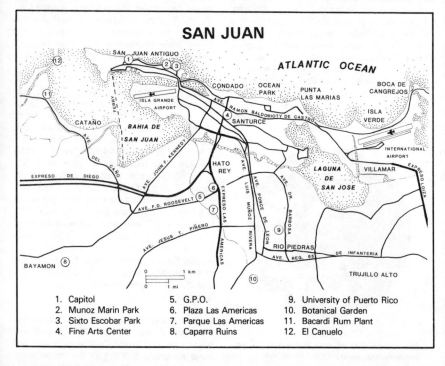

SAN JUAN

1. Capitol
2. Munoz Marin Park
3. Sixto Escobar Park
4. Fine Arts Center
5. G.P.O.
6. Plaza Las Americas
7. Parque Las Americas
8. Caparra Ruins
9. University of Puerto Rico
10. Botanical Garden
11. Bacardi Rum Plant
12. El Canuelo

pineapple: Although taken for granted today, arriving Spaniards marveled at this fruit. Indians would hang the fruit or its crown in front of their huts as an invitation to visitors. This custom was spread to the Old World by departing colonists in the 16th century. Learning of this custom from the Spanish, settlers in Virginia and New England adorned gateposts and door frames with carved pineapple decorations. Transportation of the pineapple was possible because the plant may be kept out of the ground for months but still grow when placed in moist soil. This enabled worldwide propagation of the plant, and today Puerto Rico is an insignificant producer on the world scale; the bulk of the world's pineapples are grown in Hawaii.

resemblance to a South Indian Tamil Nadu Hindu temple. Theodore Roosevelt donated the money and so received the dubious distinction of having it as his namesake. See the three sculptured heads set in back of the tower. The campus has a relaxed, laid-back atmosphere with students playing guitars and petting in the Jose M. Lazaro Library. Largest general library on the island, it contains the Juan Jiminez Room, which displays memorabilia belonging to the famous Spanish expatriate poet. A small but intriguing *museo* next to the library features archaeological artifacts as well as special art exhibitions. **Rio Piedras Market:** Located on De Diego Street. Its fairly wide aisles are numbered with signs showing which produce is being sold. Packed with fruits (pineapples, papaya, golden-skinned oranges), common and more exotic *(yuca, yautia)* vegetables, and island spices (ginger, mint, cilantro). An arcade section sells clothes. Visit in early morning when merchants and farmers unload trucks and pack booths. Savor the atmosphere.

food: Many cheap places to eat. Esquina Universidad, on the corner of Ponce de Leon and Gandara, is a popular student hangout. The owner here addresses students according to what island town they come from. But for even cheaper food during daylight hours, turn L onto Paseo de Diego from Ponce de Leon and find a sign marked SE SRVEN ALUMUEDOS. Upstairs, a lady serves fixed portions of meat and salad and all the beans and rice you can eat. There's also the usual assortment of fast-food places including a Taco Maker at Ponce De Leon 1000. Energy, a health food store and restaurant, is at Ave. Diego 2 (open Mon. to Sat. 0900-1500; tel. 764-2623). Sun y Cream, at Ponce de Leon 1004, is a cheap Chinese restaurant ($1.25 and up) which also serves ice cream. Tomas Ice Cream, across the street, is an attractive student meeting place with 85-cent cones.

entertainment: The Casals Festival takes place at the Performing Arts Center in May. The University also offers a cultural activities series which features ballet and classical music performances ($5) and avant-garde films. For information contact Dr. Francis Schwartz, Actividades Culturales, at 764-0000, ext. 2563/2567. Cine Teatro Rio Piedras, in addition to plays and concerts, offers films for $1.50 at 1230 and 1430 and all day on Wednesdays. Student price ($2) available for all other shows.

bookstores: Centro de Informacion y Servicios a la Mujer Reunion (tel. 751-5820) is a feminist bookstore on Calle Amalia Marin across from Burger King. Liberia La Tertulia, corner of Amalia Marin and Gonzales, and Libreria Hispanoamericano are open Mon. to Saturday. Other bookstores are located in Plaza Las Americas, Hato Rey.

Agricultural Experimental Station: Operated by the University of Puerto Rico. Still in Rio Piedras but way off in the boonies, take the no. 19 bus from Ochoa terminal in Old San Juan. Pack a picnic lunch. The Botanical Garden here is open Mon. to Fri. 0900-1630, and Sat. and Sun. 1000 to 1700; tel. 751-6815. There's no admission charge to visit this enchanting area, which includes an orchid garden with exotics like dendrobiums, epidendruns, and vandas and a palm garden featuring 125 species. Broad paths traverse an incredible range of vegetation, from a flaming African tulip tree and croton bushes to endless varieties of palms and ferns. Woody lianas hang from trees. Cool off in one of several libraries and check in the Forest Service office for detailed info about El Yunque.

practicalities: The General Post Office is on Roosevelt Avenue. Take a no. 8 bus from Plaza Colon, Old San Juan. Plaza Las Americas, a gigantic shopping mall, is a playground for the affluent; branches of Galerias Botello and Bell, Book, and Candle (bookstore) are located upstairs, while Thekes Bookstore is on the first floor. The British Consulate is located in Rm. 1014, Banco Popular Center, and the Canadian Consulate is located on the 16th floor of the Pan Am Building.

BAYAMON

A suburban municipality of San Juan, Bayamon has shifted from being an agricultural to an industrial community. More than 200,000 people and some 170 factories make their home here. Official tour guides wear elaborate cowboy garb because of Bayamon's nickname—*ciudad vacquero* or "cowboy city." Although it originated with

Los Vacqueros, the name of its winning baseball and basketball teams, the name is not inappropriate given the town's colorful atmosphere. **getting there:** Take bus no. 46 from San Juan.

sights: Just before Bayamon on Rte No. 2, km 6.4 at Guayanobo, are the ruins of Caparra, the first colonial settlement on the island. Established by Ponce de Leon in 1508, it was abandoned for the Old San Juan site 12 years later. Only the masonry foundations, uncovered in 1936, remain. To the rear, a small museum contains Taino artifacts and tools, weapons, and tiles found at the site. (Open Mon. to Fri. 0830-1200, 1300-1630.) Inside the municipality itself, directly across from the City Hall, the immaculately landscaped grounds of Central Park contain a country house which functions as a small museum, and the only locomotive train remaining in Puerto Rico, which runs through the grounds. This museum also displays artifacts excavated during archaeological digs at the site. Junghanns Park, several blocks to the W, features trees from all over the world which were planted by the local botanist of the same name. Adjacent to Bayamon's plaza and in the heart of the historical zone, the former city hall contains the Bayamon Art and History Museum. This recently restored neoclassic building is painted in shades of blue, pink, and yellow. Follow the *paseo* along to the Barbosa Museum (open Mon. to Fri. 0800-1200, 1300-1700). The interior of the house contains antique furniture, a small library, and memorabilia relating to Jose Celso Barbosa, journalist, physician, and political head of the pro-statehood Republican Party. Many other prominent Puerto Ricans have resided in Bayamon, including the realist-impressionist painter Francisco Oller.

events and festivals: An artisan's festival is held each May. Also held in early May is the traditional *fiesta patronales,* titled *Fiestas de Cruz.* Although this event has its origin in the 18th C., many of the original traditions connected with it have been lost. Once held in a local house, the main event (carrying the cross up the nine steps) now takes place along the Paseo Barbosa. Traditionally, a nine-step altar is prepared and lavishly adorned with flowers and royal palm leaves; candles are placed on each step. After the recitation of *El Rosario Cantao de la Santa Cruz* each night, the cross is moved up one step until, on the ninth night, it reaches the top. Traditional refreshments like *guarapo de cana* (sugarcane juice) are served at the end of each night's service.

shopping and crafts: Local craftspeople sell their wares in Central Park each Sunday. A feminist-run handicraft center, El Centro Feminista, is located at Calle F No. 8 Hnas., Davilas, Bayamon. Ariadina Saez, Calle 6A QQ19, Urbanizacion Cana, carves wooden flower replicas. **information:** Call Bayamon Tourism Office at 780-3056, ext. 280/281.

FROM SAN JUAN

San Juan can serve as an excellent base for becoming acquainted with the island, especially if you are renting (or have) your own vehicle; a good portion of the island may be comfortably explored in a day's excursion. Destinations like El Yunque, Loiza Aldea, and Humacao make good daytrips. There are also many small towns like Gurabo, Guaynabo, and Cidra which offer the visitor with limited time an inside look at Puerto Rican life. Aguas Buenas to the S is noted for its caves. Caguas (pop. 173,961) is the largest inland town on the island. Reserva Forestal de Vega Alta is located past Vega Alta on Rte. 2. Farther on is Manati. Founded in 1738, it has a number of attractive Victorian houses. Here, Hacienda La Esperanza, a 2,265-acre restored sugar plantation was once one of the largest on the island. Transformed into a living historical farm by the Conservation Trust of Puerto Rico, it may be visited with their permission. The entire U.S. supply of Valium and Librium is also produced in this town. Six beaches—Playa Mar Chiquita, Playa Tortuguero, Playa Chivato, Playa de Vega Baja, Playa Cerro Gordo, Playa de Dorado and a freshwater lagoon (Laguna Tortuguero)—lie along a series of winding roads along the coast to the N (find them using a good local roadmap). East of San Juan, near Fajardo and within easy reach of the sideroad to El Yunque, is Luquillo, the most famous beach in Puerto Rico. At the end of each day (1700), a white ambulance with screaming siren runs along the beach. Admission to the beach is free, but parking costs $1. On the eastern outskirts of San Juan are the Club Gallistico cockfighting pit and public beach at Isla Verde and, farther on, the Roberto Clemente Sports City. Dedicated to the memory of the famous Pittsburgh Pirate baseball demigod who died in a 1972 aircrash, *Ciudad Deportiva* has facilities for teaching sports to deprived children. Open daily 0900-1200, 1400-1900, it's on Calle Icurregui off the Los Angeles Marginal Rd. in Carolina. A bit farther, near Pinones along Carr. 187 lies Boca de Cangrejos ("Mouth of the Crabs")—a fishing village with a yacht club and tour boat launch: Sat., Sun. and holidays from 1200 *La Paseadora* tours the Torrecilla Lagoon amidst mangrove swamps and amongst the cries of the sanctuary's birds.

by bus: Buses leave from Puerto Rican Motor Coach station, Recinto Sur 327, Old San Juan, at even hours from 0600-1800. The route traverses Bayamon, Dorado, Vega Alta, Manati, Cruce Davila, Arecibo ($3), Hatillo, Camuy, Quebradillas, Isabela, Aguadilla ($5), and Mayaguez ($6). It's a four-hour trip from San Juan to Mayaguez. An alternative is to take one of the many *publicos* which travel all over the island and leave from numerous points scattered around Old San Juan and Rio Piedras. Hitchers will do well to take transport out of the urban congestion to a place where a thumb has room to breathe.

internal flights: Executive Air Charter flies to Mayaguez. Crown Air flies daily to Dorado, Palmas Del Mar, and Aguadilla. Vieques Air Link flies from San Juan's Isla Grande to Vieques six times daily and once on Sun. ($23 OW). Flamenco flies to Culebra from Isla Grande and Vieques.

for St. Thomas: Aerovirgin and Oceanair fly for $31 OW, $62 RT; $45 RT if you return the

PUERTO RICO AND THE VIRGIN ISLANDS

fers a $142, 17-day excursion fare. One-way fares are the same as RT excursion fares!

for Jamaica: Air Jamaica and Air British West Indies fly here. The $191 OW mileage ticket (or $292 RT excursion fare) includes stopovers in the Dominican Republic and Haiti. You may fly any of the airlines servicing the Santo Domingo/Port-au-Prince route and then continue on to Montego Bay and Kingston with Air Jamaica. As this includes the Montego Bay/Kingston internal flight, it's not a bad deal.

for the southern Caribbean: San Juan is a good jumping-off spot from which to explore this area. Arrow has $106, 17-day excursion fares to St. Maarten. Arrow flies to Georgetown, Guyana, for $428 RT. Air France offers 17-day excursion fares to Guadeloupe ($265), Barbados ($277), and Trinidad ($321).

for Latin America: Mexicana flies to Mexico for $240 OW and $426, 30-day RT excursion. Viasa flies to Caracas for $270 OW. Lufthansa flies to Bogota for $298 OW with a $411, 17-day excursion fare available. Iberia flies to San Jose, Bogota, Quito, Guayaquil, Lima, and Madrid; excursion fares available.

for the continental United States: Most cities are readily accessible through direct or interconnecting flights. Airlines include Delta, Capitol, Arrow, and Eastern. (See "Getting There" under "Introduction.")

same day, and a $99 RT "couple caper" which means that two people must travel together (i.e. $50 RT each). Once in St. Thomas, take a ferry to St. John from Charlotte Amalie ($4) or Red Hook ($2). **for St. Croix:** Oceanair has same-day return fares for $66. Regular fare is $38 OW and $76 RT. **for the British Virgin Islands:** Crown Air, and Air British Virgin Islands fly to Beef Island Airport, Tortola ($55 OW, $110 RT), and to Virgin Gorda.

for the Dominican Republic: Eastern flies for $114 RT, Dominican offers a $110 RT fare, and ALM flies on Mon. and Fri. with a 17-day excursion fare. Special monthly pass fares may be in effect. **for Haiti:** Air France and Air Jamaica offer three-day excursion fares for $104 and $108 respectively; Air Jamaica of-

NORTHEASTERN PUERTO RICO

LOIZA ALDEA AND ENVIRONS

Named after the Indian princess Luisa who died fighting beside her lover, the Spaniard Mejia, this area is the sole remaining center of Afro-Hispanic culture on the island. The *municipo* itself is divided into four parts—Pinones, Plaza, Mediana Baja, Mediana Alta. Its history dates back to the 16th C. when African slaves were brought in to work the sugarcane fields and pan for gold in the river. They were supplemented by escaped and recaptured slaves from other islands. Today, the majority of the 40,000 population are freed descendants of these Yoruba slaves. The local leadership is trying to deny the presence of African influence in the area, attempting to substitute Indian instead because there's no political capital to be gained from being black in Puerto Rico. The town itself was founded in 1719, and its San

Patricio Church (begun 1646) is the island's oldest active parish church. Loiza is one of the three poorest municipalities in Puerto Rico.

getting there: Possibly the most exciting part of the trip. Take the no. A7 bus from Old San Juan's Ochoa bus station to the end of the line in Pinones where many stalls serve traditional, African-influenced foods. From Pinones onward the feel of Africa is in the air. Hitch a ride and continue on the battered, sand-covered asphalt road which runs six miles along unspoiled white sand beaches (nicknamed the "lovers' lane of Puerto Rico"). Then cross the Espiritu Santo River on *El Ancon,* a hand-pulled, floating steel platform. An alternate but less spectacular route is to take a *publico* from Rio Piedras plaza.

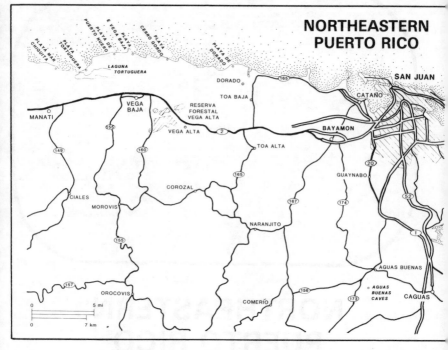

NORTHEASTERN PUERTO RICO

FIESTA PATRONALES DE LOIZA

Loiza's ten-day tribute to Santiago (St. James) is the most famous fiesta on the island. Saint James, first of Christ's disciples to be martyred, made a comeback during the Middle Ages when, descending from the skies on horseback, he slaughtered many Moors, thus ensuring a Spanish victory. His popularity with the *conquistadore* crowd confirmed by this action, he became their patron saint in the Old World as well as the New. Yoruba slaves were forbidden by their Catholic masters to worship the god of their choice, the omnipotent Chango, god of thunder, lightning and war. Noting the resemblance between their god and the Catholic saint, they worshipped Chango disguised as Santiago. In the early part of the 17th C., a fisherman on his way to work found a statuette of a mounted Spanish knight hidden in a cork tree, and he took it

home. When he returned to the house, the statue was nowhere in sight. Returning to the tree he again found it secreted, and brought it back home only to have the same thing happen. After the third occurrence, he took the statue to the local priest who, identifying it as Santiago, blessed it. The statue ceased wandering, and the local patron saint festivities commenced. Today, there are three images, the latter two brought from 19th C. Spain. Homage is paid to each image on separate days. The original, primitively carved statue, known as *Santiaquito* or "Little James," has been dedicated to children. The others are dedicated to men and women respectively. *Mantenedoras* (caretakers) take care of each of the three statues; they organize raffles and collect donations. Strings of *promesas* (silver charms), hanging from the base of the statues, are gifts from grateful devotees. These *promesas* are fashioned in the shape of the part of a body to be cured.

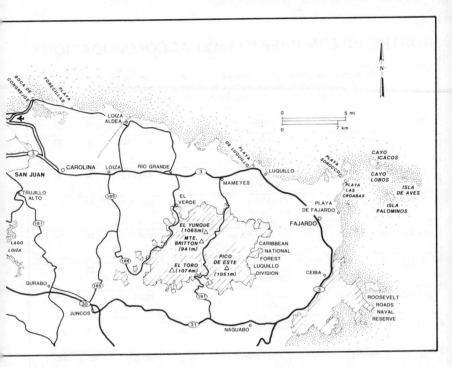

the festival: For nine days before the fiesta begins on 25 July, the *mantenedora* of Santiago de los Caballeros holds prayer sessions at her house during which elderly women and children chant rosaries and couplets honoring the saint. On the first day of the festival, a procession led by a flag-bearer proceeds to Las Carreras, the spot where the original statue appeared. Stopping at the houses of other *mantenedoras* along the way, the statues are brought out and both carriers and flag bearers kneel three times. The Loiza festival is famous all over Puerto Rico for the beauty and uniqueness of its costumes: *Vejiantes,* who represent devils, wear intricately crafted, colorfully painted coconut masks adorned with horns along the tops and sides. *Locas,* female impersonators with blackened faces, exaggerated bosoms, and wearing clothes that don't match, pretend to sweep the streets and porches along the way. *Caballeros,* who represent Santiago, wear brightly colored clothes,

ribbons and bells, and a soft wire mask painted with the features of a Spanish knight. *Viejos* wear shabby clothes and masks made from shoe boxes or pasteboard. Recently, the festival has been modified; outsiders, who know little of the traditions involved, now make up the majority of the participants. Consequently, the festival has become something of a carnival with *salsa* music replacing the indigenous *bomba y plena.* The festival is also becoming confused with Halloween: in 1982, E.T. won the prize for best costume.

crafts: The Ayala family, Carr. 187, km 6, hm. 6, in Mediana Alta, makes and sells the best festival masks. At Carr. 951, km 7, hm. 3, lives potter Ricardo Rivera.

from Loiza: Return to the plaza to catch a *publico* back to San Juan, or return via ferry and repeat the same process.

NORTHEASTERN PUERTO RICO ACCOMMODATIONS

Rates given are lowest and off season (mid-April through mid-December).
A range of prices may be in effect. Room tax is 6% additional.
Key: ★ = Price changes to $31.80 Friday to Sunday.

NAME	ADDRESS	TELEPHONE	S	D
Centro Vacacional U.I.A.	Carr. 187, km 8.8 Loiza Aldea	876-1446	30	30
El Verde	Carr. 186 Rio Grande	781-1237	34	34
Hotel la Ceiba y Fuente	Carr.959 Rio Grande	887-7511	48	52
Parador Martorell	6A Ocean Drive Luquillo	889-2710	25	34
Delicias	Puerto Real Beach Fajardo	863-1818	25	30
Family Guest House	Carr. 987 Fajardo	863-1193	25	28
Banana's	Flamboyan, Barrio Esperanza Vieques	741-8700	28	28
La Casa del Frances	Barrio Esperanza Vieques	741-3751	55	60
Ocean View ★	Calle Plinio Peterson Vieques	741-3696	17	32
Sea Gate Guest House	Barriada Fuerte Vieques	741-4661	35	35
Posada La Hamaca	68 Castelar St. Dewey, Culebra	742-3516	20	25
Seafarer's Inn	6 Pedro Marquez Oceanfront, Culebra	742-3171	15	20

EL YUNQUE
CARIBBEAN NATIONAL FOREST

Forty km SE of San Juan, the Luquillo Mountains rise abruptly from the coastal plain. Although El Toro at 3,526 ft. (1075 m) is actually the highest, the area is called El Yunque after the 3,493-ft. (1,065 m) peak. The Indian name *yuque* (white land) was transformed by the Spanish into *yunque* (anvil) which the peak does resemble when viewed from the north. Luquillo is a corruption of the supreme being Yukiyu, who the Indians believed lived among the mountainous summits. The only tropical forest in the U.S. National Forest system, its 27,846 acres contain 75 percent of the virgin forest remaining in Puerto Rico, the headwaters of eight major rivers, four distinct types of forest, and a wealth of animal and plant life.

getting there: Easily accessible by car, it's less than an hour drive from San Juan. Follow Rte. 3 from which Carr. 186 and 191 branch off. While 186 traverses the W boundary of the forest, 191 cuts through its heart. Hiking trails branch off this road. A landslide has closed 191 to traffic at km 13.5 so it's no longer possible to pass through to the south. Hitching along 186 and 191 can be slow, and there's no public transportation through the forest.

history: First protected under the Spanish Crown, the 12,400 acres of Crown Forest were proclaimed the Luquillo Forest Reserve by President Theodore Roosevelt in 1903. Since the creation of the first Forest Service office in the area in 1917, the reserve area has continued to grow; the name was changed to Caribbean National Forest in 1935.

flora: Encouraged no doubt by the more than 100 billion gallons of water that fall on the forest each year, the vegetation proliferates. There are four different types of forest which support 250 tree species, more than in any other National Forest. Only six of these 250

can be found in the continental United States. On the lower slopes is the *tabonuco* forest. Nearly 200 species of trees can be found here along with numerous small but attractive orchids. The dominant tree, the *tabonuco,* can be recognized by its whitish bark which peels off in flakes. Growing in valleys and along slopes above 2,000 ft. is the *colorado* forest. These short, gnarled trees often have hollow

El Yunque's colorado *forest*

trunks. Many are 1,000 years or more old. In one difficult-to-reach area is a 2,500-year-old *colorado* tree with a circumference of 23 ft., 10 inches. The palm forest, at the next level, is composed almost completely of *sierra* palms complemented by a few *yagrumos*. Masses of ferns and mosses grow underneath as well as on the trees. Limited to the highest peaks and ridges, the dwarf forest, composed of trees 12 ft. high or less, has vegetation (mosses, liverworts) which grow on the ground, tree trunks, and even on leaves.

fauna: Many rare species are found here, including the green, blue, and red Puerto Rican parrot *(Amazona uttata),* a protected species. Once common throughout the island, less than 50 now survive within the forest confines. Other birds, like the Puerto Rican tanager, the bare-legged owl, the quaildove, and the scaled pigeon, although rare elsewhere, are common here. Snakes are scarce, poisonous ones nonexistent; *coqui* frogs croak from every corner, and small fish, shrimp, and crayfish live in the streams.

the rare Puerto Rican parrot,
Amazona uttata

hiking: Among the 50 km of hiking trails, the principal trails include the El Yunque, Mt. Britton, Big Tree, and El Toro (Tradewinds). Trailheads are located on Carr. 186 at km 10.6 and on Carr. 191 at km 13.5. While La Coca Falls and Yohaku Lookout Tower are on or near 191, you must hike to reach La Mina Falls or Pico El Yunque and Los Picachos Lookout Towers. From the top of El Yunque on a clear day it's possible to see St. Thomas or even as far as the British Virgin Islands. Reach El Toro (392 ft., 1,074 m), one of the most remote peaks in the area, by the trail of the same name which begins near the aviary and workers' housing area along Carr. 191 at km 13.5. Follow the ridge W to the summit before descending to Cienega Alta, a forest ranger station located along Carr. 186. An alternative is to begin hiking at km 20, five or six km from Florida. Bring food (there's only one restaurant), waterproof clothing, hiking boots, and a compass. The trails are well maintained, but no fresh drinking water or toilet facilities are available. Although locals drink out of the mountain streams, it's not advisable unless the water has been treated first. Mamayes, along Rte. 3, is the last place to buy food.

practicalities: Best place to orient yourself is at the Sierra Palm Interpretive Service Center at km 11.6 on Carr. 191 (open daily 0930-1700). Obtain additional information by calling the Carolina Field Office at 877-2875, or by writing to Caribbean National Forest, Box B, Palmer, Puerto Rico. Detailed topographical maps are available from the U.S. Geological Survey, 1200 South Eads St., Arlington, VA 22202. Buy Puerto Rican snacks at stands along Carr. 191; meals are served at El Yunque Restaurant inside the park at the Service Center. Camping is permitted in most areas of the forest; permits are available at the Service Center. Other accommodations relatively close to El Yunque include Parador El Verde (tel. 781-1237), Carr. 186, km 17.6, which has a swimming pool and charges from $33.80 for rooms and Parador Martorell (tel. 889-2710), 6A Ocean Drive, Luquillo, which charges $25 s, $34-36 d.

boats at Fajardo

El Yunque's rainforest

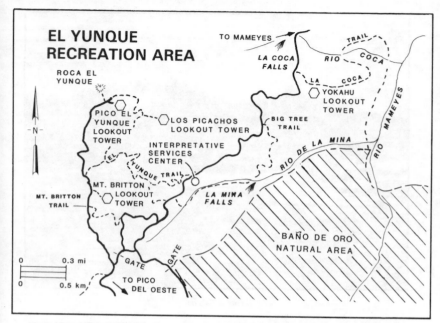

EL YUNQUE RECREATION AREA

ROCA EL YUNQUE

TO MAMEYES

LA COCA FALLS

RIO COCA

LA COCA TRAIL

YOKAHU LOOKOUT TOWER

PICO EL YUNQUE LOOKOUT TOWER

LOS PICACHOS LOOKOUT TOWER

BIG TREE TRAIL

INTERPRETATIVE SERVICES CENTER

YUNQUE TRAIL

RIO DE LA MINA

RIO MAMEYES

-N-

MT. BRITTON TRAIL

MT. BRITTON LOOKOUT TOWER

LA MINA FALLS

BAÑO DE ORO NATURAL AREA

0   0.3 mi
0   0.5 km

GATE   GATE

TO PICO DEL OESTE

FAJARDO

A small, sleepy town, it only comes alive during its patron saint festival (Santiago Apostol) every 25 July. *Publicos* go to the outlying areas of Las Croabas ($0.50) and La Playa-Puerto Real ($0.50) from the plaza. There's nothing much in Las Croabas either except Soroco Beach and a few restaurants. La Playa has a customs house, post office, and ferry terminal.

accommodations: Pitch a tent within the confines of Soroco Beach for $6 per tent. Cheapest place to stay is Express Guest House near Delicias Hotel for $18 s and $30 d. A "married" couple can share a room for $20.

Also try Family Guest House. (Also see "Accommodations" page 74.)

from Fajardo: *Publicos* for Luquillo ($0.50), Rio Piedras ($2.50), Juncos, Humacao, etc. leave from the town plaza. **for Culebra:** Ferry leaves on Sat., Sun. and holidays at 0900, Mon. at 0915 via Vieques. Cargo ferry departs Tues. to Sat. at 1600 daily at 0915 and 1630. Cargo ferry departs Mon. to Fri. at 0700 and 1100 ($2, takes one hour, 30 min.). Five flights daily with Vieques Air Link ($11 OW, $22RT). **for St Thomas;** Jennie Tours departs for Charlotte Amalie from Marina Puerto Chico (on the way to Las Croabas) on Sat. and Sun. at 0900. ($20 OW, $35 RT). Returns at 1630. **for Icacos:** Rent a sailboat or sail your own to this deserted island. Camping permitted.

VIEQUES

Seven miles off the eastern coast of Puerto Rico, this paradisical island has a special, distinct magic. Its name comes from the Taino word *bieques* ("small island"). Horses roam freely all over the island, dotted with the ruins of pineapple and sugar plantations and more than 40 magnificent beaches. Undoubtedly, Vieques would have become one of the major tourist destinations in the Caribbean were it not for the fact that over 70 percent of its 26,000 acres was arbitrarily confiscated by the U.S. military in 1941. Locals have suffered much at their hands: noise from air and sea target bombardment, annoying in itself, was devastating when coupled with the structural damage to buildings and the dramatic decrease in the fishing catch caused by sea pollution. Population plummeted from 14,000 in 1941 to the present 8,000; many left to find work in San Juan, St. Croix, or elsewhere. Bombing has now ceased, much of the land has been let out for grazing purposes, and military manuevers have been substantially reduced (though Vieques was the site of a rehearsal for the 1983 Grenada invasion). A cultural festival is held in Isabel Segunda every February.

history: First explored in 1524 by Capt. Cristobal de Mendoza, former governor of Puerto Rico, Vieques was occupied at various times by the British and French until it was formally annexed by Puerto Rico in 1854.

getting there: A bumpy but beautiful hour-long trip by launch from Fajardo. Pass by Isleta Marina, Palominos, Lobos, Isla de Ramos, and other small islands. Passenger ferries leave daily from La Playa at 0915 and 1630. Cargo ferries (which also carry cars and bicycles) leave Mon. to Fri. at 0700 and 1100.
by air: Vieques Air Link flies from San Juan's Isla Grande ($23 OW, six times daily), Fajardo ($11, five times daily), Humacao ($18, twice daily), and St. Croix ($25, twice daily).

ISABEL SEGUNDA

An exceptionally attractive town with many shops selling flowers and a 121-year-old church. Locals ride horses through the main streets while dogs sleep placidly under cars. The town plaza has a bust of Simon Bolivar, who paid a visit to Vieques in 1816, and a 19th C. city hall.

Fort Isabella Segunda: The last Spanish bastion undertaken in the Caribbean (1843), this fort, which dominates the town, was never finished. To get there turn R at the plaza

ISLA DE VIEQUES

and follow the hill up. Meticulously restored with beautifully finished wooden staircases, cannon, etc. Inside a watchman naps to the sound of a blaring radio. **others:** Puntas Mulas Lighthouse is nearby. Davies Base is just outside town. At the entrance obtain permission to visit the beautiful and isolated Green, Red, and Blue beaches, imaginatively named by the Navy. According to legend, a 16th C. island chief hid the sacred treasures of his tribe from the *conquistadores* in a large cave at the top of Mt. Hirata, highest point on the island. The roar you hear inside the cave is his ghost. Archaeolgical digs are being conducted at La Hueca. Mosquito, the long pier on the isolated NW coast, was built to shelter the British fleet in the event England fell to Germany in WWII.

accommodations and food: Many small

Isabel Segunda's Punta Mula lighthouse stands near the relaxed and placid town.

but not especially cheap hotels in town including Hotels Alvarez, Depakos, Carmen, and Vieques. The Ocean View (tel. 741-3696), on Plinio Peterson, charges $16.96 s, $31.80 d, Mon. to Thurs., and $31.80 s or d on weekends. Small cafeterias abound. The Panaderia, on the main street, has sweets made using local fruits and *parcha* juice. Also try El Yate, Starboard Light Cafe, Ocean View Restaurant, and Boricua Bar. A very attractive ice cream and frozen banana place is across the street. Also try El Yate, Starboard Light Cafe, Ocean View Restaurant, and Boricua Bar — all near the center of town.

ESPERANZA

Second largest community on the island. Taxis ($1) meet arriving ferries. The 1963 film, *Lord of the Flies,* was filmed here; see the hangar-like structure that remains. Many eccentric expatriates live in this area. Meet garrulous but personable Irving who runs La Casa Del Frances. Or, rather, he'll meet you. There's a *balneario* at Sunbe (Sun Bay) beach, a long, gorgeous stretch of palm trees and placid ocean. Hike to Navio and Media Luna beaches nearby. The latter has a cave at one end. There's also a dive shop ($30 s tank, $45 d) and night excursions to the phosphorescent bay.

accommodations and food: It's possible to camp at the *balneario* at Sun Bay ($4 per tent). Note, however, that this beach is notorious for thieves — *never* leave anything unattended. Villa Posada Parador has the cheapest rooms at $16 s, $20 d, as well as delicious, authentic, reasonably priced food (like fish *asopao*, $3). Fresh, piping-hot traditional Puerto Rican bread is available early mornings at Gerena Bakery. Colmado Lydia, next door, is well stocked with provisions. Banana's (Flamboyan, Barrio Esperanza, tel. 741-8700), charges $55 per room and up. Sea Gate Guest House (Barriada Fuerte, tel. 741-4661) charges from $35 per room, including free airport pickup and delivery. Irving's La Casa de Frances (Barrio Esperanza, tel. 741-3751) charges from $55. Also try Duffy's.

CULEBRA

This miniature archipelago, consisting of the seven-by-four-mile island of Culebra, and 24 other islands, cays, and rocks, is completely unspoiled and set apart from the world. Twenty-two miles E of Fajardo, much of the land, which includes dry scrub and mangrove swamps, has been designated as a National Wildlife Refuge.

getting there: Cheapest and best is to take a *publico* from Rio Piedras to the dock at Fajardo. Then board the ferry, which takes a scenic two hours to Dewey on Culebra. A passenger ferry ($2.25) leaves on Sat., Sun., and holidays at 0900 and Mon. at 0915. Cargo ferries leave Tues. to Sat. at 1600. (The difference between cargo and passenger ferries is chiefly that the passenger ferries leave on time.) A ferry also runs from Vieques to Culebra ($2) on Sat. and Sun. at 1100, and Mon. at 1230. An alternative is the 20-min. flight from San Juan's Isla Verde Airport ($23 OW).

history: Under Spanish rule, Culebra and surrounding islands were designated as Crown lands. Transfer to the U.S. in 1898 specified that these lands be used for their "highest and best use." Accordingly, an executive order Roosevelt signed in 1903 surrendered the lands to Navy control. Eight years later, Roosevelt, after reconsidering the matter, ordered that the lands serve the secondary purpose of a "preserve and breeding ground" for native seabirds. In 1936, the Navy (perhaps assuming noise improves fertility among nesting seabirds) began strafing and bombarding Culebra and surrounding islands. Even today, Flamenco Peninsula, a tern nesting area, is dangerous to explore on foot because of unexploded bombs. After long years of protest, both by locals *and* by the commonwealth government, bombing was finally halted in 1975. Since then, the local population has swelled to more than 2,000.

flora and fauna: The Culebra group has a huge sea bird population; several species have developed large breeding colonies on Flamenco Peninsula and surrounding offshore cays. Of the more than 85 species, the most numerous is the sooty tern which arrives to nest between May and October. The sooty

This cartoon from a 1971 issue of Claridad, an independentista newspaper, depicts an invasion of the island by militants to the evident chagrin of the officer who, holding a bombing permit and shouting through a megaphone, insists on the U.S. Marines' proprietary rights. The use of Culebra and Vieques as target ranges and bombing sites is an emotional issue in Puerto Rico. Although bombing was halted in 1975, much land that could be well put to better uses remains in the hands of the military.

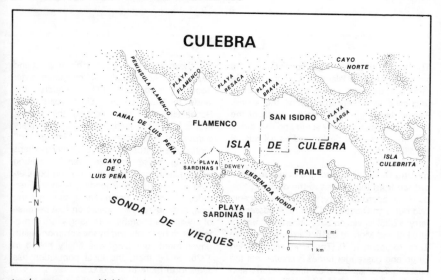

tern's eggs are highly prized by local poachers. There are four other species of terns, three of boobies, the laughing gull, Caribbean martin, osprey, and other birds. Brown pelicans, an endangered species, live in the mangrove trees surrounding Puerto de Manglar on Culebra's E side. Small herds of cattle stroll amidst the bombed wrecks of Army tanks. The seldom-seen Culebra giant anole (a huge lizard), resides in the forested areas of Mount Resaca. Four species of marine sea turtles breed on Culebra's beaches: the Atlantic loggerhead and green sea turtles, the hawksbill, and the leatherback. Leatherbacks may reach a length of 6.5 feet (two m) and weigh up to 500 kg. These turtles have been exiled from one Caribbean beach to another by poachers and developers. Here too, despite the threat of stiff penalties under the Endangered Species Act, local poachers value the eggs as a protein source and an aphrodisiac. As a well-developed, interdependent ecosystem, Culebra's flora is inseparable from its fauna. Mangrove forests surrounding the coasts provide a roosting ground for birds above the water while sheltering sea anemones, sponges, and schools of small fish among the tangle of stiltlike roots in the shallow water. Nearly 80 percent of Culebra's coastline is bordered by young and old coral reefs. Multicolored miniature mountain ranges of brain, finger, elkhorn, and fire corals shelter equally colorful and numerous schools of tropical fish.

crafts: Amparo Riviera Rios, Barriada Clark Casa No. 274, carves *coqui* frog replicas and makes articles with snail shells. Rosa Garcia de Feliciano, Calle Escudero 63, makes ceramics and articles from snail shells.

from Culebra: Passenger ferries depart Sat., Sun., and holidays at 1500 and Mon. (via Vieques) at 1330. Cargo ferries depart Tues. to Sat. at 0700. Flamingo Airways flies daily to San Juan's Isla Grande Airport; it may be possible to board morning mail flights to St. Thomas if there's space.

Dewey: When the Navy moved onto Culebra in 1903, locals living in settlements scattered all over the island were forcibly resettled in the newly created town of Dewey (or Puebla), built on what had formerly been a swamp. This small town has five *colmados* (grocery stores) and a couple of hardware stores. No movie theaters or (thankfully) video arcades. Only time the town comes to life is during the

BIRDS OF PUERTO RICO

tropic bird

frigate bird

brown pelican

hummingbird

oyster catcher

tern

black-crowned night heron

red-footed boobie

Fiesta de La Virgen del Carmen on 17 July. Bring your mask and snorkel because the real life is under the water. A pair of binoculars will also come in handy for viewing bird life.

accommodations and food: Currently, camping has been prohibited on Flamenco Beach because of the risk of damaging turtle nesting sites. It's possible to camp on Zoni, a totally isolated beach on the island's E side, but you have to be completely provisioned, including water. Seafarer's Inn, 6 Pedro Marquez (tel. 742-3171), $15-20 s, $20-30 d. Posada la Hamaca, Calle Castelar 68 (tel. 742-3516) is $20 s, $25 d. Punta Aloe Villas (tel. 725-2438) charges $70 s or d. Villa Boheme at Ensenada Honda (tel. 742-3508) has rooms available for $290 d per week, including use of kitchen, car, boats, and windsurfers.

Culebrita: Can be reached only by fishing boat or private yacht. Its century-old stone lighthouse overlooks a large bay and lagoon. Along with neighboring Luis Pena Cay to the W, it is a wildlife refuge site open to the public for daytime use. (Other cays require special use permits available from the Fish and Wildlife Service, Box 510, Boqueron, P.R. 00622.) Heavily covered with vegetation including gumbo-limbo trees, frangipani, and bromeliads, the island provides haven for many rare and endangered species of animals and birds. Red-billed tropic birds live in cliffs along the island's E shore while mangrove swamps are home to birds and marinelife. A 1980 plan, now discarded, would have transferred ownership to the Puerto Rican government so that the island could have been converted to recreational use, a move which would have been ecologically disastrous.

SOUTHEASTERN PUERTO RICO

Roosevelt Roads: Located near the town of Ceiba, this is the most important American base in the Caribbean, home of the Atlantic Fleet Weapons Range, the most advanced technical training area in the entire Atlantic. "Springboard," the full NATO fleet annual exercises, are conducted from here.

Humacao: A small inland town whose *fiesta patronales* takes place around 8 December. Palmas Botanical Gardens, 130 Candalero Abajo, has 208 acres (84 ha) of plants and trees plus a greenhouse. Cayo Santiago, a small island off the coast, contains a large colony of rhesus monkeys which are being specially bred for scientific experiments by the U.S. Public Health Service. No visitors permitted.

accommodations: Cabins are rented out at Centro Vacacional Punta Santiago by Fomento for $20 per night (see "Accommodations" under "Introduction").

Reserva Forestal Carite (Guavate): This relatively small (6,000 acres) but refreshingly cool (average temperature 72 degrees F) and moist forest reserve contains sierra palms, teak, and mahogany. It borders Charco Azul, a 30-foot-wide cool blue pool and undeveloped Lago Carite (which features an abandoned housing project). A bit of dwarf forest surrounds the communication tower which mars the 3,000-ft.-high Cerro La Santa peak. The reserve also includes Nuestra Madre—a Catholic retreat, Campamento Guavate—a minimum security penal facility, four picnic areas, and a camping spot. Permission to camp must be obtained in advance from the Department of Natural Resources in Puerto de Tierra, San Juan.

Arroyo: A small town on the W coast founded in 1855. Calle Morse, the main street, was named for the inventor Samuel Morse who arrived in 1848 to oversee installment of telegraph lines. His visit was undoubtedly the most thrilling event that has occurred here before or since the town's foundation. Several 19th C. houses, with captain's walks on the roofs, were built by New England sea captains who settled here. *Publicos* are the only regular

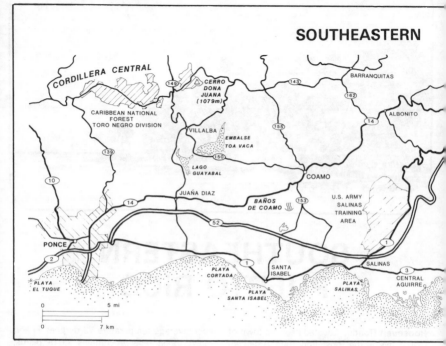

SOUTHEASTERN

transport. **accommodations:** Cabins at Punta Guilarte are rented out by Fomento to "bona fide family groups" for $20 per night. There is a two-night minimum stay, and they must be booked 120 days in advance. (For more information see "Accommodations" under "Introduction.")

Aibonito: Aibonito (from Artibonicu, "River of the Night," the Taino name for this region), a small but colorful town set in a valley and surrounded by mountains, has a Mennonite community, well-tended flower gardens, and boasts Puerto Rico's lowest recorded temperature (40 degrees F in 1911). Once an important tobacco and coffee growing area, Aibonito is now known for its poultry farms and processing plants as well as its factories which produce pharmaceuticals, clothing, electronic goods, and hospital equipment. The town's best-known celebration is its Flower Festival. Taking place from the end of June through the beginning of July, colorful

flowers (including gardenias, anthuriums, and begonias), gardens, and exhibits occupy 10 acres.

sights: Standing next to the town plaza, the twin-towered San Jose Church dates from 1825; it was reconstructed in 1978. Now notable only for its spectacular view, Las Trincheras ("The Trenches") marks the spot where the last battle of the short-lived American 1898 invasion was fought—a skirmish which took place the day after the armistice had been signed! Another famous panoramic landmark is La Piedra Degetau, a large boulder overlooking the town and on the site of the Farm of Federico Degetau Gonzales, former Resident Commissioner in Washington, D.C.

Barranquitas: At 1,800 ft., Barranquitas is not only one of the highest towns on the island, but also one of the most beautifully situated. Viewed from the massive volcanic

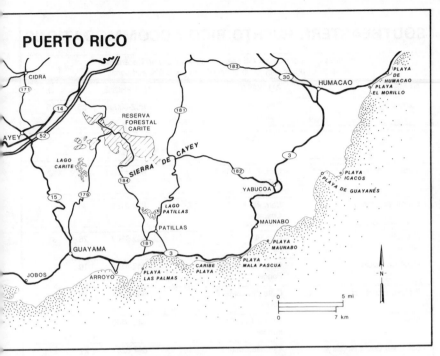

PUERTO RICO

rocks that cradle it, it resembles a Spanish medieval print. The Catholic church towers above houses which seem to have been built right on top of each other. Its chief claim to fame is as the birthplace of Puerto Rican statesman Luis Munoz Rivera (see "History" under "Introduction"). At the Museo Biblioteca, in the wooden house where he was born in 1859, a small museum displays letters, pictures, newspaper clippings, a car used in his funeral procession (in 1915), furniture and other items. *Mauseleo de Don Luis Munoz Rivera,* Calle Munoz Rivera, located next to the tomb where Don Luis Munoz are buried, documents his funeral vividly with objects and papers relevant to his demise. Also present are the skeleton of a 12-year-old Taino lad and religious relics. Barranquitas celebrates its *fiesta patronales,* San Antonio de Padua, around 13 June. The National Crafts Fair is held here in July.

vicinity of Barranquitas: Indian relics have been found in a number of caves near the town. Nearly inaccessible, the deep gorge of San Cristobal Canyon located along the road to Aibonito is the most spectacular on the island. Precipitous cliffs, densely covered with vegetation, plunge 500 ft. to a rocky valley where the Usabon River races over boulders, dropping 100 ft. at one point. Catch a glimpse from Carr. 725 (and side road 7715), 156, and 162. Best of these is from the San Cristobal Development on Carr. 156, km 17.7. An unmarked trail leads into the gorge from here.

COAMO

This small town has its old church set in a plaza enlivened by flowering bouganvillea. Once the site of two flourishing Taino Indian villages, only a solitary Indian remained at the time of the town's founding in 1579. As the third oldest town on the island (after San Juan and San German), its name, San Blas de Ilecas

SOUTHEASTERN PUERTO RICO ACCOMMODATIONS

All rates given are lowest, off season (mid-April to mid-December);
A range of prices may be in effect. Room tax is 6% additional.

NAME	ADDRESS	TELEPHONE	S	D
Palmas del Mar	Carr. 923 Humacao	852-6000	65	75
Caribe Playa	Carr. 112 Patillas		38	38
Villas del Abey	Carr. 3, km 153.4 Salinas	853-4730	26	32
Banos de Coamo	Carr. 46, km 1 Coamo	825-2186	35	40
El Coche	Carr.14 Ponce	842-9607	26	31
Hotel Comercio	Calle Comercio Ponce	842-4120	10	10
Professional Hotel	Calle Concordia 64 Ponce	840-0201	15	20
Melia	2 Calle Cristina Ponce	842-0260	41	45
San Jose Guest House	47 Calle Cristina Ponce	842-0281	21	27

de Coamo, was derived from the patron saint of a major landowner—an expatriate from Illecas, Spain.

sights: Its Catholic church is decorated with paintings by internationally renowned Puerto Rican artists Jose Campeche and Francisco Oller. The latter's "Cuadro de las Animas" features a blonde (rumored to be Oller's girlfriend) being tortured in purgatory. One of the church's three bells—said to have sounded so loudly that its vibrations killed fish off the coast and shattered lamps and glass in nearby homes—has been silenced by public pressure for over a century. An elegant two-story mansonry mansion, built by Clotilde Santiago, the town's wealthiest and most powerful farmer and entrepreneur during Spanish rule, still stands at one corner of the plaza. Converted to a museum, it now houses historical memorabilia, gold-plated bathroom fixtures, and mahogany furniture. Call City Hall (tel. 825-1150) to make an appointment to see the museum. The town's major landmark, however, is not a building but a group of hotsprings. First used by the Indians, the springs gained an international reputation by the end of the 19th century. Some assert that they are the Fountain of Youth Ponce de Leon had heard about from the Indians before leaving to search for it in Florida. To reach them, take the road outside of town going toward the Banos de Coamo Parador, a government-run inn recently built on the site of the Coamo Springs Hotel, which once sheltered the likes of Franklin Delano Roosevelt. Proceeding past the *parador*, turn L to find the springs.

accommodations: Only choice is Banos de Coamo, outside town on Carr. 46, km 1; $35 s, $40 d.

PONCE

Set between the blue of the Caribbean and the green of the Cordillera Central mountain range, Ponce is a city of many names. It is known as "La Perla del Sur" (The Pearl of the South), "La Ciudad Senorial" (Manorial City), and "La Ciudad de las Quenepas" (City of the Honeyberries). Ponce has played host to many prominent islanders, including opera tenor Antonio Paoli, composer Juan Morel-Campos, and painter Miguel Pou. Though it's the second largest city in Puerto Rico (pop. 200,000), Ponce has much more the feeling of a small town than bustling metropolitan San Juan. From the impressive art museum to the colorful firehouse on its main plaza, the city has much to offer the visitor. Established in 1692, Ponce was named after Juan Ponce de Leon y Loaiza, the great-grandson of Puerto Rico's first governor, Ponce de Leon. Originally, Ponce was a town with only two entrances: one would enter either via a mountain road passing by the Church of La Guadalupe or along the road that borders the S coast. Point of entrance was La Ceiba de Cuatro Calles (Ceiba of the Four Streets) which led, as it still does today, to the main streets of Commercio, Cruz, Salud, and Mayor. During 1877-78 when it was granted the title of *Ciudad* (city), Ponce was already the social, military, and commercial center of the S coast.

getting there: Approachable by bus from Utuado ($2) or Adjuntas, or by *publico* from Rio Piedras, Santurce, Mayaguez, or other neighboring towns.

SIGHTS

Ponce's beautiful plaza with its fountains and gardens is dominated by the sugar-white Cathedral of Our Lady of Guadalupe. Built in

Ponce's firehouse, the Parque de Bombas

1670, it was destroyed several times by earthquakes. In the center of Plaza Las Delicias, a bronze Luis Munoz Rivera, first elected governor of Puerto Rico, gazes out over the banks, travel agencies, and video game parlor that surround the plaza. Also in the center of the plaza is the Fountain of the Lions, a monument dedicated to eight brave citizens who risked their lives in 1899 to extinguish a fire in the munitions depot that might have spelled disaster for the city, and a monument to Juan Morel Campos, known as the father of the

Puerto Rican *danza* (see "Music and Dance" under "Introduction"). Born in Ponce in 1857, his *danzas* are still played in Puerto Rico and many of his symphonic works have received international recognition. Situated just off the plaza is Ponce's gaudy landmark the *Parque de Bombas* or firehouse. Painted red, green, black, and yellow, it has become the symbol of the city. Sole survivor of several buildings constructed for an agricultural fair held in 1882, it was donated to the homeless firemen in 1885 and has been in active use ever since.

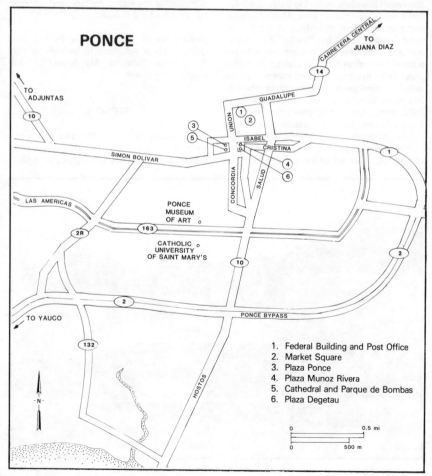

PONCE

TO JUANA DIAZ

TO ADJUNTAS

GUADALUPE

UNION

ISABEL

CRISTINA

SIMON BOLIVAR

CONCORDIA

SALUD

LAS AMERICAS

PONCE MUSEUM OF ART

CATHOLIC UNIVERSITY OF SAINT MARY'S

TO YAUCO

PONCE BYPASS

HOSTOS

-N-

CARRETERA CENTRAL

1. Federal Building and Post Office
2. Market Square
3. Plaza Ponce
4. Plaza Munoz Rivera
5. Cathedral and Parque de Bombas
6. Plaza Degetau

0   0.5 mi

0   500 m

Enter and see the second-floor exhibits. From one of the balconies, the municipal band entertains on Sun. nights.

Ponce Museum of Art: Ponce's most renowned attraction is the Ponce Museum of Art, on Ave. Las Americas across from Universidad Catolica Santa Maria. Open weekdays 1000-1200 and 1300-1600, Sat. 1000-1600, Sun. 1000-1700, closed Tues.; $1.50 admission. Designed by architect Edwin Stone and financed by conservative multimillionaire industrialist and former Governor Don Luis Ferre, this block-long building uses natural light to lend a spacious effect to its hexagonal galleries. It contains the best collection of European art in the entire Caribbean. From an original 400 works, the collection has grown to include more than 1,000 paintings and 400 sculptures. Three sculpture gardens branch off the main floor, and two dynamic, 18th C. polychromed wooden statues carved in Toledo, Spain, representing Europe and America, greet the visitor near the entrance. Besides portraits and the representative works of Puerto Rican master painters like Jose Campeche and Francisco Oller, the first floor also contains a 15th C. Siamese *bodhisattva* bust, intricate Incan pottery, and fine hand-blown decorated glass pieces. The second floor holds many fine sculptures and old European thematic religious paintings: plenty of blood, breasts, and skulls. See St. Francis at prayer and Pero feeding Cimon with her breast. Also works by masters like Van Dyck, Reubens, Velazquez, and Gainsborough are included. When visiting the museum weekdays, allow for the fact that it closes one hour for lunch, and everyone must leave the building.

others: La Ceiba de Ponce, an enormous 300-year-old silk cotton tree, overhangs Calle Comercio about one km E of the plaza. Once a meetingplace for the Taino Indians, it was recreated in one of Franciso Oller's paintings. El Vigia Hill, on Rte. 1 near Calle Bertoly, is a famous lookout point surrounded by homes of the wealthy upper class. In the distant past, a watchman, noting the arrival of a visiting merchant vessel, would raise a flag which in-

interior of museum

dicated its nationality. On a clear day, it's possible to see Caja de Muertos offshore, a small island named for its coffin-like shape.

Tibes Indian Ceremonial Center: Located in a suburb of Ponce; take a *publico* ($0.50) from the vicinity of the *mercado* to get there. (Open daily 0900-1630; $1.50 admission.) Predating the Caguana site near Utuado, it was discovered by Luiz Hernandez, a local resident, in 1974. Archaeological evidence suggests two distinct periods of occupation: during the latter phase of the Igneri culture from A.D. 400-600, and within the pre-Taino period from A.D. 600-1100. Both cultures were similar in terms of diet and lifestyle; cultural differences were due to an influx of new blood from outside or transitions in style over time. The older Igneri period is characterized by animal-shaped amulets, ceramic vessels, and axes. The majority of the 182 graves excavated here, which contained the remains of children along with ceremonial offerings, date from this period. Other ceramics, and objects such as frog-shaped amulets, *cemi* figures, and adzes, are from the later pre-Taino period. ***bateyes:*** Ten ceremonial *bateyes* have been reconstructed. Petroglyphs, with animal and human faces, have been chiseled on some of the stones which delineate the *bateyes*. The largest *bateye*, measuring 111 by 118 ft., is bordered with walkways containing riverbed stones. (The area of Tibes derives its name from these stones; *tibes* is the Taino word for smooth, riverbed stones.) These *bateyes*, known colloquially as ballparks, were multipurpose in use. While some were used for a game resembling soccer, others were used for *areytos*, ceremonial dances in which Indians, drinking beer made from fermented cassava and inhaling hallucinogenic *cajoba* seeds through a two-pronged pipe, would commune with the gods. There are no records as to what they talked about, but presumably they touched on politics, food, and sex. One elliptical *bateye* is surrounded by triangles, which suggests that it represents the sun. The major archaeological find at Tibes, an adult male skeleton discovered within the foundations of a walkway bordering one of the *bateyes*, has been dated at A.D. 790, which has pushed back the date of the earliest known Indian stone constructions by 400 years. Besides the *bayetes*, a small Taino village nearby has been faithfully recreated. There is also a small museum, and bilingual guides are available.

PRACTICALITIES

accommodations: Many hotels are clustered around the main square. Hotel Comercio, Calle Comercio, is cheapest at $10 per night s or $25 per week (tel. 842-4120). Hotel Belgica, Calle Villa, has $10 rooms available, but these are used only for short-time prostitution; you must take a $12 room. Professional Hotel, Calle Concordia 64, charges $15 s, $20 d, a/c with bath, (tel. 840-0201). San Jose, Calle Cristina 45, is $21.20 s and $26.50 for

bateye *at Tibes Ceremonial Center*

Don Q's Seralles Mansion on El Vigia hill

matrimonia, $31.80 d, $37.10 t (tel. 342-0281). El Coche, Rte. 14, has rooms for $20.20 s and $25.50 d. Also try Hotelio Argentino, Calle Luna, Hospedaje Mi Hogar ($20/week), Calle Sol 66, and the Texan Hotel near the bypass.

food: Streets are literally packed with cafeterias and restaurants. Cafeteria Chealy, Calle Isabel, serves a 99-cent breakfast special. Max's Cafe Villa has great seafood (squid, shellfish) and meat sandwiches. Cheddy's Pizza on Calle Union has a cafeteria. Try Scissor's Restaurant near Perla Cheater. Find fast-food places along Ave. Las Americas.

entertainment: Ponce's discos include La Nueva Discoteca, Calle Aurora, and Cowboy, Calle Commercio. Latin music can be found at El Sol Restaurant, Ave. Munoz Rivera, in front of Santa Maria Shopping Center. For movies try the Rivioli on Calle Leon, Ponce Twins, Calle Constacia, and El Emperador at the bypass.

events: The annual patron saint festival of Nuesta Senora de Guadalupe, held from 6-16 Dec., centers on the main plaza. *Salsa, merengue,* and jazz bands play, and *bomba y plena* dancing is supplemented by *aguinaldo* music. A variety of foods are served, and *artesanias* sell their wares. *Feria Regional de Artesanias,* a crafts fair, is held each Feb., and the *Festival de Bomba del Bo. San Anton* is held in November.

crafts and shopping: Antonio Rodriguez Acosta, Calle Martin Corchado 33, makes *torneros* (morter and pestles). *Santero* Domingo Orta works at Calle Lorencita Ferre, Final 139, Sector El Tuque. Juan Alindato, Puerto Viejo No. 18, Playa de Ponce, makes *caretas* (masks). Onofre Riviera Torres, Callejon Nueva Atenas 10, manufactures maracas. Ponce's modern *mercado* is an air-conditioned showplace with fruit and vegetables, spices, bottles of pure honey, gigantic avocados, and drinking coconuts ($0.65). Shop 138 has pigs' tails, ears, and snouts for $1 a pound—a great buy! Feet are even cheaper at $0.55 a pound; best quality assured. There's also Nirvana

Laundry which undoubtedly offers heavenly service. *Botanicas* (shops selling spiritualist literature and goods), tailors, and other shops are upstairs. At No. 49, charming handmade stuffed cloth black *madama* dolls start at $6.

services: Ponce Tourism Office (tel. 844-5575), corner of Cristina and Mayor, is open Mon. to Fri. 0800-1630. At the small municipal library nearby, shorts are *verboten* under pain of expulsion by the resident guard.

from Ponce: Numerous *publicos* and very occasional buses depart from the areas surrounding the plaza and *mercado* for local destinations and Guayama ($2.50), Yauco, Coamo, etc. Get an early start or you'll feel like a roast chicken while waiting for them to fill up. Linea Atlas Trans Island (tel. 842-1065/4375), with offices on the plaza, will take you to Rio Piedras ($6), Santurce ($8), and directly to Isla Verde Airport ($15). The first of nine *publicos* daily departs at 0400. Either reserve a seat or just hunt one up when you're ready to leave.

SOUTHWESTERN PUERTO RICO

YAUCO

Built on a hillside W of Ponce, this small town still has its step streets, old houses, great coffee, and a distinctly Spanish-American atmosphere. The Coffee Festival is held here in Feb., while the festival of patron saint Nuestra Senora del Rosario comes around 7 October.

history: Originally known to the Indians as Coayuco, the surrounding area was settled by the Spanish, becoming an independent municipality in 1756. Haitian French, Corsicans, and other immigrants began arriving in the early 1800s. Sugarcane and cotton gave way to coffee cultivation. Low in caffeine but rich in taste, Yauco's coffee became famous in Europe for its exceptional quality, soon commanding a high market price. The loss of European markets after the Spanish-American War, combined with the devastation caused by a hurricane in 1899 and competition from mass-producing countries like Brazil and Colombia, sadly led to the decay of the local coffee industry.

practicalities: La Casa Roig, Calle Betances 10, has rooms; $4-6 s, $7-15 d. Richard's Hotel, Calle 25 July, has rooms from $4. *Publicos* go to Ponce ($1.50), Guanica-Guayanilla, and Sabana Grande.

Guanica: Reserva Forestal Guanica, several beautiful beaches, and the place where the Americans landed during the 1898 invasion are all situated around this pleasant town of 9,000. The reserve itself is one of the finest examples of cactus-scrub-subtropical dry forest in the world. It has recently been designated by the United Nations as a "Man and the Biosphere Reserve." Vegetation inside the reserve includes *aroma* (acacia) and *guayacan* *(lignum vitae)* trees as well as 700 other species. The *guabairo* (Puerto Rican whippoorwill) survives on the island only in this

SOUTHWESTERN PUERTO RICO

above, clockwise: sugarcane cutting, Dominican Republic (Roger LaBrucherie); coffee beans, Dominican Republic (R. LaBrucherie); coffee harvesting, Padre las Casas, Dominican Republic (R. LaBrucherie); rum distillery near Ponce, Puerto Rico (R. LaBrucherie); sugarcane harvesting near Ponce, Puerto Rico (R. LaBrucherie)

above, clockwise: Condado area of San Juan, Puerto Rico (Roger LaBrucherie); Government Hill, St. Thomas, USVI (USVI Division of Tourism); Main Street, Charlotte Amalie, St. Thomas, USVI (USVI Division of Tourism); lamp on building, Old San Juan, Puerto Rico (R. LaBrucherie); boys in front of store near Arecibo, Puerto Rico (R. LaBrucherie)

reserve. Be sure to catch the view of Guanica and the bay from the top of the stone tower. **accommodations:** Copamarina (tel. 842-8300), on Carr. 333, charges $34 s, $42 d.

Sabana Grande: Founded mostly by Spanish nobility and members of venerable Spanish families, the locals here set up their own government during the Spanish-American War. It lasted only a few days. The *fiesta patronales* of San Isidoro Labrador takes place around 15 May. This small community is chiefly noted for the miracle which occurred here. One day in 1953, a group of schoolchildren chanced upon the Virgin Mary while pausing at a brook near the town. After chatting a few minutes with the children, the Virgin promised to return on 25 May. When a group of 130,000 devotees arrived on that date at the spot, the Divine Lady failed to show up. However, many of the chronic ailments and diseases of those present were reportedly cured on the spot. Many eyewitness reports attest to serious diseases cured by the healing power of the brook where the Virgin was seen. Numerous small shrines and a large chapel have been erected to commemorate the miracles that took place here.

SAN GERMAN

Second oldest and certainly the most attractive town on the island, San German retains its quiet colonial charm and distinguished architecture. The atmosphere is distinctly Mediterranean. Local legend insists that the swallows of Capistrano winter here. The town is named after Spain's King Ferdinand's second wife, Germaine de Foix, whom he married in 1503. Today's population are descendants of the pirates, Corsicans, smugglers, poets, priests, and politicians of days past. Although the pirates and sugar plantations may be gone forever, a feeling from that era still lingers in the town.

sights: Two rectangular plazas in the center of town face each other, separated only by the city hall, a former prison. Martin Quinones

entrance to Porta Coeli

Plaza boasts San German de Auxterre Church. Built in the 19th C., its wooden vault, painted in blue and grey, simulates a coffered ceiling. The second plaza, Parque de Santo Domingo, now bordered with black iron and wooden park benches, was originally a marketplace. The Church of Porta Coeli ("Gate of Heaven"), the town's main attraction, rises dramatically from the end of the plaza (open Wed. to Sun. 0900-1600). Twenty-four brick steps lead up to the white walls of the entrance. Originally constructed by Dominican friars in 1606, it is believed to have been connected by tunnels to the main monastery which no longer exists. Restoration was completed in 1982. While the palm wood ceiling and tough, brown *ausobo* beams are original, the balcony is a reconstruction. It's set up to resemble a working chapel rather than a museum, but Mass is held here now only three times a year. Treasures gathered from all over have been placed along its sides. Exhibits range from choral books from Santo Domingo to a surly

17th C. portrait of St. Nicholas de Bari, the French Santa Claus. Others include a primitive carving of Jesus found in San Juan, several lovely 19th C. Senora de la Monserrate Black Madonna and Child statues, and a representation of San Cristobal with a part from one of his bones inserted.

SOUTHWESTERN PUERTO RICO ACCOMMODATIONS

All rates given are lowest, off season (mid-April to mid-December); a range of prices may be in effect. Room tax is 6% additional

NAME	ADDRESS	TELEPHONE	S	D
La Casa Roig	10 Calle Betances Yauco	856-1941	5	15
Copamarina	Carr. 333 Guanica	842-8300	34	42
Parador Oasis	Calle Luna San German	892-1175	35	39
Boquemar	Carr. 101 Cabo Rojo	851-2158	31	43
Cabo Rojo Guest House	Calle Munoz Rivera 24 Cabo Rojo		10	20
Cuestamar	Carr. 307, km 7.4 Cabo Rojo		40	40
El Combate Guest House	1st St., Parcelas El Combate, Cabo Rojo	754-9061	30	30
Perichi's Beach Colony	Carr. 102, km 14.2 Barrio Joyuda, Cabo Rojo	851-3131	35	39
Posada Porlamar	Carr. 304 Lajas	899-4015	25	35
Viento y Vela Guest House	Carr. 304, km 3.2 Lajas	899-4698	30	30
Villa Parguera	Carr. 304 Lajas	899-3975	48	48
El Sol	Calle Sol Este 9 Mayaguez	834-0303	28	36
Hotel Lugo	58 Calle Mendez Vigo Mayaguez	832-9485	8	12
Hotel Sultana	Calle Maquila 57 Mayaguez		15	20
Hotel Venezia	62-0 Calle Mendez Vigo Mayaguez	833-1948	8	15
Hacienda Juanita	Carr. 105, km 23.5 Maricao	838-2550	25	30

near Porta Coeli: The residence of Mrs. Delia Lopez de Acosta contains decorative murals on the inside. The Perichi home on Calle Luna is another classic. Mrs. Olivia Perez's home on Calle Esperanza fulfills the fantasies associated with having a home in the tropics. The lovely grounds of Inter American University are on the edge of town just off the road to Cabo Rojo.

accommodations: Hospedaje Porta Coeli, Ruiz Belvi's 34, is three doors from Porta Coeli. If full, try Hotel Matos in Barrio Minillias, or Motel Rosal on Rte. 2. Oasis is a classically styled hotel on Calle Luna (tel. 892-1175/1345), $34.68 s with a/c, $32.92 d, $46.92 t; extra cot $6. La Pension is a guesthouse located on the grounds of Inter American University; for information or booking contact Javier Boscio, Prof. of Social Sciences, Inter American University, San German, P.R. 00753.

Hormigueros: This town, whose name means "ant hill," owes its name to the unique topography of the region. Originally a *barrio* of San German, later of Mayaguez, it became a distinct town in 1874. Hormigueros is home to the Shrine of Our Lady of Monserrate, a majestic yellow church which towers above the town. According to a 17th C. legend, a peasant working in the field where the church now stands saw an enraged bull charging toward him. After pleading with Our Lady of Monserrate to protect him, the bull stumbled and fell; the man managed to escape and the church was erected in thanksgiving. In commemoration of the miracle, the devout arrive on a religious pilgrimage, and each 8 Sept., climb the long bank of steps leading to the church on their hands and knees. See the oil painting by Jose Campeche, which portrays the miracle, on a wall inside the church.

Cabo Rojo: A small town and convenient jumping-off point for Mayaguez or destinations to the south. Founded in 1772, the San Miguel Arcangel Church was erected in 1783 next to the plaza. It reached its peak of prosperity in the 1800s, when immigrants from Spain and other Mediterranean countries,

fleeing revolutions in Europe, arrived to take up sugarcane cultivation. Today, the canefields have been displaced by pasture for cattle. Cabo Rojo's *fiesta patronales* takes place around 29 September. Joyuda Beach, with its 18 seafood restaurants, is off Carr. 102 to the northwest. To the W, nearly half the island's fish are caught at Puerto Real. When it served as Cabo Rojo's port (1760-1860), merchandise and slaves from St. Thomas and Curacao were off-loaded here. At Ostiones, a point of land protruding to the N of Puerto Real, is an important Indian archaeological site.

accommodations: Cabo Rojo Guest House, 25 Munoz Rivera, has fine, very clean rooms, $10 s, $20 d, $25 t. Frank Moralles' house at 46 Carmelor resembles a yellow castle. Common refrigerator, $12 s, $20d, $25t. (Also see "Accommodations" chart page 98.)

statue of La Senora de la Monserrate inside Porta Coeli

BOQUERON

Located S of Cabo Rojo and W of San German is the small town of Boqueron, and the western branch of the Bosque Estatal de Boqueron (Boqueron Forest Reserve). Herons perch on mangroves in the bird sanctuary here. The town itself is well known for its *balneario* (public beach), as well as its oysters and other types of seafood. Cabo Rojo Lighthouse is on Carr. 303. It stands along a spit of land between Bahia Salinas and Bahia Sucia. Beneath the lighthouse, jagged limestone cliffs at Jaguey Point drop 2,000 ft. into the sea. Once inhabited by the lighthouse keepers and their families who occupied the two wings at its base, it is now electrified and automatic. This lighthouse was built in 1881 under Spanish rule in response to pressure from local planters. Behind it lies the Sierra Betmeja, low hills which date back 130 million years. The Salinas salt beds are nearby; salt harvested here is sent off to the Starkist plant in Mayaguez. El Combate, a fishing village to the N of the salt beds, has an unmistakable 19th C. aura about it. Farther to the N at Guaniquilla are Buye and La Mela beaches; the neighboring lagoon at Guaniquilla Point harbors strangely shaped boulders which protrude from and dominate the still waters of the sometimes dry lagoon. Birds squeal and cry overhead. Pirate Roberto Cofresi, who terrorized the coast during the early 19th C., hid out in a cave nearby.

accommodations: The government agency Fomento rents out cabins to "bona fide family groups" (i.e., parents and children) for $20 per night. There is a two-night minimum stay, and they must be booked 120 days in advance. (For more information see "Accommodations" under "Introduction.") Camping is available around the Cabo Rojo area: Villa Plaza at Denigno Obejo Plaza is on Carr. 301 at km 6.9 (tel. 851-1340). Villa La Mela is at Carr. 307, km 35, Cabo Rojo (tel. 851-1391/2067). Mo-jacascade Camp is at Carr. 301, km 10.1, Playa Combate, Cabo Rojo (tel. 745-0305).

LA PARGUERA

Located off Carr. 304 is the eastern branch of Bosque Estatal De Boqueron, commonly referred to as La Parguera, after the town of the same name. This area contains what is probably the most famous marine attraction in Puerto Rico. La Bahia Fosforescente (Phosphorescent Bay) contains millions of luminescent dinoflagellates, a microscopic plankton. Any disruption or disturbance causes them to light up the surrounding water. Pick a moonless night and take one of the twice-nightly boats (times vary) departing

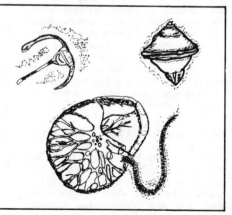

The dinoflagellates which produce luminescence are a variety of protozoan known as "whippers," single-celled animals with one or more tiny projecting flagellum—*lashes or whips*. Because multibillion-member blooms of dinoflagellates drain the surrounding water of dissolved oxygen, they poison the water for fish. Dinoflagellates luminesce only when disturbed; the glow of the species on the far right, *Noctiluca miliaris*, dims in radiance when anesthetized, and these microscopic unicellular creatures have been found to possess a time clock which limits the intensity of their flashes to the late-night hours.

from Villa Parguera's pier ($2). Dip a hand in the water and watch as sparks of liquid silver run through it. (Bahia Mondo Jose, nearby, also has a large population of dinoflagellates.) The small town lights up on weekends when there's live entertainment. Offshore are more than 30 mangrove cays. Check on transport out to Mata de la Cay, two miles offshore. Visible from the outskirts of town is Isla Cueva. It's commonly known as Monkey Island because 400 monkeys reside there. Originally from India, they are allowed to pursue their favorite pastimes freely among the trees. Occasionally, a group of scientists arrives to check up on their habits. Rosada Beach is E of town. **accommodations:** Expensive. Cheapest is Posada Porlamar, Carr. 304, with rooms for $25 s, $35 d, $42 t, extra person $5.

MAYAGUEZ AND VICINITY

Despite its reputation as a center of industry, this western port, the third largest city on the island, still retains much of the grace and charm suggested by its lovely name, taken from *majagua*—the Indian name for a tree plentiful in the vicinity. In addition to its zoo and agricultural research station, Mayaguez is a good place to base yourself for day trips to Maricao, San German, and the many beaches and small towns in the area.

getting there: Easily reached by *publico* from San German or Ponce and by bus from San Juan ($6), Arecibo, Aguadilla, or Rincon.

sights: Almost completely destroyed by an earthquake in 1917, one of the premier sights in this largely rebuilt city is the impressive Plaza de Colon, with its monstrous statue of Columbus, surrounded incongruously by statues of Greek maidens. The old post office building is on Calle McKinley nearby, as is the Yaguez Theater. In 1977 this theater was purchased by the federal government and declared a Historical Monument. Renovated, expanded, and modernized at a cost of $4.5 million, it presents all types of stage productions and is a center for artistic, cultural, and educational activities in the community. The Mayaguez Zoo is home of innumerable reptiles, birds, and mammals, presented both in cages and in simulated natural habitats. See everything from Bengal tigers to *capybara*, world's largest rodents. Located on Carr. 108 at Barrio Miradero; open Wed. to Sun. 0900-1600, $1 admission; tel. 832-8110. Much closer to town is the tropical Agricultural

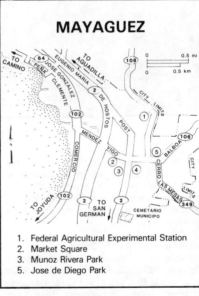

1. Federal Agricultural Experimental Station
2. Market Square
3. Munoz Rivera Park
5. Jose de Diego Park

Research Station on Carr. 65, between Calle Post and Carr. 108, located next to the University of Puerto Rico at Mayaguez. (Open Mon. to Fri. 0730-1200, 1300-1630. Free admission; tel. 832-2435.) Established at the beginning of this century on the site of a former plantation, the grounds present a dazzling array of exotic vegetation ranging from a cinnamon tree from Sri Lanka to pink torch ginger to the traveler's tree. While you're here be sure to check out the Parque de los Proceres (Park of the Patriots) across the street.

Red mangrove forests near Mayaguez

events: Mayaguez's festival honoring her patron saint, *La Virgen de la Candelaria,* around 2 Feb. each year, is among the most spectacular on the island. The annual crafts fair is held at the beginning of each Dec. at the coliseum.

accommodations: Cheap, clean, and spacious is Hotel Venezia, 62-0 Calle Mendez Vigo (tel. 833-1948). Rooms with fans or a/c are priced at $8 s, $15 d, and $21 t. Also good is Hotel Lugo, 58 Mendez Vigo, (tel. 832-9485); $8 s, $12 d. Next step up the price ladder is Hotel Sultana, Maquila 57; $15 s, $20 d, $24 t, all rooms a/c. Hotel Plata's a/c rooms cost $18 s, $24 *matrimonia,* and $34 d. El Sol, 9 El Sol, is $28 s, $36 d, tel. 834-0303. Hotel Embajador, 11 de Augusto Oeste, charges $30 s, $32 d, $42 t. La Palma (tel. 876-1446), also on Mendez Vigo, charges from $28 s, $36 d. More a run-down boarding house than a hotel, Miranda is at 265 Post, conveniently located next to the municipal cemetery in case you're in town to visit a dead relative or attend a funeral. Inquire about rooms at the ice factory below.

food: Plenty of small, cheap lunchrooms, fast-food places, and restaurants. Veggies can eat at Appleseed's Restaurant near Hotel Venezia.

entertainment: Pretty dull even on weekends. Best thing to do is walk around and watch the kids hanging out and trying to be cool just as they do in any other town large or small on the island and everywhere else in the world. See if Teatro Yaguez has a show on. Funkiest local hangout is Maravillosa Music Club on Calle Jose de Diego.

from Mayaguez: *Publicos* leaving for surrounding towns depart from the area around the plaza. If heading for Maricao, get an early start. The Puerto Rico Motorcoach station for points N and Old San Juan ($6) is on Calle

Jose de Diego. Departures at 0600, 0900, 1100, 1300, 1500, 1700, 1800. A pleasant six-hour trip along Rte. 2, climbing up and down slopes, and passing by Anasco, Aguada, Isabela, Quebradillas, and other points en route.

MARICAO (MONTE DEL ESTADO)

Maricao is a small coffee-trading center near Monte del Estado, a forest preserve which, confusingly, is also called Maricao. The preserve is one of the driest areas on the island. At the Maricao Fish Hatchery, more than 25,000 fish are reared and schooled yearly in preparation for their journey to lakes and fishponds. Open daily 0730-1200, 1300-1600. A trail, starting at km 128 on Carr 120, leads from Maricao ridge down to the hatchery.

accommodations: Apply for permission to camp at the Dept. of Natural Resources, Puerto Del Tierra, San Juan, tel. 724-3724/3623. Cabins at the Centro Vacacionales hold six and cost $20 per night. Maricao or Monte del Estado also has picnic grounds, an observation tower, and a swimming pool. Climb the stone tower for a commanding view of SW Puerto Rico. On a clear day, you can even see the cliffs of Mona Island off in the distance. More expensive is the Hacienda Juanita, Carr. 105, km 23.5. Facilities include swimming pool, tennis and other ball courts, and hiking trails.

MONA

Least known and least accessible of all Puerto Rico's offshore islands, Mona lies in the southern center of the Mona Passage. Viewed from the air, this 20-sq-mile island appears as a perfectly flat oval surrounded by offshore coral reefs. Situated 50 miles to the W of Mayaguez, the only ways to reach it are by fishing boat from Mayaguez, private plane, or yacht. Nine miles of rough trails lead from the S shore through the dense foliage to the nor-thern, rock-littered mesa, which gives way on three sides to a sheer 200-ft. drop to the sea below. The plateau is covered with low-lying trees and orchids, and the indigenous rock ig-uana *(cyclura)* scuttles furtively between rocks. Some grow as long as four feet. The only other land animals—wild boars, bulls, and goats—are descendants of livestock kept by the long-vanished pirates. The only native food is prickly pears. Water is in short supply so bring your own.

history: Mona's history is steeped in romance, much of which carries over into the present. Discovered by Columbus during his second voyage in 1493, it later became a port of call for Spanish galleons. Ponce de Leon stopped here to secure a supply of cassava bread on his way to take up his command of Puerto Rico. By 1584, most of the native In-

Iguanas, prized by man for their eggs and succulent flesh; Mona I. is one of the few places where it still survives in the Caribbean.

dians had been exterminated. A network of stalactite and stalagmite-filled underground caves, containing pools of spring water used to supplement the average annual rainfall of 41 inches, served as a home for pirates for nearly three centuries. Fireplaces, cooking utensils, fragments of sabers, and chains have been found inside. On the W end of the plateau are the ruins of a lodge which date from the 1930s and '40s when Mona was a popular weekend getaway for sports fishermen. Legend has it that the remains of a Spanish galleon lie just off the lighthouse and radio beacon, manned by the U.S. Coast Guard on the E end of the island.

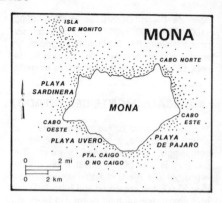

NORTHWESTERN PUERTO RICO

RINCON

Although the name of this small town means "corner" (which suits its location perfectly), the town is actually named for Don Gonzalo Rincon, a 16th C. landowner. He granted a hill, known as *cerro do los pobres* ("hill of the poor"), to local settlers. When the town was founded years later, they named it for their benefactor. There are a half-dozen bathing beaches in this area, including Punta Higuero, where the World Surfing Championships were held in 1968. A reef to the N of town has a marina and charter boats available to take divers over to the National Wildlife Refuge surrounding Desecheo Island.

sights: Rincon's Catholic church, facing the E end of the plaza, is built on the very site which Santa Rosa de Lima, the town's patron saint, recommended when she appeared in a vision. A small chapel dedicated to her — containing plastic flowers and a model boat — stands on a ridge just beyond the intersection of Carr. 414 and Ramal 414. Pico Atalaya ("lookout peak"), easily recognizable because of its communication tower, commands a great view of the environs. A silver water tank, the sole reminder of a railroad which passed from San Juan to Ponce between 1907 and the early 1950s, stands on Cambija Street. The ruins of the storehouses and residences of the Corcega Sugar Mill (constructed 1885) remain behind trees where Corcega Beach meets Carr. 429. Rincon's lighthouse, rising 98 feet (30 m) above the sea at Higuero Point, was built by the Spanish in the early 1890s. Today, the electric 26,000-candlepower rotating beacon is unmanned. At the end of the road passing by the lighthouse are the rusting remains of the Boiling Nuclear Superheater Plant. BONUS, as it was so quaintly named, was the first nuclear energy plant in Latin America. It began operation in April 1964, but closed down a decade later after leaks occurred.

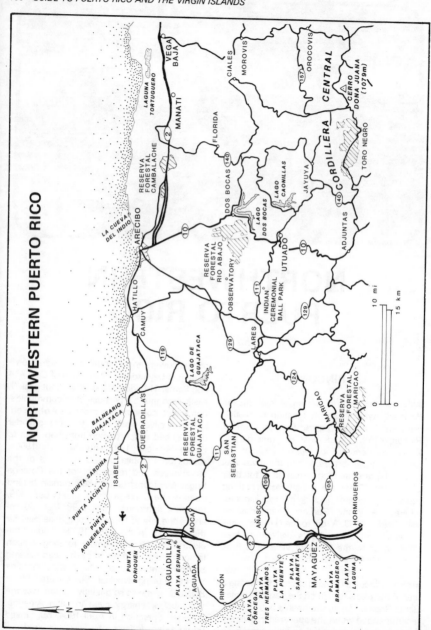

NORTHWESTERN PUERTO RICO

accommodations: Cheapest is La Primavera. on Carr. 429; from $15 s and $20 d. More expensive is Villa Antonio Beach Resort at Carr. 115, km 12.3 (tel. 823-2645/2285); $25 s, $32 d; apartments start at $25 and cabins from $50. Camp at your own risk at Playa de Corcerga, Rte. 2 Salida 115.

AGUADILLA

Located on Carr. 111 along the W coast, this small town boasts fine beaches, intricate lace, and fascinating historical sites. Christopher Columbus first stepped onto Puerto Rican soil somewhere between Aguadilla and Anasco on his second voyage in 1493. Since then it's undergone numerous changes! Recently the population (52,000) has declined owing to the economic depression caused by the phasing out of Ramey Air Force Base. Beaches (great snorkeling) extend from Crash Point to the north. (Crash Point receives its name from the launches kept here to pick up crews in the event of a plane crash around Borinquen Point.) Aguadilla is famous for its *mundillo* (finely embroidered lace) which was introduced to the area by immigrants from Belgium, Holland, and Spain. Bosque Estatal de Guajataca and Lago de Guajataca are located 30 km to the E of Aguadilla.

sights: Ramey Air Force Base has been converted into Punta Borinquen, a tourist complex with complete sports facilities. Playuelas Beach is divided by what was once the pier and docking facilities for submarines and fuel tankers. Punta Borinquen Lighthouse, located W of town, has been designated a historic site worthy of preservation by the National Register of Historic Places. Severely damaged by the 1918 earthquake, this tower, built in 1870, was incorporated into Ramey Air Force Base as a picnic area. Near the city's N entrance, between the foot of Cerro Cuesto Villa and the beach, lies the Urban Cemetery, established on what had once been a sugarcane hacienda. Although the 1918 earthquake destroyed many of the old tombs, those remaining are finely sculpted Italian marble. Borinquen Archaeological site, the only signifi-

cant Indian site in the region, was excavated by Dr. K.G. Lathrop of Yale in the 1920s. Objects found include human skulls, shells, animal bones, and potsherds. Fort Concepcion is the only remaining building from the Fuerte de la Concepcion mlitary complex which was protected by a moat, walls, and guard and sentry houses. Extensively remodeled, it now houses schoolrooms. A statue of Columbus, built in 1893, stands inside seaside Columbus Park. El Parterre Park contains *ojo de agua,* a natural spring which once served as the water supply for arriving sailors.

accommodations: Rent cabins at Punta Borinquen off Carr. 107 for $60 per night (tel. 890-6128/6330). Camp freely but insecurely at Playa Crashboat, Rte. 2, Salida 458, Aguadilla. Parador Montemar (tel. 891-5959), Carr. 107, km 125.4, has rooms $45 s, $55 d.

events: In honor of the world-famous composer, the Rafael Hernandez Festival is held yearly from 22 to 24 October; his music is interpreted by soloists and orchestras. Festivities surrounding the town's *fiesta patronales* go on for the two weeks around the main feast day of 4 Nov. on the main plaza. Music is performed and local specialties are cooked. Another lively time is the *Velorio de Reyes* (Three Kings Celebration). Initiated 30 years ago by a wealthy local family, a religious ceremony with music, prayers, and chants takes place on the plaza on the evening of 6 January.

from Aguadilla: Arrow Air flies three times a week from Punta Borinquen Airport to New York City.

ARECIBO AND VICINITY

This simple but refreshing town on the Atlantic is more of a transit point or base for exploring the rest of the area than a destination in itself. The town comes alive during the annual feast of San Felipe Apostol on or around 1 May. A good jumping-off point for the beaches to the E or the mountains to the south. **getting there:** Halfway point on the main San Juan-Mayaguez bus route. Buses ($3) pass through every two hours. Another approach would be from Ponce via Utuado, but allow for plenty of time.

sights: The town's name is derived from Aracibo, an Indian chief who had a settlement here, and a cave (La Cuevo del Indio) four miles E of town that was used for Indian ceremonies before the arrival of the Spaniards. Bear petroglyphs adorn the walls.

accommodations and food: Highly recommended is Hotel Plaza, Ave. Jose de Diego 112 (tel. 878-2295) $8.48 s, $21.20 d, $31.30 t. Campsites are at San Isidro Village, Rte. 2 km 85, Hatillo or at Punta Maracaya Camping Area, Justo Rivera, Rte. 2 km 84.6 (tel. 878-7024/2157). Plenty of cafeterias around.

Arecibo Observatory: Hitch a ride on Sun. out to this amazing concrete, steel, and aluminum anachronism located to the S of town when it's open to visitors from 1400-1630. Reach it via roads 10, 651, 635, 625; a special access road leads up to it. The 600-ton platform, largest of its kind in the world, is a 20-acre dish set into a gigantic natural depression. Using this telescope, Cornell University scientists monitor pulsars and quasars and probe the ionosphere, moon, and planets. Unlike other radio telescopes which have a steerable dish or reflector, the dish at Arecibo is immobile, while the receiving and transmitting equipment, which hangs 50 stories in the air, can be steered and pointed by remote-control equipment on the ground. Although it costs $3.5 million annually to operate this facility, it has been responsible for several major discoveries, including signals from the first pulsar and proving the existence of the quasar.

forest reserves: Lying to the E of Arecibo near Carr. 682, Cambalache Forest Reserve, a

NORTHWESTERN PUERTO RICO ACCOMMODATIONS

All rates are lowest, off season (mid-April to mid-December);
a range of prices may apply. Room tax is 6% additional

NAME	ADDRESS	TELEPHONE	S	D
La Primavera	Carr. 429 Rincon		35	35
Villa Antonio Beach Resort	Carr. 115, km 12.3 Rincon	823-2645	25	32
Villa Cofresi	Carr. 115, km 12.3 Rincon	823-2450	40	49
Parador Guajataca	Rte. 2, km 103.8 Quebradillas	895-3070	52	55
Parador Vistamar	Carr. 113, km 7.9 Quebradillas	895-2065	37	42
Hotel Plaza	Ave. Jose de Diego 112 Arecibo	878-2295	9	21
Hacienda Gripnas	Carr. 527, km 2.5 Jayuya	721-2884	25	30
Hotel Cerro Gordo	Carr. 690, km 4 Vega Alta	883-4370	30	30

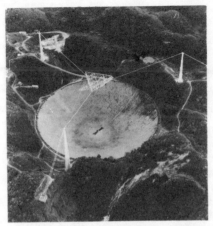

The dish of the Arecibo Observatory is the largest of its kind in the world.

914-acre (370 ha) subtropical forest, has 45 different species of birds. Great for hiking and picnicking. The same is true of Guajataca Forest Reserve with its limestone sinkholes and haystack hills. Sandwiched between Quebradillas to the N and San Sebastian to the S, Carr. 446 slices it in half. Cabralla, one of the longer of the 25 miles of hiking trails, ends at Lago Guajataca. Maps are available at the ranger station. Camp Guajataca here may be rented on weekends when available; for information contact the Puerto Rico Council of Boy Scouts in San Juan at 767-0320. Rio Abajo State Forest is S of Arecibo. Elevations reach 1,400 feet. Here, the most rugged karst formations are found. This 5,080-acre forest was established in 1935. Although balsa, mahogany, pine, and other trees are found here, it is dominated by Southeast Asian teak. A recreational center and picnic ground is open 0800-1800. In all of these reserves, camping is permitted with permission obtained from the Dept. of Natural Resources in San Juan 15 days in advance.

Dos Bocas Lake: Located at km 68 on Rte. 10 at the junction of the roads to Jayuya and Utuado from Arecibo and lying parallel to Rio Abajo. Its name means "Two Mouths." This long, beautiful, and winding reservoir was created in 1942. Three launches run scheduled (0700, 1000, 1400, 1700) two-hour trips around the lake. Although these free trips are provided as a service for local residents, visitors are welcome to join. A one-hour trip to Barrio Don Alonso leaves daily at 1240.

UTUADO AND VICINITY

This small, sunny mountain town is a stronghold of traditional *jibaro* culture and is one of the best places to experience Puerto Rican mountain culture. Local buses run from Jayuya, Arecibo, and up from Ponce via Adjuntas. *Publicos* also ply these routes as well as connecting with other towns in the area.

sights: Near Utuado is Caguana Indian Ceremonial Park and Museum, the most important archaeological site in the Caribbean, (open daily 0900-1700; museum open Sat. and Sun. 1000-1600). To reach it, take a bus or *publico* ($1) or hitch 12 km E along Carr. 111 to Lares. Originally excavated by the famous archaeologist J.A. Mason in 1915, the park has been restored and established under the auspices of the Institute of Puerto Rican Culture. Don't expect much; although a loyal band keep up the grounds, the funds needed for guides and markers have not been supplied because the government is intent on downplaying local culture in order to prepare a suitable image for statehood. The 10 *bateyes* (ball courts) are situated on a small spur of land surrounded by fairly deep ravines on three sides. The largest rectangular *batey* measures 60 by 120 ft. (20 by 37 m). Huge granite slabs along the W wall weigh up to a ton. A few are carved with faces (half-human, half-monkey) which are typical of Taino-Chico culture. One has deep, cuplike, haunting eyes. La Mujer de Caguana, most famous of all the petroglyphs, is a woman with frog legs and elaborate headdress. Originally, all of the slabs were decorated with reliefs, but these have

Dating from A.D. 1200, this bateye was once the scene of Indian athletic competitions.

been lost due to erosion. The *bateyes* are bordered by cobbled walkways. This site dates from A.D. 1200. Although the ball game played in these arenas was indigenous to the entire Caribbean, the game reached its highest degree of sophistication in Puerto Rico. Two teams of players, thick wooden belts lashed to their waists, would hit a heavy, resilient ball—keeping it in the air without the use of hands or feet. These balls still survive in the form of stone replicas. Other examples of petroglyphs are found in Barrio Paso Palma and Salto Arriba, Utuado.

Caguana petroglyph

festivals and crafts: San Miguel Arcangel, the town's patron saint, has his festival on and around 29 Sept. every year. A crafts fair and Jayuya Indian Festival are held here in November. Don Carmelo Martell, Ave. Esteves 48, makes fine *cuatros* (10-string guitars). Emilio Rosado, Calle Hopital, Parcela 63, Bda. Maestro, carves masterful wooden roosters. Rafael Valentin Reyes, Barrio Judea A-B2, Sector La Playita, makes *holajateria* (crafts from tin).

accommodations and food: The modest Riverside Hotel charges $25 per week. Negotiate with the manager for longer stays. Many places to eat in town.

FROM UTUADO

Yellow buses and *publicos* ply over steep hills to Jayuya, and, via Lake Dos Bocas, to Arecibo. **for Ponce:** A magnificent, steep and cool, lushly vegetated road leads through the mountain town of Adjuntas down to Ponce and the sea below.

Lares: *Independentista* town in the heart of coffee country where the famous *Grito de Lares* rebellion (see "History" under "Introduction") was raised in 1848. A white obelisk in the plaza lists the names of the revolt's heroes. Annual *independentista* rallies are still held here on 24 Sept. in commemoration of the event. Locked amidst limestone hills, the town is cool and relaxed. Lares' *Fiesta Patronales de San Jose* happens around 19 March.

Jayuya: Another small mountain town with strong Indian cultural influences. The only industry here is Travenol, an artificial kidney factory. Jayuya's patron saint festival *(Nuestra Senora de la Monserrate)* takes place on and around 3 September. Held yearly in the public plaza since 1969, the Jayuya Indian festival features parades, craft markets, presentation of Taino sports and dance, and a band which performs using indigenous musical instruments. Small carvings of faces, frogs, and spirals are inscribed on the surface of a large boulder in the Saliente riverbed inside Barrio Coabey. *Sol de Jayuya* ("Sun of Jayuya"), found in Zama Province, is one of the most spectacular indigenous murals in Puerto Rico; it's essentially a sun equipped with eyes and mouth which reflects suprise or fear. Los Tres Picachos (3,952 ft., 1,201 m), near Jayuya, is the second highest mountain in Puerto Rico. Only place to stay in town is Hacienda Gripinas, a *parador* set on the site of a 19th C. coffee plantation, $25 s, $30 d. From the *parador* climb to the top of Cerro Punta inside Toro Negro State Forest.

Adjuntas: Small mountain town on the road to Ponce. Stay at Monte Rio, end of H St., $15.90 s, $25.50 d. *Fiesta Patronales* for San Joaquin and Santa Ana is held 21 August. Lago Garza, a volcanic lake nearby, is said by locals to contain a giant monster with a 15-ft. wingspan.

Bosque Estatal de Toro Negro: To the E of Adjuntas en route to Barranquitas. One of the most magnificent reserves on the island (open 0800-1700). Also known as Dona Juana Recreation Center. Climb Cerro Dona Juana (3,341 feet, 1,016 m) and Cerro Punta, which at 4,390 ft. (1,338 m) is the tallest peak on the island. Hikers can also explore Inabon Falls in the heart of the reserve. Inside the reserve is a swimming pool, barbeque pits, and observation tower. Enter from Carr. 143, km 32.4.

accommodations: Camping is permitted inside the reserve if applied for 15 days in advance at the Department of Natural Resources in San Juan. Rooms are rented on a daily, weekly, or monthly basis at Quinta Dona Juana within the reserve.

Bosque Estatal de Guilarte: Divided among six areas of land and located along Carrs. 518 and 525 to the SW of Adjuntas, this reserve has Monte Guilarte, one of the few peaks on the island which remain unmarred by radio or TV towers. To the NE and lying off of Carr. 525, Charco Azul is the local swimming hole.

THE
UNITED STATES
VIRGIN ISLANDS

INTRODUCTION

Featuring spectacular beaches, panoramas, and climate, the U.S. Virgins have been part of the United States for over half a century, yet many Americans have never even heard of them. These islands (pop. 100,000)—with their largely black but composite society—have a distinct culture and history of their own. The three main islands—St. Thomas, St. John, and St. Croix—are easily accessible from neighboring Puerto Rico.

THE LAND

Located 1,500 miles (2,413 km) SE of New York and 1,000 miles (1,069 km) S of Miami, the United States Virgin Islands are bounded on the N by the Atlantic Ocean and on the S by the Caribbean. Covering 132 sq miles (342 sq km) of land area, these islands—of which St. John, St. Croix, and St. Thomas are the main ones—are volcanic in origin. Well exposed and only slightly deformed rocks give a nearly complete record of evolution dating back more than 100 million years. Primary growth having vanished long ago, vegetation is largely secondary; there are few streams and water is frequently in short supply; and except on St. John, soils are thin and number among the stoniest in the world. No minerals of any value are found here save salt and blue green stone or blue bit, an excellent building material. A ridge of high hills runs almost the entire length of St. Thomas. Although its rocks are chiefly sedimentary, limestone reaching up to the peak of Crown Mountain (1,550 ft., 471 m) tells a story of cyclical earthquakes, submergence, and upheavals. Saint John, terminating in a narrow curving neck enclosing a series of bays, rises abruptly from the sea with Bordeaux Mountain (1,277 ft., 389 m) being the highest point. Coral Bay, on the S side of St. John, is the best harbor in the islands. Saint Croix, a fraternal rather than identical triplet, lies 32 miles (59 km) to the S separated by 1,000- to 2,400-fathom trenches. Its topography is quite different from the other islands. The N upland contains Mt. Eagle (1,165 ft., 355 m), the S side is a broad coastal plain while the E end is rough, arid scrubland.

climate: Rarely does it rain on these islands (average rainfall is only 50 in. per year). When it does, it usually lasts only a few minutes. May, Sept., and Oct. are the wettest months. During the day, temperatures range in the 80s, dropping to the 70s in the evening.

FLORA AND FAUNA

Occasionally used as a Christmas tree in the Virgin Islands, agave americana or the century plant lives about ten years, not the 100 its name suggests. As the plant blooms for its first and last time in its last year, the canary-yellow bilbils wilt and cast their seed to the winds.

PLANT LIFE

These islands feature an amazing variety of plantlife, from lichen and mosses to fruit trees and orchids. Considering its tiny area, St. John has an extraordinary diversity of tropical foliage. There are 260 different species of plants, vines, shrubs, and trees. A century-old botanical survey of St. Thomas found 1,220 plants in its 32 sq miles. Saint Croix also has a wide diversity of foliage: in addition to numerous trees and shrubs, it has 42 varieties of orchids and nearly twice as many varieties of morning glories. More common trees on all the islands include the umbrella tree, cinnamon bay, various species of fig, palm, breadfruit, flamboyant, false almond, West Indian ebony, buttonwood, horseradish tree, fiddlewood, boxweed, yellow cedar, and mahogany. Fruit trees include the mango, soursop, tamarind, coconut, guava, sugar apple, and the genip. The guana tail and the penguin are shrubs frequently used as hedges. The penguin, a type of bromeliad with sharp end spines on its leaves, resemble the pineapple. The four o'clock is a small shrub with trumpet-shaped purple blossoms which open at 1600 each day. The *ceiba* or silk-cotton tree was once believed by slaves to walk at night. The bright yellow blossom of the yellow cedar is the territorial flower.

forbidden fruit: The mangrove and *manchineel* grow near the sea. The *manchineel* secretes an acid which may be deadly. Said to be the original apple in the Garden of Eden, biting into this innocuous-looking yet highly poisonous fruit will cause your mouth to burn and your tongue to swell up. In fact, all parts of this tree are potentially deadly. Cattle standing under the tree after a torrential tropical downpour have been known to lose their hides as drops fall from leaves. Other tales tell of locals going blind after a leaf touched an eye. Slaves wishing to do away with a particularly despicable master would insert minute quantities of juice into an uncooked potato. Cooked, these small doses were undetectable but always fatal if served to the victim over a long period of time. If you see some of these trees, stay well away!

name game: Many of the imaginatively named species have colorful stories behind their names: The "love plant" was so named because an aspiring suitor would write his lover's name on the leaf; if it remained for a time, it meant that he could count on acceptance of his proposal. The "catch and keep" sticks to everything it touches while the "jump up and kiss me" is well endowed with small, seductive blossoms. The trunk of the "monkey-don't-climb tree" bristles with thorns, while the "nothing nut" is so named because that's exactly what it's good for. The pods of the "woman's tongue" tree clatter on and on in the breeze like gossiping housewives. Other unusually named plants include the "jumbi-bread" vine with its knife-shaped miniature red blossoms, the "stinking toe," "bull hoof," "poor man's orchid," "powder puff," "crown of thorn," "lucky nut," "burning love," and the "lady of the night."

others: Guinea grass, which covers many island hillsides and provides feed for livestock, was originally introduced by mistake. Brought over as birdseed for the governor's pet birds, who rejected them, the seeds were tossed out and the grass began to proliferate on its own accord. Many other plants have had utilitarian uses: while switches for beating slaves were made from the tamarind tree, calabash gourds were perfectly suited for bailing devices, eating utensils, and dishes. Natural herbs and herbal remedies were made from the sandbox, mahoe, and other trees, shrubs, and plants.

U.S.V.I. CLIMATE CHART	Daily Average Air Temp. °F	Rainfall Days
January	77	4.3
February	77	1.9
March	78	2.0
April	79	7.5
May	80	1.3
June	82	2.9
July	84	5.6
August	84	4.1
September	83	6.6
October	83	5.6
November	80	5.4
December	78	3.8

ANIMAL LIFE

Save for the now-extint agouti, a rodent once considered a delicacy by local Indians, very few land animals existed here before the coming of Europeans. Today, monkeys and wild boars have disappeared, though a few scattered deer still remain. Introduced in legend rather than fact, werewolves were once hunted by slaves who believed in this European folktale. Doubtless the legend was kept alive in order to cover up for the master when he went on a sexual rampage. Unique to St. Croix is the husbandry of Senepol cattle. More than a half century ago, a Cruxian plantation owner named Nelthrop was kicked by a cow. Determined to create a new and improved version, he crossed the African Senegal with the English Red Poll. The result was a new breed that is hairless, shortlegged, requires less water, and is disease resistant. The mongoose, introduced to kill snakes, has just about done in the reptile population. Lizards include several varieties of ground and tree lizards; the colorful herbivorous iguana, whose tail has long been considered a culinary delicacy, is on the way out. Although centipedes and scorpions live on these islands, they maintain passive, nonaggressive attitudes towards humans unless they are disturbed.

birds: There are over 200 species of birds, including brightly colored wild parakeets, pelicans, and egrets. Since most of the swamps have been drained, the sea bird population has dwindled. Land birds include hawks, doves, sparrows, thrushes, West Indian crows, wild pigeons, canaries, yellow breasts, and several varieties of hummingbirds.

sealife: Divers and snorkelers will find a dazzling array of coral, fish, and sponges of all colors of the rainbow. Delicate in appearance only, yellow or purple (depending on diet) sea fan, a coral with fanlike branches, is so strong that it will support a man's weight without tearing. Normally the size of a pinhead, the sea jewel *(valonia)* is the largest single-cell animal in existence. Saclike and round in appearance, it reflects the colors of whatever's nearby. A kaleidoscope of fish include the doctorfish, grouper, old wife, one-eye, silver angelfish, sergeant fish, marine jewel, and trunkfish.

HISTORY

The original inhabitants of the Virgin Islands were members of the Ciboney tribe. Little is known about them and few reminders remain save some archaeological sites. Later joined by the Arawaks, both tribes were conquered and enslaved by invading Carib Indians. During Columbus' second voyage, the admiral sighted East Point on St. Croix. Christening the island Santa Cruz (Holy Cross), his fleet anchored in Salt Bay. After putting ashore in a small boat, the island's first tourists made the village rounds. On the way back, Columbus' boat was attacked by a canoe full of Caribs, who immediately fled at the strange sight of white men, firing arrows to cover their escape. Continuing on his voyage, Columbus and his men passed a great number of islands, cluster after cluster, some verdant, others naked and sterile. The islands, seemingly thousands of them, with their combinations of glistening white and azure rocks were, he supposed, filled with jewels and precious stones. Accordingly, he named the islands *Santa Ursula y las Once Mil Virgines* (Saint Ursula and the 11,000 Virgins).

colonization: After Columbus' visit, not much attention was paid to the islands, except in frequent raids by Spaniards as they carted off natives to slave in Dominican gold mines. These raids led to the complete extermination of the local population. By 1625 the Dutch and English were settled on St. Croix.

In that year, a Danish West India Company was formed by a Dutchman. However, control of St. Croix passed from English to Spanish to French hands while Danish plans remained on the drawing board. Finally, a second Danish West India Company, organized by a group of court insiders, was chartered on 11 March 1671, and a decision made to settle on St. Thomas. A little more than eight months passed before the Company had two ships on the way. One was forced to turn back; the other, waylaid by inclement weather, managed to limp into the harbor of what was to become Charlotte Amalie more than six months after the date of departure. It had been a horrendous voyage for the *Pharoah:* only six of the 239 who had boarded in Copenhagen survived. Other ships followed, some with clergy to provide spiritual guidance. However, of the first priests sent over, most simply couldn't adapt and one had to be sent home for drunkenness. ("Kill devil," as the local unaged rum was called, was potent stuff indeed!) By 1679 there were 156 whites and 176 slaves on St. Thomas. Tobacco, indigo, cotton, and dyewood were the main exports to Denmark. A series of vile rascals reigned as Danish West Indies Company presidents. Making St. Thomas a haven for privateers, pirates, and all manner of shady operators from all parts of the Caribbean resulted in visits from Bluebeard, Blackbeard, Captain Kidd, and other such "Brethren of the Coast." The har-

On his second voyage Columbus and his men passed a great number of islands, cluster after cluster, some verdant, others naked and sterile. The islands, with their combinations of glistening white and azure rocks must be, he supposed, filled with jewels and precious stones. It seemed to him he was sailing among thousands of islands. Accordingly, he named the islands "Santa Ursula y las Once Mil Virgines" (Saint Ursula and the 11,000 Virgins.) Prior to sainthood, Ursula was a proper British princess. Arranged to marry a foreign king, she begged a pleasure cruise from her father as a wedding present. This three-year, 11-ship voyage came to a brutal end when, arriving in Cologne just as it was being sacked by the Huns, Ursula and her comrades were raped and slain.

bor was also renowned for its slave market: buyers would come from as far away as Curacao and the Carolinas. Saint Croix, purchased from France in 1733, was also a base for the "Triangle Trade." New England ships would buy rum, carry it to Africa, use it to buy slaves, and return to sell the slaves and buy more rum. Of a total of 123,000 slaves brought over between 1733-82, about 70,000 were re-exported while the rest were retained. In 1764 Charlotte Amalie was declared a free port for intracolonial trade. Its neutrality attracted privateers of all nations who arrived to sell their booty. In 1815 this trade was extended internationally.

emancipation: Denmark's King Frederick VI appointed Peter von Scholten governor in 1827. An unusual man, versed in creole and comfortable among slaves, von Scholten lived with Anna Heegard, the daughter of a freed slave. Perhaps under her influence, he began urging freedom for all slaves. In 1847 he implemented the policy of "gradualism," whereby slave children born during the succeeding 12 years were to be free at birth. All slaves would then be free at the end of the 12-year period. Resentment by slaves against the system, however, continued to build. Receiving word of a planned slave rebellion, von Scholten emancipated the slaves on 3 July 1848, on his own initiative, from Fort Frederick in Christiansted. The rebellion began in Fredericksted before the news reached there. After the news arrived, however, the violence turned into a jubilant celebration. Brought back to Copenhagen for trial, von Scholten was acquitted. Emancipation led to dire poverty for freed slaves and to labor riots on St. Croix in 1878 during which most of Fredericksted burned.

sale to United States: During the U.S. Civil War, the danger of having an unprotected

IMPORTANT DATES IN UNITED STATES VIRGIN ISLANDS HISTORY

1493: Columbus discovers St. Croix and the other Virgin Islands.

1625: The Dutch and English settle on St. Croix.

1650: The English are driven from St. Croix by Puerto Rican Spaniards. The French take over from the Spanish.

1651: Chevalier de Poincy, Lt. General of the French West Indies, buys St. Croix from the bankrupt French West Indies Company.

1653: Ownership of St. Croix is transferred to the Knights of Malta.

1665: Erik Neilson Smith, a Danish sea captain, is granted a charter from the Danish king to colonize St. Thomas and is named royal commandant and governor. Saint Croix is purchased from the Knights of Malta by the French West Indies Company.

1666: Schmidt takes possession of St. Thomas only to die 6 months later; he is replaced by Lutheran pastor Kjeld Slagelse.

1667: Saint Thomas is captured by the English, who soon abandon it.

1668: Slagelse and most of the island's Danish inhabitants return home.

1671: Danish King Christian V issues a new charter to the West India and Guinea Company.

1672: Danes, under Gov. Iverson, formally take possession of St. Thomas.

1673: The first consignment of African slaves arrives on St. Thomas.

1674: The king of France takes over St. Croix as part of his dominions from the French West Indies Company.

1681: Taphus (Charlotte Amalie) is founded on St. Thomas.

1684: Saint Thomas formally takes possession of St. John.

1685: Saint Thomas is leased to the Brandenburgh Company to carry on commerce for 30 years.

1691: Saint Thomas is leased to George Thormohlen, a Bergen merchant, for 10 years.

1694: Thormohlen's lease ends in a lawsuit.

1696: French settlers abandon St. Croix.

1716: Export and import duty is reduced to 6 percent *ad valoreum.*

1717: Planters from St. Thomas occupy St. John and begin cultivation.

1724: St. Thomas is formally declared a free port.

1726: The first Supplication Day (to pray for "aid against hurricanes") is held.

1730: Taphus is renamed Charlotte Amalie.

1733: Saint Croix is purchased from France by the Danish West Indies Company; slaves on St. John openly rebel.

1734: The St. John insurrection is put down.

1735: Danes formally take possession of St. Croix; Christiansted is established.

1751: The town of Fredericksted is established.

1764: Saint Thomas and St. John again granted free port status.

1792: Denmark outlaws slave trade.

1801-2: Britain again occupies the islands.

1804: Much of Charlotte Amalie is swept by fire.

1806: Two more fires devastate Charlotte Amalie.

1807-15: Britain again occupies the islands.

1825: Yet another fire sweeps through Charlotte Amalie.

1826: Another fire on St. Thomas.

1831: Still another fire on St. Thomas.

1848: Slaves on St. Croix are emancipated by Governor-General Peter von Scholten after demonstrations.

1867: A treaty is signed in Denmark for the sale of St. Thomas and St. John to the U.S. for $7.5 million.

1870: The treaty of sale is rejected by the U.S. Senate.

1872: Charlotte Amalie once again becomes the administrative seat of the islands.

1892: Poor economic conditions, coupled with a lack of stable currency, cause a rebellion on St. Thomas.

1898: The U.S. again attempts to purchase the islands.

1902: A second treaty, granting the islands to the U.S. in exchange for $5 million in gold, is signed; it is rejected by the Danish parliament.

1916: Treaty selling the islands to the U.S. for $25 million is signed.

1917: Treaty of sale is ratified and the islands formally become part of the U.S.

1927: U.S. citizenship is granted to most island residents.

1931: Jurisdiction of the islands is transferred from the Navy to the Dept. of the Interior; President Hoover visits the U.S.V.I.

1936: The first Organic Act is passed.

1940: Population shows an increase for the first time since 1860.

1946: First black governor of the islands, William Hastie, is appointed.

1950: Morris De Castro, first native-born governor, is appointed.

1954: Revised Organic Act passed.

1956: National Park on St. John approved by U.S. Congress.

1959: The Revised Organic Act is amended.

1968: Passage of the Virgin Islands Elective Governor Act permits the U.S.V.I. to elect a governor.

1969: Dr. Melvin Evans, first native black governor and last appointee, takes office.

1970: Dr. Melvin Evans elected governor.

1972: Hon. Ron de Lugo elected as first Congressional delegate from the Virgin Islands.

Atlantic coastline, along with the strategic value of having a Caribbean colony, became clear. Saint Thomas was seen as a Caribbean Gibraltar: a floating fortress, surrounded by impregnable coral reefs, strategically located, and with harbors eminently suited for naval vessels. Negotiations, opened secretly by Secretary of State Seward in Jan. 1865, were delayed by Lincoln's assassination, but finally culminated in a treaty signed on 24 Oct. 1867, which provided for the sale of St. Thomas and St. John for $7.5 million, or a half-million more than Seward had paid for Alaska. As a stipulation of the treaty, a referendum among the local populace was held in 1868; a majority of the 12 percent of the population who qualified for suffrage voted in favor, and the sale was considered by both nations to have been approved. However, although the treaty passed in the Danish Rigsag, it failed to pass a U.S. Senate divided and impassioned by President Johnson's impeachment. In the 1890s private American operators, attracted by the possibility of a 10-percent commission, negotiated with the Danes. Interrupted by the Spanish-American War, negotiations resumed again in 1900 at which time a Standard Oil vice-president joined the group. Boasting that he had 26 senators under his control, he claimed he could deliver a treaty for the price of a Standard depot on St. Thomas. Meanwhile, the islands being an expensive financial liability, the Danes were hoping to swap them with Germany in exchange for the return of North Schleswig. The Treaty of 1902, from which any mention of citizenship was deleted, arranged for the sale of all three islands at this time for a bargain basement $5 million. Although the treaty was passed in the U.S. Senate, it failed by one vote in its Danish counterpart—largely because the U.S. refused to hold a plebiscite. Fresh negotiations dragged on again until the beginning of WW I. Faced with the prospect of the Kaiser's armies marching into Copenhagen, American naval strategists began to fear for the safety of the Panama Canal. Negotiations began again under President Woodrow Wilson. Seizing advantage of the situation, the clever Danes, reluctant to negotiate at first, pushed the price up five times to $25 million. The U.S. accepted the offer without attempting to bargain, and a treaty was signed on April 14, 1916. At $290 an acre, the islands represent the most expensive U.S. government land purchase in history.

United States takeover: On 31 March 1917, the Stars and Stripes were raised by the U.S. Navy, ending 245 years and six days of Danish rule. Packing up everything moveable—from furniture to the rope attached to the Government House flagpole—the Danes were happy to leave. At the time of the U.S. takeover conditions were absolutely abhorrent. A high death rate was coupled with a high rate of infant mortality. Agriculture was confined to cultivation of small crops of yams and sweet potatoes. Malaria, typhoid, leprosy, diptheria, and elephantiasis were widespread. There were four miles of roads on St. Thomas, no high school, and only 19 elementary school teachers. The brutality of the slavery system, one of the harshest in the Western Hemisphere, was transformed after emancipation into an almost complete neglect of the plight of the poor. As the islands were acquired by the U.S. purely for their strategic value rather than out of any concern for the inhabitants or for economic reasons, the most expedient thing to do was to transfer them to military rule and worry about status, citizenship, human rights, and such other troublesome issues sometime in the indefinite future. Under the Navy, all of the authoritarian local laws remained in force. This surprised locals who, having not opted for Danish citizenship, assumed they would be automatically granted American citizenship. The Navy found a strange world. White Naval officers, many of them from the South, were astounded to find themselves dealing with high-ranking local blacks. Run-ins between locals and intoxicated Marines frequently resulted in violence. A succession of Southern Caesars as military governors, hard-core white supremacists all, fanned the flames.

civilian administration: The 14 years of Naval control ended on 18 March 1931 as control passed to the U.S. Department of the Interior and Paul Pearson was sworn in as the first civilian governor. President Hoover, visiting eight days later, declared, "Viewed from every point except remote naval contingencies, it was unfortunate we ever acquired these islands." Although the Jones Act had granted citizenship to Puerto Ricans in 1917, Virgin Islanders were denied this because the treaty of purchase spoke of citizenship "in" the U.S. as opposed to citizenship "of" the U.S. Citizenship was finally granted in 1927 to most residents, but not until 1932 was this privilege extended to all. The Basic Organic Act, passed in 1936, gave the vote to all citizens who were able to read and write English, and made the U.S. Con-

stitution operative in the Virgin Islands. In addition, all federal taxes collected were to be held for use by local governments in the Islands. Pearson, known as the "Experimenting Quaker," although unpopular with both the left and right, continued as governor under President Franklin Roosevelt. During the New Deal, the Public Works Administration instituted the Virgin Islands Company (VICO), a public corporation which grew and refined sugarcane, distilled and marketed rum, and controlled water supplies and power production. Rum was produced and sold under the brand name "Government House," bearing a label personally designed by Roosevelt. Unlike its mainland counterparts, VICO (later renamed VICORP) wasn't such a good idea, as the Virgin Islands are not particularly well suited to sugarcane cultivation.

the governors: President Truman appointed William H. Hastie to be the islands' first black governor in 1946. He was succeeded by Morris F. Castro in 1950 who, in turn, was replaced by Archie Alexander. Alexander resigned in 1955 under the guise of ill health after allegations of conflict of interest and misuse of government funds had been made against him. In 1954 Congress passed the revised Basic Organic Act which established a unicameral legislature and allowed all federal excise taxes collected from rum sales to be returned to the Islands. A succession of governors ruled until President Kennedy—under pressure from his father, who had been a friend of the rum distilling Paiewonsky family—appointed entrepreneur Ralph M. Paiewonsky governor. A bill providing for the direct election of governors became law on 23 Aug. 1968. Selected by President Nixon, Dr. Melvin H. Evans became the last appointed governor on 1 July 1969. In the first gubernatorial elections, held in Nov. 1970, Cyril King was elected. After the death of Melvin King (no relation) in Jan. 1978, Juan Luis became acting governor and was subsequently elected in Nov. 1978 and re-elected in 1982.

GOVERNMENT

As citizens of the nation and residents of an unincorporated territory under the U.S. flag, at four-year intervals, Virgin Islanders elect their own governor (currently Juan Luis), legislature, and a nonvoting representative to Congress. The legislature, the backbone of the local government, is a unicameral body of 15 members who are elected to two-year terms. Its main powers and duties derive from the 1954 Revised Organic Act. Although the system may sound ideal, the realities have been different. In the U.S.V.I., politics has always been politics. For years the autocratic legislature has been dominated by the Unity Democrats. Party of the creoles, it has allowed the entry into the political process of only a few Continentals and Puerto Ricans, while the vast number of alien residents remain unrepresented. Party politics is confusing and crossing of party lines while voting is common.

constitution: It's been in the works for a while. On 4 Nov., 1981, Virgin Island voters rejected the latest draft of their proposed constitution. This is the fourth constitution rejected since 1964. The first constitution failed to pass Congress; the second (1972) was approved by Congress only by an insubstantial margin; and the third (1979) was also rejected by the voters. The latest constitution defined a "Virgin Islander" as one born on or with one parent born on the islands—a designation which would have conferred no special benefits. The original draft contained a specification that the governor must be a native. After residents from the States complained, it was removed. Regarding the modest voter turnout for the election (47 percent), Judge Henry Feuerzeig—who helped draft and actively campaigned for the constitution—pontificated: "Constitutions aren't sexy. You can't identify with them as you can with a candidate."

ECONOMY

No other Caribbean island or island group has ever undergone such a fast-clipped transformation, ethnic or economic, as did the U.S. Virgin Islands during the 1960s. Although the entire population of the U.S.V.I. was only 100,000 in the late '70s, the government budget was larger than that of San Juan with its one million people! The islands have the highest per capita income in the Caribbean (about US$7100 per year), but they're also plagued by prices higher than Stateside without wage levels to match. The presence of Continentals, while stimulating to the economy, has served to drive up land values and cause considerable resentment. Although businesses on the main shopping street of Charlottte Amalie are owned by six island families, more than 95 percent of the businesses island-wide are owned by mainland whites. Meanwhile, unemployment among local youth is 40 percent or higher. The average family—with the help of food stamps—is just making it.

government: Surprisingly, the largest employer in the U.S.V.I. is the territorial government. Its more than 13,000 employees give the islands the highest ratio of bureaucrats to taxpayers of any area of the United States. Although the government employs a full *third* of the working force and receives more per capita in federal funds than any state or territory save the District of Columbia, it has been ponderously slow to deal with practical concerns such as power plants, desalinization plants, and new roads, and stories of corruption are legendary.

industry: Although no industry exists on St. Thomas or St. John, Harvey Alumina has constructed a $25 million alumina processing plant on St. Croix's S shore. And though the government claimed the rationale for the plant's allocation was to "alleviate unemployment," it—like the neighboring Hess refinery—has actually employed few locals.

tourism: This economic sector is the major income earner. Hotels increased from 11 in 1946 to 84 in 1982. Tourists have come because of the duty-free (seven percent) shopping available, as well as the sense of security offered by islands that are part of the United States.

agriculture: Nearly totally neglected. Even cows and goats are not milked; the milk just goes to the calves and results in a lack of fresh milk — reconstituted milk is imported instead!

FESTIVALS AND EVENTS

With 23 official holidays, Virgin Islanders have plenty of time off — perhaps more than anyone anywhere else in the world! Various public holidays are marked by special celebrations and events peculiar to the U.S.V.I.: New Year's Day features a children's parade in Fredericksted. Three Kings Day, which follows on 6 Jan., constitutes the finale of St. Croix's Christmas Festival with a colorful parade of costumed children and adults. Transfer Day, 31 March, celebrates the transfer of the islands to the U.S. in 1917. Easter is marked by church services; outdoor sporting events are held on Easter Monday. The Rolex Regatta usually comes in mid-April, as does St. Thomas' Carnival which takes place during the last eight days of April. Parades and ceremonies are commonplace throughout the islands on Memorial Day, and yacht races are featured on St. Croix. A special ceremony marking Danish West Indies

Emancipation Day takes place in Fredericksted, St. Croix, on 3 July, because the proclamation was first read there. All three islands celebrate this day with parades and ceremonies: Cruz Bay, St. John, features a miniature version of St. Thomas' Carnival. Also in July, many residents of these islands attend services marking Hurricane Supplication Day and pray that no hurricanes will visit them (it's worked for more than half a century now). Special festivities are held on all three islands on Labor Day just as they are held on the mainland. Columbus Day is also known as Puerto Rico/Virgin Islands Friendship Day; a traditional boat trip from St. Croix to the Puerto Rican island of Vieques is made on this day. Liberty Day, 1 Nov., commemorates the establishment of the first free press in 1915. The Virgin Island Charterboat League Show takes place in mid-November. Veterans Day, 11 Nov., features parades and ceremonies.

U.S.V.I. PUBLIC HOLIDAYS

1 Jan.: New Year's Day
6 Jan.: Three Kings Day
15 Jan.: Martin Luther King's Birthday
Feb.: Lincoln's Birthday (movable)
31 March: Transfer Day
March/April: Holy Thursday, Good Friday, Easter Monday (movable)
May: Memorial Day (movable)
June: Organic Act Day (movable)
3 July: Emancipation Day
4 July: U.S. Independence Day

July: Supplication Day (movable)
Sept.: Labor Day (movable)
Oct.: Columbus Day — Virgin Islands/Puerto Rico Friendship Day, Hurricane Thanksgiving Day (movable)
1 Nov.: Liberty Day
11 Nov.: Veterans Day
Nov.: U.S. Thanksgiving Day (movable)
25 Dec.: Christmas Day
26 Dec.: Second Christmas Day

PRACTICALITIES

getting there: Even if you don't intend to visit San Juan, it's necessary to switch planes at San Juan International Airport. From San Juan it's a short hop by small aircraft to either St. Thomas or St. Croix. While discount OW fares are not available, shop around for various RT excursion and "circle" (San Juan-St. Thomas-St. Croix-San Juan) fares. These—like everything else—are cheapest off season. Eastern flies direct only from Miami: $169 OW, $218 RT excursion. They also offer RT fares via Miami from Atlanta ($436 RT) and New York ($359 RT). All of these APEX fares require ticket purchase seven days in advance, one Sat. night spent in the islands, and a maximum stay of 60 days. American flies from Dallas/Fort Worth on Sat. and Sun. Lowest fares available ($511 RT to St. Thomas and $519 RT to St. Croix) are seven-day APEX with a 30-day maximum stay. In any case, you'd do well to check out the lowest RT fare to San Juan from New York and Miami and then figure on another $70 RT to St. Thomas and St. Croix. In the fall, you might try crewing aboard yachts departing from along the U.S. Eastern Seaboard for St. Thomas, and catch a return passage in the spring. Jennie Tours has boats on Sat. and Sun. from Marina Puerto Chico (on the way to Las Croabas near Fajardo on Puerto Rico) at 0900 ($20 OW, $35 RT; returns at 1630). For St. John it's best to take a ferry from Red Hook, St. Thomas. The only way to get to St. Croix is by flying from San Juan, Vieques, or St. Thomas. Virgin Islands Seaplane Shuttle, which lands near the harbor area, connects all three islands.

getting around: Local taxis—shared or unshared—are expensive. Be sure to decide the price before entering. Inefficient and limited local bus service is available on St. Thomas and St. Croix. Hitching is easiest on St. John. **by ferry:** Those available run between Fajardo, Puerto Rico and Charlotte Amalie, St. Thomas, and from St. Thomas to St. John. **hitchhiking by yacht:** Hitchhiking by boat through the Caribbean can be easy if you have the time and money to wait for a ride and are at the right place in the right season. Best time to head there is about mid-Oct. just before the boat shows and the preparation for the charter season. Along with those at English Harbor on Antigua, the marinas on St. Thomas (at Red Hook and at Charlotte Amalie) have the greatest concentration of boats and the most competition for work of any island in the Caribbean. Many times it's easy to get a ride from one island to another.

The ferry running between St. Thomas and St. John functions much as a bus does in rural areas. Here, a school team departs.

CAMPING IN THE VIRGIN ISLANDS (AMERICAN AND BRITISH)

NAME/ADDRESS	TELEPHONE	RATES, FACILITIES, AND SPECIFICS
Larry's Hideaway 10-1 Hull Bay St. Thomas	774-8955	$10 s, $20 cabin year round. Extra person $15. Facilities include horseshoe pitching, volleyball court, snorkeling, and surfing
Cinnamon Bay Box 720 Cruz Bay, St. John	776-6330	Bare sites: $9 pd for 1-9 10 by 14 tents: $32 d ($41, 15 Nov.-1 May) $6 pp add'l. 15 by 15 ft. cottages $40 d ($50, 15 Nov.-1 May) $6 pp add'l. Equipment for rent. Commissary. Kitchen facilities; restaurants.
Maho Bay Camps Box 310 Cruz Bay, St. John	776-6626	3 rm cottages $40 d ($50, 15 Nov.-1 May). Luxury camping. Kitchen facilities; restaurants.
Brewers Bay Campground Box 185 Road Town, Tortola		Bare sites $5 pd for 2; add'l persons $1. Tents; $14 d pd. add'l persons $2.50. Restaurant, commissary, tours, snorkeling.
Tula's N & N Campground Little Harbour, Jost Van Dyke (Box 8364, St. Thomas, USVI 00801)	774-0774	Bare sites: $15 pd for 3 8 by 10 ft. tents; $25 d 9 by 11 ft. tents: $35 d

Just hang around the docks or pubs and ask! As far as working on yachts goes, it's hard work and long hours, and you must have a real love for sailing and boats and the sea. Depending upon whether you are working on salary or for piece work, the salary may or may not be how many hours are actually involved. Usually you are constantly doing something from early morning until late at night. Some boats may be more lax than others, but it generally involves pretty continuous work. Check out *Sail* magazine or *Yachting* for the addresses of charter companies. However, it's really unnecessary to write: most people are employed on the spot.

accommodations: These islands make their living from tourists and housing is tight, so the cost of lodging is correspondingly high—from $35 d to up to $400 or more per night. It's cheapest to visit these islands off season (mid-April through mid-December). Camping (bare sites and rented tents) is available on St. John and (rented tents only) on St. Thomas.

food: Mostly high prices and a dearth of local cuisine. *Souse, calaloo,* and *fungi* have been supplanted by hamburgers, hotdogs, and Kentucky Fried Chicken. Owing to frequent personnel changes, quality of food in restaurants tends to be inconsistent. Most are high priced; local establishments tend to be expensive because the locals dining there tend to make their living off of the tourist dollar as well. There are no street vendors, but there are a few bakeries in the main town where you can buy bread. If you want to eat well here, you'd better plan on parting with a lot of green. Even food in the supermarkets runs 25-35 percent higher than Stateside on the average so it's best to bring what you can.

shopping: Shops are open Mon. to Sat. 0900-1700; they close for official holidays.

Hotel shops close at 2100. These islands still maintain the minimal Danish import duty of seven percent, which has made them into a "duty-free" shopper's paradise. Charlotte Amalie and Christiansted are the two main shopping centers. Returning American citizens, under existing customs regulations, can lug back with them up to $600 worth of duty-free goods. (Items sent by post may be included in this tally. Obtain a Customs Form 255.) One gallon (or five fifths) of liquor may be brought back as well as five cartons of cigarettes. Pre-1881 antiques and local handicrafts are also duty free. **money and measurements:** Monetary unit is the US dollar; measurements are the same as those used in the States.

broadcasting and media: Local TV, largely consisting of recycled pap from the States, is available for those addicts who positively must watch. Imported newspapers are available but exhorbitant. *The San Juan Star* is available on St. Thomas and St. Croix. Saint Thomas has *The Daily News,* St. John has the weekly *Tradewinds,* while St. Croix has the *Avis.*

visas: All visitors from abroad (except U.S. citizens and Canadians) require a U.S. visa. It's

---

UNITED STATES VIRGIN ISLANDS
DIVISIONS OF TOURISM

SAINT THOMAS
Box 6400
Charlotte Amalie, St. Thomas, USVI 00801
(809) 774-8784

SAINT JOHN
Box 200
Cruz Bay, St. John, USVI 00830
(809) 776-6450

CHRISTIANSTED, ST. CROIX
Christiansted, USVI 00820
(809) 773-0495

FREDERIKSTED, SAINT CROIX
Frederiksted Customs House
Strand Street, USVI 00801
(809) 772-0357

PUERTO RICO
1300 Ashford Avenue
Condado, Santurce, PR 00907
(809) 724-3816

NEW YORK CITY
1270 Avenue of the Americas
New York, NY 10020
(212) 582-4520

MIAMI
7270 NW 12 St., Ste. 620
Miami, FL 33126
(305) 591-2070

CHICAGO
343 South Dearborn Street, Ste. 1108
Chicago, IL 60604
(312) 461-0180

LOS ANGELES
3450 Wilshire Blvd.
Los Angeles, CA 90010
(213) 739-0138

CANADA
11 Adelaide St., W., Ste. 406
Toronto, Ontario M5H 1L9
(416) 368-4374

UNITED KINGDOM
25 Bedford Square
London WC1B 3HG
(01) 637-8481

WEST GERMANY
Freiherr Vom Stein Strasse 24-26
D-6000 Frankfurt Am Main 1
West Germany
(0611) 725200

DENMARK
5 Trommesalen DK-1614
Copenhagen V
(01) 223379

best to obtain a multiple-entry visa and, if possible, do so in your own country, as U.S. embassies and consulates tend to be persnickety about issuing visas to citizens of countries other than the one they're stationed in.

health: Good but expensive medical care is available. Make sure you have adequate health insurance. Hospitals and clinics are located in or near the island's main towns. (See individual sections for listings.)

conduct: Many people (especially illegal aliens from the West Indies) do not appreciate having their pictures taken without their permission. There is a great deal of racial tension and animosity on these islands so do nothing to make the situation worse. Saint Thomas and St. Croix have very high crime rates. Getting mugged on these islands is a very real possibility so exercise caution while walking around the streets at night. Too many cruise ship passengers have caused too much resentment by flashing too much money around. Try to avoid this and keep valuables safely locked up. If camping on St. John, don't leave valuables in your tent.

services and information: VITELCO, the local phone company, is notorious for its bad service. It costs 25 cents to use the pay phone to call any of the three islands. As bad as VITELCO is, WAPA (the Water and Power Authority) is worse. For information about local events, be sure to pick up current copies of *St. Thomas This Week* and its St. Croix equivalent.

ST. THOMAS

Most populous and popular of all the U.S. Virgin Islands, this three-by-13 mile self-styled "American Paradise" (to quote the license plates) hosts one million tourists a year. Flanked by the Atlantic to the N and the Caribbean to the S, its 32 sq miles are hilly and rugged. Hills, running up to 1,500 ft., give incredible views. The island, although commercialized, still retains substantial charm. If at times it seems to be overbearing, just remember that, throughout its history, St. Thomas has always been a place where money and property have come before human beings.

history: Arriving in 1666, the first Danish settlers found an abandoned island. To guard the harbor, Ft. Christian was constructed in 1674. First known as "Tap Hus," in 1691 the town was renamed Amalienborg (later Charlotte Amalie) after the Danish queen. In 1755, after the dissolution of the Danish West Indies Company and purchase by the Danish government, the capital was transferred to Christiansted, St. Croix. A series of fires between 1804 and 1832 destroyed two-thirds of the town before a strict building code was enacted. In 1837 a Lutheran Church census discovered at least 140 nationalities on St. Thomas. Most residents spoke two or more languages; church services were given in three languages and newspapers were printed in several. During this period, Charlotte Amalie was the third largest city in the Danish monarchial realm. After the emancipation of slaves in 1848, the island was transformed from an agricultural community into a supply depot for blockade runners and privateers from the South, and the U.S. men of war that chased them. Capital status was restored to Charlotte Amalie in 1871. During the last quarter of the 19th C., St. Thomas became a coaling depot for European steamship companies. When the U.S. Navy took possession of the island in 1917, they dredged a large channel between St. Thomas and neighboring Hassel I. to allow them an alternate escape route in case of attack. Since the end of WW II, tourism has become the chief industry of St. Thomas.

CHARLOTTE AMALIE

Most of the 51,000 St. Thomians live in this small but attractive town. Although cruise ships rather than slavers visit the harbor these days, the smell of history is still in the air. The shops lining the streets running parallel to the harbor were originally pirate warehouses. As a reminder of the colonial past, street signs affixed to corner buildings are in both English and Danish, and cars drive on the left side of the streets. The three main streets are Dronningen's Gade (Main Street), Norre Gade (North Street), and Vimmelskaft's Gade (Back Street). A series of interlocking alleyways (converted into shopping malls) runs from Dronningen's Gade down to Waterfront Drive, a four-lane thoroughfare paralleling the waterfront. By all means, avoid this town when cruise ships unleash their passengers and it becomes a struggle just to walk.

arriving by air: From San Juan a beautiful flight takes you past Icacos, flying directly over Culebra with Vieques in the background. Houses on St. Thomas appear as white fungi on a patch of green moss. The aircraft terminal is a large, crowded hangar. A branch of

the Chase Manhattan Bank is open Mon. to Thurs. 0900-1300, Fri. 0900-1400. Turn R at the gate and wait for the maroon-striped Manassah Bus ($0.50) operating every 20 min. from 0600-2130 and gives you a criss-cross tour of the island before passing through downtown Charlotte Amalie. If proceeding directly to St. John, get out at the Grand Union shopping plaza on the other side of town and hitch or wait for the Red Hook bus ($0.25) from there.

getting around: Manassah Bus Service (tel. 774-5678) runs to the airport, Red Hook, and Bordeaux (five times daily). Daily truck buses leave the Market Place for Red Hook ($2) hourly from 1115-1715 and return from Red Hook from 0715-1815. A harbor shuttle operates between Charlotte Amalie waterfront, Yacht Haven Marina ($1.50) and Frenchman's Reef Hotel ($2.50) hourly from 0900-1700. Other island destinations are reachable only via expensive shared meterless taxis. (Obtain a price list from the tourist office.) Hitching is possible, but locals are not as accommodating as their St. Johnian neighbors. Jeeps, cars ($40 per day), and motorbikes can be rented on a daily or weekly basis.

SIGHTS

Best way to see this town is on foot when no cruise ships are in the harbor. If you can ignore the touristic, sales-minded atmosphere that prevails downtown, there's plenty to see. You're sure to find your own attractions in addition to the ones listed below.

Virgin Islands Legislature: This lime-green building with white shutters, constructed in 1874, served as the Danish police barracks before housing the U.S. Marines. It became a school in 1930 and then the legislature building in 1957. For a unique glimpse of local politics in action, check out the heated, virulent debates which take place inside.

Fort Christian Museum: Enter along Veterans Drive. Built shortly after the arrival of the first colonists, this imposing red landmark, in neoclassic style, is the oldest building on the island. Completed in 1672, the masonry ramparts and bastions were added in the 18th C.; the fort was completely renovated in 1871 when Charlotte Amalie regained its status as capital. A building of many uses, the fort has housed the governor, the artisan community, and in times of natural disaster during its early history, the entire population. It has also served as the local branch of the Lutheran Church, as a site for pirate executions, and (in its present function) as a jail. The small museum occupies a few fluorescent-lit cells in the basement. Note the archaeological artifacts, shells, old mahogany furniture, and display of household utensils which includes a hollow glass rolling pin which could be filled with water to keep dough from sticking. Open Mon. to Fri. 0930-1700, Sat. and Sun. 1230-1700. Free admission.

Emancipation Park: These small public gardens near the fort mark the spot where Governor von Scholten proclaimed the emancipation of the slaves in 1848. A bell on the SW corner is a replica of the United States' Liberty Bell.

Frederick Lutheran Church: One of the most beautiful architectural treasures on St. Thomas, this, the oldest church on the island and the second oldest Lutheran building in the Western Hemisphere, is located uphill from Emancipation Park along Norre Gade. Built in 1793, it was renovated in 1826 and 1973. Bethania Hall, which serves as the Parish Hall, is adjacent to the church. A Danish manor, it was built as the private residence of one Jacob S. Lind in 1806. The nearby Grand Hotel dates from 1840. Once the headquarters for the social elite, it now houses shops and restaurants. Farther down Norre Gade is the Moravian church, which dates from the nicely numbered year of 1888.

Government House: Atop the hill on Kongens Gade. Stand in the small park across the road and view the impressive architecture and the black limos parked outside. Inform the

Charlotte Amalie today

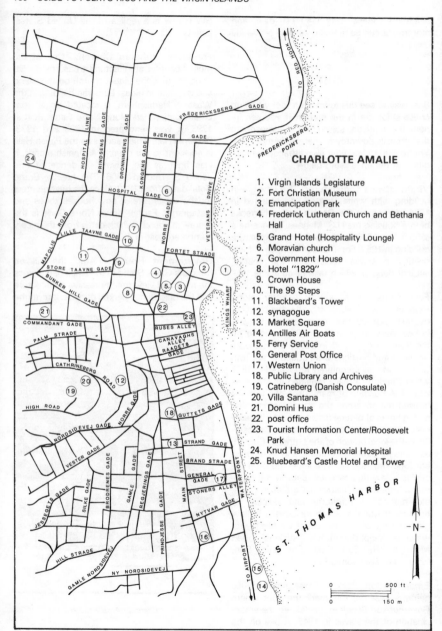

CHARLOTTE AMALIE

1. Virgin Islands Legislature
2. Fort Christian Museum
3. Emancipation Park
4. Frederick Lutheran Church and Bethania Hall
5. Grand Hotel (Hospitality Lounge)
6. Moravian church
7. Government House
8. Hotel "1829"
9. Crown House
10. The 99 Steps
11. Blackbeard's Tower
12. synagogue
13. Market Square
14. Antilles Air Boats
15. Ferry Service
16. General Post Office
17. Western Union
18. Public Library and Archives
19. Catrineberg (Danish Consulate)
20. Villa Santana
21. Domini Hus
22. post office
23. Tourist Information Center/Roosevelt Park
24. Knud Hansen Memorial Hospital
25. Bluebeard's Castle Hotel and Tower

guard at the entrance as to your mission, and he'll escort you around the areas available to the public. Now the official office-residence of the elected governor of the U.S.V.I., this elegant brick-and-wood three-story mansion was built in 1867. Inside, large paintings depicting Transfer Day and Salt River, St. Croix, adorn the staircase walls, while two paintings by St. Thomas-born Camille Pissarro hang in the ballroom upstairs. Beautiful view of the harbor from the window. (Open daily during working hours.) Farther up the same street to the W is Hotel "1829" which is a good example of 19th C. architecture.

Crown House: Climb either of the two step streets along Kongens Gade to reach here. Now privately owned, this 18th C. mansion once functioned as the governor's residence. Recently remodeled, it's filled with antique furniture. This mostly stone two-story house has a Dutch gambrel hipped roof. Peter von Scholten lived here when he was governor of St. Thomas in 1827. Inside, note the handsome ceiling, carved woodwork, the 18th C. Chinese wall hangings, and the French chandelier which is said to come from Versailles. Admission includes a guide and a hit of rum. Open Mon. to Sat. 1000-1700.

99 Steps and Blackbeard's Tower: The step street perpendicular to Blackbeard's Tower is the 99 Steps, most famous of the town's step streets. As you climb, count to see how many there actually are. Note the multicolored bricks: they arrived here as ship's ballast; the yellow ones are from Denmark, the reds come from England, France and Spain.

Synagogue of Beracha Veshalom Vegimulth Hasidim: On Crystal Gade. Take the stairs up to the entrance. Rebuilt in 1833 on the site of previous temples, this building was constructed in a mixture of Gothic Revival styles in 1833. Still in use today, it's the oldest synagogue on the island and the second oldest in the Western Hemisphere. Sand on its floors commemorates the exodus of the Jews from Egypt.

interior of synagogue

market square: The site of what was once the largest slave market in the Caribbean, located along Kronprindsens Gade near the library. Here, locals sell a vast variety of fruit and vegetables ranging from tannia to okra to cassava. Its roof was imported from Europe.

accommodations: Sky-high, especially in season. (High-season prices are listed in parentheses below.) Only campsite available is Larry's Hideaway (tel. 774-8985), located on the N coast at Hull Bay, which charges EP $10 s or $15 d; cabins are $20. Facilities include pool tables, volleyball courts and horseshoe pitching. Guesthouses are the next least expensive alternative: most reasonable of these is the Beverly Hill which charges EP $20.75 s, $35.75 ($40) d. Domini Hus (tel. 774-2661) charges CP $18-20 s ($20), $25-30 ($30) d. Ramsey's (tel. 774-6521) charges EP $22-24 ($28) s, and $28-30 ($35) d. Estate Thomas (tel.

776-4974) charges EP $22.50 s ($25) and $30 ($35) d. Villa Santana (tel. 774-1311), on Denmark Hill, charges EP $25-30 ($45-50) s, and $30-40 ($45-50) d.

food: Tends to be expensive. Quality is always changing due to fluctuations in restaurant personnel. Buy food in the markets and have a picnic. Cafe Portofino has good pizza. The Shanghai on Back Street serves Chinese food. Try the salad bar at the Chart House in French Town. The Sunshine Cafe near Coki Beach serves a good vegetarian lunch. Shabazz Restaurant along Rte. 38 has natural foods.

events: Chief among these is Carnival. Revived in 1952, it is usually held during the last eight days of April. The parade, which takes place on the last Sun., features the King and Queen of Carnival, *Mocko Jumbie* ("imaginary ghosts") mounted on 17-ft.-high stilts, and local contingents of steel and calypso bands, dance troupes, and floats. Local

Main Street commercialism

delicacies are served in Market Square, and events are held inside Lionel Roberts Stadium (near Bluebeard's Hill). Another major event is the Hook In and Hold On (HIHO) board sailing race usually held in late June. Every St. Patrick's Day local Irish residents hold a parade.

shopping: Know your Stateside prices before arriving if you intend to save money on duty-free goods. Things tend to be expensive and "local crafts" are usually the productions of expatriate Continentals. Saint Thomas' Crafts Cooperative on Back St. handles rag dolls manufactured on nearby islands. Take advantage of liquor-tasting bars to get plastered even if you don't intend to buy any liquor. If you do intend to buy some, lowest liquor prices are at Al Chen's in Havensight Mall. Impoverished window shoppers may feast their eyes on the gems and jewelry displayed at Columbia Emeralds at Royal Dane Mall, the Illas Lalaounis counter set inside A.H. Riise, Cardow's, and at H. Sterns Jewelers. All are located on Main Street. Also check out Blue Carib Gems and Rock Factory in Bakery Square. Down Island Traders, also in Bakery Square, has a variety of teas, spices, and unique fruit jellies. *Batiks* are sold at Java Wraps on Main Street. Paperback Gallery, inside Palm Passage, is the island's largest bookstore (open Mon. to Sat. 0900-1700.)

services and information: Get information from the tourist bureau on one side of Emancipation Park. Staffed with volunteers, the Hospitality Lounge inside the Grand Hotel (facing the same park) dispenses advice and checks luggage ($1). The Virgin Islands Public Library and Archives, Main St., are open Mon. to Fri. 0900-2100; a quiet place to pass the time. Banks are open Mon. to Thurs. 0900-1430, Fri. 0900-1400, 1530-1700. Knud Hansen Hospital is located near downtown. Its emergency room is open 24 hours a day.

FRENCHTOWN

Town within a town, this small community in the SW part of Charlotte Amalie is home to one of the smallest but most conspicuous ethnic groups in the Virgin Islands—descendants of the French Huguenots. Also known as Carcenage because old sailing boats careened here for repairs, the brightly painted houses have immaculate, packed-dirt yards. Local watering hole is the Old Normandy Bar.

ST. THOMAS ACCOMMODATIONS

All rates given are lowest; a range of prices may be in effect. Room tax is 6% additional.
KEY: ★ = Continental Plan (CP) applies. ★ ★ = $3.00 pp pn energy charge.
★ ★ ★ = 10% service charge. ☆ = 2½ % energy charge applies.

NAME / ADDRESS	TELEPHONE	HIGH S	HIGH D	ROOM RATES DATES	LOW S	LOW D
Island Beachcomber Box 1618	774-5240	80	85	20 Dec.- 5 April	65	70
Virgin Isle Hotel ★ ★ ★ Box 3188	774-1500	110	115	16 Dec.- 4 April	70	80
Windward Passage Box 640	774-5200	85	90	12 Dec.- 30 April	65	
Galleon House Box 6577	774-6952	35	40	1 Dec.- 30 April	25	40
Harbor View ★ Box 1975	774-2651	70	90	1 Dec.- 1 May	40	60
Inn at Mandahl ★ Box 2483	774-2100	100	110	14 Dec.- 19 April	55	59
Limestone Reef Water Island	774-2148	64	69	15 April- 30 April	45	50
Mafolie ★ Box 1506	774-2790	52	64	1 Dec.- 30 April	38	46
Villa Olga ★ Box 4976	774-1376	86	94	20 Dec.- 14 April	54	62
Beverly Hill Contant #105	774-2693	21	36	15 Dec.- 15 April	21	35
Bunkers' Hill View #9 ★ ☆ Commandant	774-8056	35	45	15 Nov.- 15 May	30	35
Danish Chalet ★ Box 2205	774-5756	35	45	1 Dec.- 30 April		
Estate Thomas Box 1212	776-4974	25	35	1 Dec.- 30 April	23	30
Island View ★ ★ ★ Box 1903	774-4270	37	46	1 Dec.- 30 April	26	34
Maison Greaux ★ ★ Box 1856	774-0063	26	30	15 Dec.- 5 May	22	26
Miller Manor Box 1570	774-1535	33	40	15 Dec.- 1 May	24	28
Ramsey's Box 9168	774-6521	28	35	30 Nov.- 14 April	22	28

ST. THOMAS

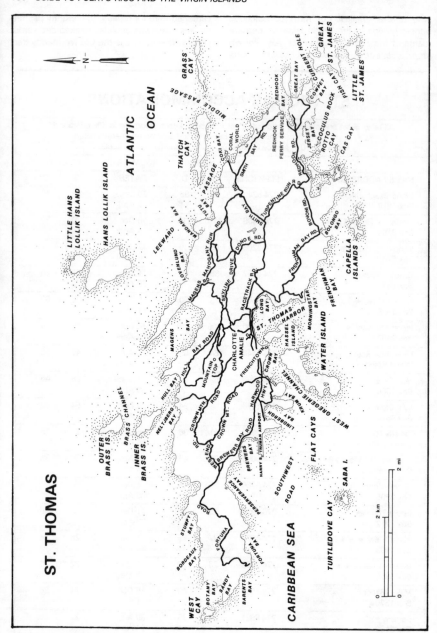

history: Centuries ago, Protestant French Huguenots, fleeing religious persecution in Catholic France, were among the earliest settlers in the Caribbean. They arrived on several islands, including miniscule St. Barths (St. Bartolemy). In 1848, two members of the La Place family migrated to the site of Frenchtown and to sleepy Hull Bay along the N coast. Emigration began in force between 1863-1875, when economic conditions on St. Barths worsened and many sought to flee that tiny, rocky wart of an island.

the people: Some 1,500 strong, the "Frenchies" are a tough people renowned for their fishing and fighting abilities. The two French communities speak different dialects of archaic W. Indian French and retain their cultural distinctions; there has been little intermarriage or even sociability between them. Traditional dress was unique and resembled that found in their native Brittany: women's heads were adorned with the *ealeche,* the traditional shoulder-length headdress; men wore black and calico shirts with their denim trousers rolled halfway up their legs and went barefoot. Retaining this style of dress after arrival caused the locals to make fun of them. In return, the vitriolic French spat out "cha cha" which means "go to the devil." Ironically, the locals began to refer to the community as "Cha Cha Town," a name which sticks to this day. There has been no love lost between the French and the local blacks — each side regarding the other with derision. Long the lowest socio-economic class in the U.S.V.I., in recent years the French have emigrated in droves to the mainland — where they are readily assimilated. **events:** Traditional events such as St. Anne's Day, Bastille Day, and the Christmas Day parade are still observed.

HASSEL ISLAND

This small island guarding Charlotte Amalie harbor is one of the most important historic sites in the U.S.V.I. Today, the National Park Service manages 90 percent of its 135 acres.

getting there: Access is restricted due to a

St. Thomas Carnival revelers

lack of docking facilities, unstable structures, and the potential problem of trespassing on private property. If you wish to spend more than just a short time on the island, get a visitor use permit from Red Hook Headquarters (tel. 775-2050).

history: Activities ranging from agricultural to commercial to military have gone on here. Originally a peninsula attached to St. Thomas, it became an island in the 1860s when the Navy cut through and dredged the narrow connecting isthmus. During the early 1800s, when steamships stopped at Hassel to transfer cargo and take on fuel, the island had two working marine railways, three coaling docks, and a floating drydock. Fort Willoughby was constructed during the 1801 and 1807 British occupations of the island. A U.S. Naval Station was located on Hassel I. from 1917-31; it was reactivated during WW II but abandoned thereafter. Much of the island was acquired during the 1930s by the Paiewonsky family, chiefly in order to provide water for their rum distilleries. During the 1970s, Ralph Paiewonsky wanted to develop the island but his conservationist brother Isidor opposed the move. Lucrative offers, including one of $3 million from Reverend Sun Myung Moon, were turned down. Finally, the two brothers compromised by selling the land to the Department of the Interior for incorporation in the U.S.V.I. National Park.

AROUND ST. THOMAS

Although Charlotte Amalie is the island's heart, there are a number of other settlements and scattered points of interest. Just on the edge of town atop Denmark Hill sits Catrineberg, a mansion built around 1830 in modified Greek Revival and classical Georgian styles. Visible along Skyline Drive is Luisenhoj, a giant castle built by publishing tycoon Fairchild (both are closed to the public). Offshore Water I. may be visited via a seven-min. ride from the sub base. Restored Nisky Moravian Mission, which dates from 1777, is along Harwood Highway. The Orchidarium is located in the shopping center off Harwood Highway to the W of town. Admission is charged for guided tours.

beaches: Among the more than 40 beaches on St. Thomas, Magens Bay, on the N coast of the island off Magens Rd., is on nearly every list of the world's best beaches. Surrounded by the luxurious villas of the wealthy, palm groves are set to the back. This magnifi-

cent mile-long horseshoe of sand was given to the local government in 1946 through the beneficence of publishing tycoon Arthur Fairchild, and fears are that a 50-acre resort planned by developer James Armour will have a negative effect on the environs—so get here fast! (Fifty cents admission.) More accessible Morningstar Beach, SE of Charlotte Amalie, is a family beach with beige sand and occasional surf ($2 admission). Lime Tree Hotel Beach, nearby, charges $1 admission. For a quick dip after arriving or before departing the island, Lindbergh Beach, named after the famous flier, is conveniently located across the street from the airport and near the campus of the College of the Virgin Islands. Brewers Bay Beach is said to be one of St. Thomas' best. Near Cowpet Bay, Bluebeard's Beach is no longer the exclusive property of the hotel of the same name. Coki Beach, reputed to have the island's best snorkeling, lies next to Coral World to the northeast. Semi-official nude beach is Smith Bay Beach near Point Pleasant.

The Bomba Charger *is one of the ferries that ply from St. Thomas to the British Virgins and back.*

the underwater observation tower at Coral World

Less frequently visited beaches include Bordeaux Bay (along the N coast), Stumpy Bay (nearby), and Hull Bay (with perhaps the best surfing on the island). Mandahl Beach is at the end of a very rough road along the same stretch.

dive sites: Visibility often reaches 150 ft. in the vicinity of Sail Rock, nine miles from St. Thomas harbor. Farther still is Saba I. with three different dive sites. Grain Wreck, the unmarked site of a 450-ton cargo ship, is restricted to experienced divers. The wreck of the *Warrick* (1816) rests on Packet Rock while *Cartanser Senior*, a small packet ship, is nearby. French Cap Cay is a rocky underwater promontory surrounded by a myriad variety of sealife. Tunnels, reefs and huge boulders comprise Cow and Calf, the top dive spot on the island. Several dive locales on the N coast are located near Thatch Cay and the wreck of *General Rodgers*. Another good spot is Carvel Rock.

Coral World: One of the only underwater observation towers in the Western Hemisphere, this touristic attraction is located near Coki Beach on the island's NE side. A good way for non-divers to view underwater sea life. Three nights a week a diver hand-feeds the fish. From the two-level deck, observe life on the sea floor as well as circling sharks, barracudas, and stingrays above. Marine Garden Aquariums have 21 saltwater tanks featuring zoological curiosities like purple anemones and fluorescent coral. Open daily 0900-1700;Thurs., Fri., and Sat. until midnight; $5 admission.

Drake's Seat: On Skyline Drive in the center of the island towards the N shore. Legend has it that Sir Francis Drake sat here and peered through a telescope to watch for Spanish galleons approaching what is now known as Drake's Passage. Rendered obsolete by Toyota pickup trucks, the last donkeys—a reminder of the era when they sufficed for the island's automobiles—have been shuttled up here so that tourists may have the privilege of paying to take their pictures. North coast "Frenchies" attend Our Mother of Perpetual Help Catholic Church nearby.

FROM ST. THOMAS

for St. John: Ferries run on the hour between Red Hook, St. Thomas, and Cruz Bay, St. John ($2 OW), and between Charlotte Amalie, St. Thomas, and Cruz Bay, St. John ($4 OW). Virgin Islands Seaplane Shuttle (tel. 773-1776) flies to St. John from Charlotte Amalie harbor ($39 OW).

for St. Croix: Virgin Islands Seaplane Shuttle flies for $29 OW and $58 RT. Crown Air and Ocean Air fly to Christiansted.

for Tortola: Refreshments are served on the soothing *Bomba Charger* ferry which leaves daily for Road Town and West End ($11 OW). Virgin Islands Seaplane Shuttle flies to Tortola for $19 OW, $38 RT. From St. Thomas' airport, Coral Air, Air BVI, and Crown Air fly to Beef Island. **for Virgin Gorda:** *Bomba Charger* continues on Wed. and Sun. at 0800 to Virgin Gorda and returns late afternoon. Costs $12.50 OW, $23.50 RT. **by air;** Crown Air and Air BVI fly. **for Jost van Dyke:** *Bomba Charger* runs to Harris Place on Mon. and Sat. at 0830 ($25 RT); returns Mon. at 1500 and Sat. at 1800. **for San Juan:** Crown Air, Ocean Air, and Coral Air fly daily. A ferry ($20 OW) run by Jenny Tours leaves from Charlotte Amalie for Fajardo, Puerto Rico, on Sat. and Sun. at 1630.

ST. JOHN

Only a 20-min. ferry ride from Red Hook, St. Thomas, St. John seems worlds removed from its neighbor. More than any other Virgin, St. John is someplace special. Seasoned Caribbean travelers call it the most beautiful island in the Caribbean. No one who visits can fail to be romanced by the loveliness of its scenic charms and the friendliness of its inhabitants. Unscathed by cruise ships, this small (19 sq miles) island has near-deserted beaches with wonderful snorkeling, hiking trails, and coral reefs teeming with life. Set amidst a pristine sea, the island is contoured like a maple leaf. More than half of the island's area has been placed under the aegis of the National Park Service. Though the smallest of the "natural area" National Parks of the United States, St. John nevertheless brings together within its 9,500 acres of land and 5,650 acres of surrounding water a natural ecosystem which is amazingly varied and spectacularly beautiful.

HISTORY

Arawak Indians, existing in frugal harmony with the island's resources, inhabited St. John for 1,000 years before being displaced by arriving Caribs. The latter had already departed by the time the first Europeans arrived. Given by the Spanish, the island's name refers to St. John the Apostle rather than St. John the Baptist after whom San Juan was named. Before the Danish West Indies and Guinea Company acted to take control of St. John in 1694, the island had only been visited infrequently. It was not until 1717 that the first company-operated plantation was established at Estate Carolina in Coral Bay. Settlers hoped that this area, with its fine harbor, would soon rival Charlotte Amalie in importance. At first, their optimism appeared justified; St. John became one of the most productive spots in the whole region. By 1733, 15 years after taking possession, 101 plantations were under cultivation. Seven-year tax exemptions had attracted 208 whites, who controlled 1,087 black slaves. Danes were overwhelmingly outnumbered by Dutch.

slave rebellions: St. John was used as a training ground where slaves were "broken in" before being shipped to the more sophisticated plantations of St. Thomas. A large number of the slaves were members of

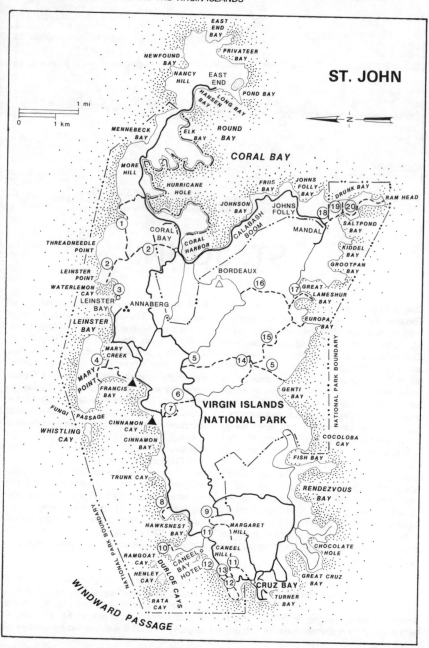

the Amina tribe; to these proud tribesmen, tilling the land was women's work and considered degrading. Akamboos, many of whom had been sold to Coral Bay planters, were equally rebellious. In 1733, Philip Gardelin, the new governor of St. Thomas and St. John, issued an 18-point manifesto. Under its terms, punishment ranging from amputation, beatings, and pinching the skin with a hot iron were prescribed for all types of infractions. Slaves were forbidden all dances, feasts, and plays; any slave caught in town after curfew faced being beaten and locked in the fort. That very same year the island was beset by a hurricane, a long drought, a plague of insects, and a fall storm. Refused rations by their owners owing to scarcity, the half-starved slaves struck decisively for freedom. At dawn on Sun., 13 Nov. 1733, slaves entered Fort Berg carrying the customary load of wood. Whipping out cane knives concealed in the wood pile, they sliced open all of the soldiers save one who had scurried under a bed. They then fired two cannon shots that were the pre-arranged signal to hundreds of slaves to rise up in revolt. All across the island, marching bands of slaves ransacked greathouses and burned cane fields. Whole families of settlers were wiped out. Within a few hours, the slaves controlled the entire island.

short-lived freedom: By late Dec., the rebels had been forced into waging a guerilla war in the hills. The British sent 70 men from Tortola, but they withdrew after being ambushed, as did a similar force dispatched from St. Kitts in February. Worried about their holdings in St. Croix to the S, the French sent two warships from Martinique which arrived in April. Finding themselves hopelessly outnumbered in mid-May, the rebels held one last feast in a ravine near Annenberg, then committed ritual suicide *en masse.* Forming a circle, each shot the one next to him until the last one shot himself. When the planters arrived, they found seven guns—all broken to pieces save one—a symbol that the struggle would continue until freedom had been won. While the ruined settlers chose to relocate, others soon arrived, and St. John became a prosperous colony once again. This lasted until the Napoleonic Wars, when British troops occupied the island in 1801 and again from 1807-13. This second occupation served to depress the economy. The perfection of the sugar beet and the 1848 emancipation resulted in falling profits. Many planters were already facing ruin when a new variety of sugarcane was introduced from Java at the end of the 19th century. After another short-lived burst of enthusiastic activity, the sugar balloon burst again, and the island wandered off in a somnolent stagger, which the transfer to U.S. ownership in 1917 left unchanged.

SAINT JOHN

1. Brown Bay Trail (1.2 miles, 2 hours)
2. Johnny Horn Trail (1.5 miles, 2 hours)
3. Leinster Bay Trail (0.8 miles, 30 min.)
4. Francis Bay Trail (0.3 miles, 15 min.)
5. Reef Bay Trail (2.5 miles, 2 hours)
6. Cinnamon Bay Trail (1.2 miles, 1 hour)
7. Cinnamon Bay Self-Guiding Trail (1 mile, 1 hour)
8. Peace Hill (Christ of Caribbean)
9. Water Catchment Trail (0.8 miles, 30 min)
10. Turtle Point Trail (0.5 miles, 30 min.)
11. Caneel Hill Trail (2.1 miles, 2 hours)
12. Lind Point Trail (1.5 miles, 1 hour)
13. Caneel Hill Spur Trail (0.9 miles, 40 min.)
14. Petroglyph Trail (0.3 miles, 15 min.)
15. Lameshur Bay Trail (1.8 miles, 1 ¼ hours)
16. Bordeaux Mountain Trail (1.2 miles, 1 ½ hours)
17. Yawazi Point Trail (0.3 miles, 20 min.)
18. Salt Pond Bay Trail (0.2 miles, 15 min.)
19. Drunk Bay Trail (0.3 miles, 20 min.)
20. Ram Head Trail (0.9 miles, 1 hour)

THE PARK

Practically synonymous with the island itself, the Virgin Islands National Park is the island's most valuable resource. Remember that this is a trust held in perpetuity and one that visitors years hence will wish to find in the same shape it is today. Act accordingly.

the making of a national park: In 1939, a National Park Service study compiled by Harold Hubler recommended that a park be established on St. John; the plan was forgot-

ruins of a sugar plantation at Annaberg

ten after the onset of WW II. Cruising around the Caribbean for six years after the war, multimillionaire philanthropist Laurence Rockefeller determined that the island had "the most superb beaches and view" of any place he had ever seen, and that St. John was "the most beautiful island in the Caribbean." He quickly bought up nearly half the island during the early 1950s and established an exclusive resort at Caneel Bay on the grounds of a ruined sugar plantation. Discovering Hubler's report, Rocky transferred his property into his Jackson Hole Preserve Corporation nonprofit tax writeoff. Jackson Hole then offered to donate over 5,000 acres, provided they retained franchise rights to the park area. Legislation signed into law by President Eisenhower on 2 Aug. 1956 authorized the federal government to accept donation of up to 9,500 acres. No local opinion was sought before a government bill was introduced in Congress in 1962 which would have authorized $1.25 million to acquire another 3,300 acres of St. John by condemnation—whether the owners acquiesced or not! This sum was contingent upon a Rockefeller offer to provide matching funds. Even the government administrator for the island first heard of the plan over the radio, and he, like other islanders,

was outraged. The bill passed (without the condemnation clause) and Rocky withdrew his offer of matching funds.

boating: Park waters are subject to regulations designed to help preserve the environment. The N and S offshore areas were added to the park in 1962. Altogether, there are 26 anchorages around the island. Overnight stays in park waters are limited to 14 days per year, and boats are not to be left unattended for periods in excess of 24 hours. Charts and maps, along with a complete list of park regulations, are available at the Cruz Bay Ranger Station.

hiking: A total of 21 trails—from brief walks to two-hour jaunts— are probably the most underutilized of all St. John's resources. Because most are steep and rocky, they give maximum amount of exercise for the time involved. In just a short time, you climb from 700 to 1,700 ft. above sea level, where you get a very different view of the island! Although NPS tours are available, the best way to go is on your own. Trees creak in the wind, squirrels scurry across paths, and shy wild donkeys scatter when approached.

CRUZ BAY

Cruz Bay, with its relaxed, ecological-minded feeling, is like a miniature version of Berkeley, California, in the Caribbean. So small that the streets are nameless, its slow pace of life is intoxicatingly contagious. Aside from the ultramodern but aesthetically pleasing Mongoose Junction shopping center, there're a few shops, a small park, and a ranger station for the park.

getting there and around: Catch the hourly ferry from Red Hook, St. Thomas ($2 OW), or from Charlotte Amalie ($4 OW). Virgin Islands Seaplane Shuttle (tel. 773-1776) flies from Charlotte Amalie harbor ($39 OW). Also accessible by seaplane from St. Croix or by ferry from Tortola and Virgin Gorda. It's easy to walk anywhere in town. To visit other parts of the island, take local transport (expensive), hitch, or rent a jeep. If hitching, stand on the outskirts of town and use your forefinger to point in the direction you want to go (St. John-

ians consider using your thumb to be rude, and you won't get a ride that way).

sights: St. John's Administration Building, known as the "Battery," was built on the foundation of an 18th C. fortification. Explore the small museum, which has everything from seashells to antique maps within the narrow confines of old prison cells (open Mon. to Fri. 1000-1400, free admission). Near the pier stands the Nazareth Lutheran Church. Gallow's Point, directly across from the harbor, served a gruesome purpose in its time. Farther out of town, along Centerline Rd. (formerly known as "Konge Vej"), stands the Bethania Moravian Church. Note the renovated 18th C. Parish Hall, the vaulted cistern behind it, and the two Dutch ovens inside the small house to the rear. Near a large green water tank, a short dirt road to the L leads to the ruins of Estate Catrineberg. One of the earliest plantations on St. John, it has

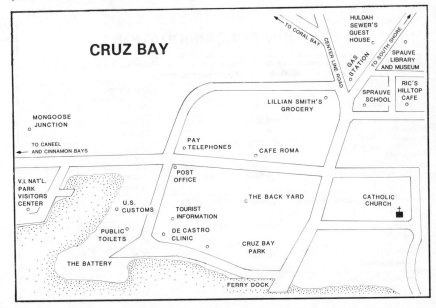

now been completely engulfed by bush. Looking carefully around the grounds you can see the remains of a horsemill and windmill. The now gunless Lind Battery, allegedly constructed in a single night by the English during either their 1801 or 1807 assaults, can be reached by the Lind Point Trail (see "hikes" below).

accommodations: Limited and expensive. Bamboo Inn, off season the cheapest, charges $21.50 s, $31 d, and $10 extra with third person sharing. Next cheapest, and least expensive in season, is Huldah Sewer's Guest House, $25 s, $35 d, $10 extra person sharing. "Camping" is available at Cinnamon and Maho Bays (see "accommodations" under respective sections), but only Cinnamon Bay has bare sites where you can pitch your own tent. If you've arrived without a reservation and the campground is full, see Victor at The Kite along the North Shore Road. Victor can generally be found in his small, open-air restaurant listening to his favorite tape—the one of himself playing music! You may camp on his private beach (toilet, no electricity) for $10 pp. If planning an extended stay on the island, remember that housing is expensive and difficult to find.

food: Prohibitively expensive, so try to bring what you can with you. If you're planning on cooking your own food at the campground and staying a while, it may be worthwhile to go all the way over to St. Thomas to shop (as the locals do) because the few local stores have a minimum amount of goods at maximum prices. Eating out can also cost you. One alternative to the restaurants is to load up on bread, cheese, and other such digestible commodities at the bakery inside Mongoose Junction. The Back Yard usually has a luncheon special for $4 and under. Cafe Roma has good pizza. Limin Inn's baked potatoes ($2.50) are a meal in themselves. Local food spots include Miss Maeda's (near The Back Yard) and Fred's. There's also a Rasta fruit stand and a lot of snack food available including conch fritters and sandwiches.

events: St. John's Carnival, now integrated with the U.S. Independence Day celebrations,

ST. JOHN ACCOMMODATIONS

All rates given are lowest; a range of prices may be in effect. Room tax is 6% additional.
KEY: ★ = $1.00 pn energy surcharge.

NAME / ADDRESS	TELEPHONE	HIGH		ROOM RATES	LOW	
		S	D	DATES	S	D
Bamboo Inn Box 96	776-6318	38	53	15 Nov.- 15 April	30	45
Bethany Condos Box 254	776-6318	50		15 Dec.- 1 May	50	
Havens with Ambiance Box 635	776-6322	100		1 Dec.- 1 May	70	
Huldah Sewer's Guest House ★ Box 24	776-6814	35	40		35	40
Raintree Inn Box 566	776-6103	65		15 Dec.- 15 April	65	
Selene's 18-44 Enighed	776-7850	65		15 Nov.- 15 April	50	
Serendip Condos Box 273	776-6646	65		15 Dec.- 30 April	45	

commemorates the emancipation of slaves on 3 July 1848. Not as large as the one on St. Thomas but equally intense in atmosphere, the Carnival begins in the first days of July, climaxing on 4 or 5 July. Constructed along the waterfront, Carnival Village has handicrafts, food and drink stalls as well as games and pony rides for children. Calypso and reggae bands from all over the Caribbean ride through town on the backs of trucks. Celebrating begins in earnest at 0430 on 4 July when St. Johnians depart their homes attired in diapers, pajamas, and other outlandish clothes for the *j'ouvert* (French for "opening" or "break of day") festivities. The parade is the highlight of the festival, and *its* highlight is the *mocko jumbie* dancers who hop, skip, and do acrobatics on stilts. They are followed by the Carnival Queen and various floats. Evening fireworks end the celebration. The biweekly St. John Festival of the Arts, a relatively new phenomenon, also takes place during the summer. Events are held in Cruz Bay's Park, Caneel's Patio, and Maho's Recreation Center. Past performers have ranged from folksinger Oscar Brand to the ultra-eclectic Joan Miller Dance Players. (Detailed information about the festival is available from Maho Bay's New York City office, 17 E. 73rd St., New York, NY 10021.) A yearly celebration, commemorating the slave uprising of 1733, takes place around Thanksgiving; it includes a candlelight procession and symposiums.

entertainment: To find out what's happening where, check local tree trunks and utility poles, as well as the bulletin board across from the bank. Frontline, an excellent ska band, plays Sat. nights at Fred's. The local fish fry happens every Fri. and Sat. evening at Pond Mouth near town. Starting at 1830 and going on until midnight or later, there are usually ska, reggae, calypso, or scratch bands playing. Old movies are shown at the Back Yard on Thur. nights. Don't miss the nightly audio-visual display put on by the moon, stars, and crashing surf.

hikes around Cruz Bay: The Lind Point trail (1.5 miles, one hour) connects the NPS Visitor Center with Caneel Bay Plantation. Just before the descent to Caneel Bay, the trail reaches an overlook at Lind Point. The Caneel Hill trail (2.1 miles, two hours) joins Cruz Bay with the Northshore Rd. entrance to Caneel Bay via Caneel and Margaret Hills. These two trails are interconnected by the Caneel Hill Spur Trail (0.9 miles, 40 min.) which crosses Northshore Rd. at an overlook of Cruz and Caneel Bays. Interlocking Centerline and Northshore roads and joining the Caneel Hill trail over a portion of its route, the Water Catchment Trail (0.8 miles, 30 min.) has a deep-forest feeling to it. About three miles from town along Centerline Rd. is the shortest hike on the island; it takes 10 min. to get to the island's strangest sight, the Christ of the Caribbean. Set amidst the ruins of the Denis Bay Plantation with its sugar mill tower, this armless but enormous concrete statue of that Jesus fellow was donated to the Virgin Islands National Park in 1975. It was built in the 1950s on the orders of a certain Col. Wadsworth, a transplanted mainlander, who dubbed the area "Peace Hill" and dedicated the statue to "inner and outer peace."

services and information: The tourist office is near The Battery. Telephones are located at the dock near the park and across from the post office. The Morris De Castro Clinic is next to the tourist office (open Mon. to Fri. 0800-1630; tel. 776-6222). In case of emergency, a doctor can be reached 24 hours a day by calling the Dept. of Public Safety (tel. 776-6262). Laurence Rockefeller's brother David has opened a small branch of his bank near the Lutheran church. A beautiful, carpeted two-story Elaine Ione Sprauve Library, a reconstruction of the Enighed Estate great house, is on the same road as Huldah Sewer's Guest House. The National Park Service office, next to the ferry pier, is perhaps the best source of information on the island. Don't procrastinate—make this your first stop. Folders, maps, and books are available. Ask for information about any of a number of activities including nature hikes, history walks, and snorkel trips. They also present films, discussions, etc., at Cinnamon Bay campground. Information can be obtained in advance by writing directly to National Park Service, Box 710, St. John, USVI 00830 (open daily 0800-1600; tel. 809-776-6201).

Cruz Bay

CANEEL BAY

Here's where good American politicians are sent on holiday. Located about two miles down the road from Cruz Bay, this elite resort is a place at which a very few select of the well-connected and well-heeled rich can relax. Insulated from the plebians by the surrounding parkland, this oasis of Florida-style architecture costs an all-inclusive $250-340 per day for each of its 130 rooms. Set on 170 acres including gardens, tennis courts, and seven beaches, the only luxury missing is golf. Although much of its original posh status has been lost to Little Dix, another Rockresort in the neighboring British Virgins, it continues to attract prominent guests, including former President Richard Nixon. Because of the nature of its clientele, it is said that Caneel Bay is for "the newly wed or the nearly dead." Worthy of note on the grounds is the ruins of the Durloe Plantation, which has been ripped apart for transformation into a bar and gift shop.

from Caneel Bay: An elitely priced ferry ($4

OW) plies four times a day between Caneel Bay and National Park Dock, St. Thomas. The Lind Point Trail (1.5 miles, one hour) goes back to Cruz Bay. Turtle Point Trail (0.5 miles, 30 min.) begins at the N end of Caneel Bay. (Register at the front desk at the main entrance before using this trail.) Farther down the main road to the E is Hawknest Bay and Peace Hill.

TRUNK BAY

Most popular and famous of all the island's beaches, Trunk Bay is named after the "trunkback" or leatherback turtle (which may reach eight ft. and weigh up to 1,000 pounds)—though it's rarely seen around here these days. Orange markers identify the snorkeling trail. No longer quite the mecca for snorkelers that it used to be, the coral has been damaged by boat anchors, souvenir hunters, and careless swimmers. Friendly fish still greet you underwater, however, and tiny "ghost crabs" still spook the beach. Watch out for sea urchins.

CINNAMON BAY

This small but pretty beach has an outlying coral reef with lots of fish, a campground, and rewarding walks in the vicinity. To get here take either one of the large taxi-buses ($2) from town, hitch, or walk.

accommodations: There are 10 bare sites, 40 erected tents, and 40 cottages available. Up to six people in two tents may occupy the bare sites ($9 per night). Picnic table and charcoal grill are provided. Canvas tents (10 by 14 ft. with concrete floor) with camp cots, two-burner propane gas stove, and utensils, are $32 d ($41 15 Nov. to 1 May; $6 extra third person). Cottages ($40 d; $50 high season; $6 extra third person) measure 15 by 15 ft., have concrete walls and floors, two screened walls, four twin beds, picnic table and grill, ice chest, propane gas stove, water container, cooking and eating utensils. Linen is changed weekly and a $20 deposit is required. Make reservations well in advance by writing Cinnamon Bay Campground, Box 720, Cruz Bay, St. John, USVI 00830 tel. (809) 776-6330, (800) 223-7637; (800) 442-8198 in New York State, (212) 586-4459 in New York City.

food: Best to bring as much of your own as possible. The commissary only has a limited and expensive supply of goods (50 cents per onion!) so it's better to shop in St. Thomas beforehand or even to bring food from the mainland. A mediocre cafeteria serves breakfast (0730-0930), lunch (1130-1330), and dinner (1730-1930); *a la carte* dishes average around $4. Cookouts on Sun. nights provide a good opportunity to socialize with fellow campers.

services and practicalities: Upon check-in (daily 1400-2000), you will be provided with a map of the campground. If arriving before that time, you may use camp facilities. Site assignments will be posted for those arriving after 2000. Check-out is 1100; luggage may be left in the office. There are four bath houses; water should be conserved. Pay telephone service is available near the registration desk. Campground office numbers are 776-6330/6458, and 776-6111, ext. 260. Bus schedule is posted near the registration desk. Films are shown Sun. nights after the cookouts. Snorkel sets may be rented for $4 per day or $15 per week. Scuba sets and underwater cameras are also available. Diving costs around $30 single tank, $55 double. Bring plenty of insect repellent to combat mosquitos, the most ferocious animals on the island.

hiking: A good place to base yourself for hiking on the island. The Cinnamon Bay Self-

overlooking Cinnamon Bay

Guiding Trail (one mile, one hour) passes by native tropical trees and the ruins of a sugar factory. The trailhead is a few yards E of the entrance road to the campground. A hundred yards E of the entrance road, Cinnamon Bay Trail (1.2 miles, one hour) goes past a stone cistern with guava trees in front to Cinnamon Bay ruins atop the hill. To the R is the estate house and to the L, buried in the bush, are the remains of the sugar factory. Built during the mid-19th C., the original estate house was destroyed by a hurricane during the early 1900s. A quarter mile farther atop a steep incline is a round platform which is the remains of one of a number of charcoal pits found in this part of the island. Still farther, along a path hemmed in by hogplum trees, is the old Danish cemetery. Tombstones here were sized according to the deceased's station in life. Look for thrasher, ani, quail dove, golden orb spiders, and the low-flying zebra butterfly.

MAHO BAY

The second campground on the island, opened in 1974. Designed with ecological conservation in mind, a series of tent cottages built on wooden boardwalks preserve the natural ground cover that prevents erosion; insecticides are not used here, and taps and toilet facilities are specially constructed to conserve water. Seeming more like tree houses than tents, these three-room canvas cottages have completely equipped dining and cooking areas. Everything you need is supplied. The small but complete commissary stocks freshly caught fish and baked bread. Prices are high. Breakfast and dinner ($7) are also served. The "Help Yourself Center" has toys, books, and groceries left by departing guests. Rates are $40 per day d ($50 15 Nov. to 1 May), plus $10 per extra person. Write to Maho Bay Camps, Box 310, Cruz Bay, St. John, USVI 00830 (tel. 809-776-6240) or to Maho Bay Camps, 17-A E 73rd St., New York, NY 10021 (tel. 212-472-9453).

hiking: At the W end of the Mary Creek paved road, the Francis Bay Trail (0.3 miles, 15 min.) passes through a dry scrub forest, and past the Francis Bay Estate House to the beach. Several hundred slaves are said to have leaped to their deaths from Mary's Point during the 1733 slave revolt rather than face recapture. Local legend maintains that the water here turns red each May.

ANNABERG RUINS

The attractive ruins of this sugar plantation sit atop a point overlooking Leinster Bay. The structures have been spruced up rather than restored, and a self-guiding tour takes you through what was once one of the 25 active sugar-producing factories on St. John. Imagine yourself back in the 18th C., when the entire surrounding area was covered in sugarcane. Comprising 510 acres and dating back to 1780, the estate was run by overseers, which is why no great house was ever built. Walk through the former slave quarters, the ruins of the village, the remains of the windmill, horsemill, boiling bench, and oven. Drawings of schooners and a street scene, which may date back to Dutch times, decorate the small dungeon. Fruit trees on the property were planted by Carl Francis, a cattle farmer, who lived here during the early 1900s.

manchineel *tree*

vicinity of Annaberg: From here it's a nice walk, via two interconnecting paths, to Coral Bay. First follow the Leinster Bay Trail (0.8 miles, 30 min.), actually the remains of an old Danish road, along the shoreline to the pebbled beach with its crystal-clear water. Watermelon Cay is off in the distance. Next follow the ruins at the other end of the bay to the beginning of the historic Johnny Horn Trail (1.5 miles, two hours). The trail climbs a ridge framed by cactus and yellow spaghetti vine. The latter covers trees and bushes and looks as if someone had scattered gallons of spaghetti in tomato sauce. The trail follows the ridges S to the paved road running past the Emmaus Moravian Church in Coral Bay. The unmaintained Brown Bay trail (1.2 miles, two hours) starts from the ridge saddle 0.6 miles along the Johnny Horn Trail. Branching to the E, it descends through hot and open valley covered with dry thorn scrub before running along Brown Bay, then ascends across the ridge above Hurricane Hole before terminating at the East End Rd., 1.3 miles E of Emmaus Moravian Church.

CORAL BAY

Quiet streets and a relaxed atmosphere mark the site of the best harbor in the U.S. Virgin Islands. More than two centuries ago Admiral Lord Nelson claimed it was large enough to hold most of the navies of Europe. (It is still sufficient for a modern fleet.) Although it was the site of the first Danish settlement on the island, it never grew to the size or prominence hoped for. Here, the action is at Redbeard's Saloon and Island Grocery where bands play occasionally. Good place to meet transplanted St. Johnians.

sights: First to greet the visitor is the Emmaus Moravian Church. Constructed during the late 1700s on the site of the Caroline Estate, this large yellow building stands at the edge of town. Judge Sodtmann and his 12-year-old daughter were murdered on this spot during the 1733-34 slave revolt; local legend maintains that a *jumbie* (spirit) appears as a ram each and every full moon to haunt the premises. The windmill nearby is another

cactus and flowers along the Johnny Horn trail

relic of the vanished estate. Further to the N past the Moravian cemetery is the beginning of the path to the top of Fort Berg Hill which sticks out onto the harbor. At the top are the ruins of Fort Berg, which slaves captured and held during the 1733-34 revolt (see "History"). The English Battery, at the foot of the fort, was built during the British occupation of 1807-14; a few rusty cannon are still lying about. (Ask permission from the owners of the Flamboyant Restaurant before exploring these ruins.)

to the east: A dramatic road, surrounded by cactus-covered bluffs, leads to Round Bay at the E end of the island. Excellent view of Tortola to the L before reaching Hurricane Hole to the R where ships still shelter during hurricanes. This area is still comparatively undeveloped and only about 40 people live at this end of the island. Even the road is a fairly recent addition. No public transport, so hitch or walk.

to the south: From the junction before Coral Bay, take the road (concrete with bits of imbedded shell) along the mangrove-lined coast, smelling strongly of brine, to the town of Calabash Boom (where there's a health clinic) and beyond. Salt Pond Bay trail (0.2 miles, 15 min.) begins 3.6 miles S of Coral Bay and leads to Salt Pond Beach. From the S of the beach, turn to the E and follow the Drunk Bay trail (0.3 miles, 20 min.) along the N of the salt pond to Drunk Bay Beach (dangerous swimming). Most of the year this bleak and rocky beach ("drunk" means "drowned" in Dutch creole) is swept by 30-mph trade winds. The seaside lavender bay pea vines, which cover the sandy soil, prevent sea erosion. At the far end of Drunk Bay, Ram Head, the oldest rock on the island (dating from the Lower Cretaceous period over 90 million years ago), overlooks a 200-ft. precipice. Follow Ram Head Trail (0.9 miles, one hour) to a blue cobble beach and on to the top. Back on the main road, sandwiched on a peninsula between Great Lameshur and Little Lameshur Bays, is Yawzi Point trail (0.3 miles, 20 min.). Years ago people afflicted with yaws (a contagious tropical skin disease resembling syphilis) were forced to live here in order to avoid spreading the disease. The Lameshur Bay trail (1.8 miles, 1.25 hours) connects Lameshur Bay with Reef Bay trail through open forest. A rock side trail, 1.4 miles before the Reef Bay junction, leads to dramatically silent, peasoup-colored Europa Pool (watch your footing). From Little Lameshur Bay, the sunny Bordeaux Mountain trail (1.2 miles, 1.5 hours) climbs 1,000 feet right up to the top of 1,250-ft.-high Bordeaux Mountain, highest point on the island. Magnificent view of the British Virgins from here. This trail dates from the time when donkeys laden with bay leaves would descend to the still at Lameshur Bay below. The oil was extracted by boiling in seawater, and then shipped to St. Thomas where it was used to produce St. John's Bay Rum, a famous cologne. From the top, the dirt road connects with Centerline Road.

REEF BAY TRAIL

Most popular hiking trail on the island, it begins five miles E of Cruz Bay. Takes two hours to negotiate. Formerly a wagon road, it was still the best road on the island as late as 1950. An incredible abundance of nature, much of it annotated by the National Park Service, grows along the sides of the trail. Descending through both wet and dry forests, the trail passes the remains of no less than five sugar estates, their stubbles of masonry foundation nearly consumed by strangler figs and wild orchids. Built of red and yellow imported brick, basalt rock, and brain coral, this attractive mosaic is still held together by local mortar of lime made from seashells, sand, molasses, and goat hairs. Stone rocks, laid over the road, still act as culverts which divert the torrential rainfall. Along the path, you may see wild pigs, donkeys, or even a hermit crab clatter across the road. The laundry pool along the gut of the trail was formerly a meeting and gossiping place for housewives. About 100 ft. away from a mango tree on the trail stands the remains of the wattle-and-daub Old Marsh House which was swept away in the Oct. 1970 floods.

Estate Par Force: Right on the trail. Built before 1780, it was remodeled in 1844. All that remains of the estate are the corral, sugar factory, and horsemill. In lieu of the unaffordable windmill, horses circumnavigating the 80-ft. stone grinding platform provided power to grind the cane.

Petroglyph Trail: Begins 1.7 miles down the Reef Bay Trail. It takes 15 min. to reach this quiet, peaceful, and secluded pool which teems with life, including wild shrimp. Situated below a small waterfall, chiseled petroglyphs were originally thought to have been the work of indigenous Indians. In 1971, a Ghanian ambassador visiting the site noted the resemblance of one of the symbols to an Ashanti one meaning "accept God." More

FISH OF THE VIRGIN ISLANDS

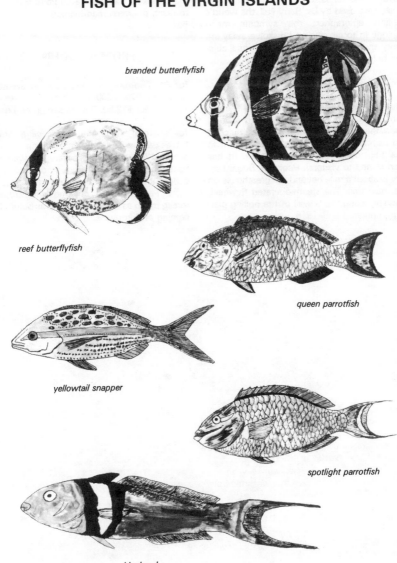

branded butterflyfish

reef butterflyfish

queen parrotfish

yellowtail snapper

spotlight parrotfish

bluehead

recently, the double spirals have been found to be identical with those found on A.D. 200 Libyan tombstones. Symbols of purification, these were used by Dr. Barry Fell, the world's leading epigrapher; the symbols mean "plunge in to cleanse and dissolve away impurity and trouble; this is water for ritual ablution before devotions."

Reef Bay Estate House and Sugar Plantation: Last stop on the trail. Made of local stone, the greathouse was originally stuccoed and painted. Its hilltop location enabled it to take full advantage of sea breezes. (It has been closed to visitors). Reef Bay Sugar Factory is about a mile beyond the greathouse on the main trail. The steam-operated flywheel, standing along the S wall of the boiling platform, operated until 1916.

from Reef Bay: Either climb back up to Centerline Rd. or retrace your steps and take the Lameshur Bay and Yawzi Point trails back to reach the main road leading back to Coral Bay.

FROM ST. JOHN

for St. Thomas: A ferry runs on the hour daily from 0700-2200. Books of 10 tickets are available for $12.50. Beer is served on board.

for Tortola: Take the *Sundance II* which leaves daily at 0830 with an extra trip on Sun. only at 1700. It's not necessary to have a RT ticket. A beautiful, panoramic ride. Sea gulls glide in the wind; cacti arc from the sides of cliffs. Pass by cays covered with tropical forest, much as the whole area was before the coming of Europeans.

ST. CROIX

Separated from the other two Virgins by distance, Saint Croix (pronounced "Croy") differs in other ways as well. It strikes a comfortable balance between the commercialism of St. Thomas and the tranquility of St. John. Although it was the last island to become Danish, it retains the strongest Danish feeling. There's a real sense of living history here. Fredericksted and Christiansted retain old architecture and streets, and ruined sugar estates dot the countryside. The large Puerto Rican population adds a Latin element.

the land: Largest and most fertile of all the U.S. Virgin Islands, it's 29 miles long by seven miles wide. Its 84 sq miles (more than twice the size of St. Thomas) are still subdivided into large sugar plots with names like "Hard Labor," "Little Profit," "Work and Rest," and "Humbug." This comparatively flat and spacious island is blessed with an abundance of vegetation. While the tropical forests of the W adjoin the arid scrublands of the E, the hills of the N contrast sharply with the long, even plateaus of the south. Although water has always been in short supply, the flat S plain is

well suited to sugarcane (unlike the other, almost entirely mountainous islands). The N is frequently lush and verdant, though the S may be brown and desolate during the drier seasons. The E end is a virtual desert.

history: Viewed by the superpowers of the time as a small pearl to be fought over, ownership of the island was disputed among English, French, and Dutch settlers. Said to have borne the flags of seven nations, there have actually been more owners than that. Between the time Columbus and his men were attacked by Indians at Salt River in November 1493 and the time the island was first settled in 1625, the original inhabitants had disappeared, presumably conscripted to work in the gold mines of Santo Domingo. The Indians had called the island "Ay Ay," and Columbus called it Santa Cruz—the name which stuck. When the dust of disputation settled in 1650, France had control; ownership was transferred the next year to De Poincy, a leading Knight of Malta. In 1653 he deeded his title to the Knights of Malta. The island was then sold to the French West Indies Company in 1665. Twelve years later, the French monarchy took possession of the island from the bankrupt Company, and in 1695, Louis XIV ordered it abandoned. The island was left to unofficial squatters until 1733, when it was sold to the Danish West Indies and Guinea Company which, in turn, sold the island to the Danish government after it too nearly went bankrupt.

Danes and English: Arriving Danish settlers found that large tracts of land had already been cleared by the French, who had set fire to the entire island. For a time thereafter, St. Croix became the richest sugar island in the Caribbean. Within 20 years, there were 1,000 people and 375 plantations. Arriving from neighboring islands, English planters soon outnumbered the Danes five to one. This one-crop prosperity lasted for 65 years, during which cane production swelled from 1.5 million pounds in 1755 to 46 million in 1812.

By 1796, more than half of the island was planted in sugarcane. In 1802 there were 30,000 slaves, but the slave trade was abolished the next year. Briefly captured by the British in 1801, the island was held by them again from 1807-15 during the Napoleonic Wars. Already in a slump due to the price drop following the introduction of the sugar beet, the abolition of the slave trade and the U.S. foreign sugar tariff of 1826 signalled the downfall of the island's prosperity. Further setbacks followed. Part of Christiansted burned in 1866, an earthquake and tidal wave hit the island in 1867, the capital was moved back to Charlotte Amalie in 1871, another severe hurricane struck in 1876, and labor riots occurred in 1878 and 1892. It was almost as though someone had it out for the island, which continued its decline after the U.S. purchase in 1917; it was only reversed following the post-WW II growth in tourism.

CHRISTIANSTED

Larger of the two towns on the island, it is by far the most fascinating town in the U.S. Virgin Islands. Founded in 1734 as a planned community by the Dutch West Indies and Guinea Company, it was made the Danish colonial capital in 1755. A discriminatory building code, effected in 1747, had the incidental effect of preserving the town's old houses for posterity. Christiansted is so well preserved that parts were designated a national historical site in 1952. There are blocks of pastel pink, yellow, and brown colonnaded buildings with high-peaked roofs.

arriving by air: Alexander Hamilton Airport, named after the famous American statesman who once lived here, is seven miles from town on the S coast. Pick up information at the tourist office counter. Shared taxis to town cost $5 pp.

getting around: It's both pleasant and easy to walk around town. Abrahamson Bus Lines has buses ($0.50) every half hour for Fredericksted. Expensive shared taxis are

available; make sure you get the correct price, and not the one reserved for gullible tourists. (Rates are fixed by the local government and are available from the tourist bureau.)

SIGHTS

Try to pick a time to explore when no cruise ship passengers have been bused in. Allow a morning for this walking tour.

Scalehouse: Built in the mid-1800s, scales stand in the entryway. Imports and exports were weighed in and inspected in this building, and troops were also quartered here. It now houses the tourist information center.

Old Danish Customs House: Begun in 1751 and completed in 1830, this elegant building now houses the National Park Service information center on the first floor and photographic displays on the second.

Fort Christiansvaern: One of the best-

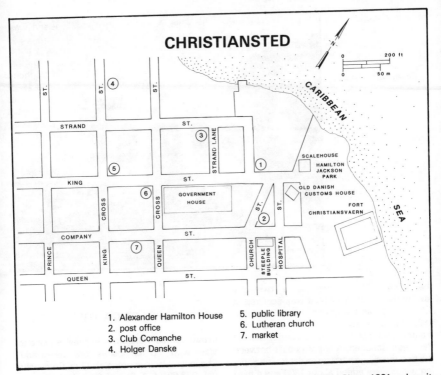

CHRISTIANSTED

CARIBBEAN

SEA

STRAND ST.

KING ST.

COMPANY ST.

QUEEN ST.

SCALEHOUSE

HAMILTON JACKSON PARK

OLD DANISH CUSTOMS HOUSE

GOVERNMENT HOUSE

FORT CHRISTIANSVAERN

CHURCH ST.

STEEPLE BUILDING

HOSPITAL

1. Alexander Hamilton House
2. post office
3. Club Comanche
4. Holger Danske
5. public library
6. Lutheran church
7. market

preserved 18th C. forts in the Caribbean, this fortification, painted red with white trim, has been restored to its 1820 appearance. Standing at the edge of the harbor, there are no outerworks. Enter through the wooden gate flanked by masonry columns. Pick up the self-guiding yellow pamphlet at the Visitor's Counter. The main courtyard is dominated by a huge flamboyant tree. Built from Danish bricks used as ballast in Danish battleships, the fort was constructed from 1732 to 1749; the walled horse yard to the E of the citadel was added in 1837. It remained the military hub of the island until it was converted into the police headquarters in 1878. Enjoy the great views from the water battery.

Steeple Building: Completed by 1753, it was once called The Church of Our Lord of Sabaoth. First Lutheran church on the island, it was originally steepleless; the present stee-

ple was added in 1794. Since 1831, when it was taken over by the government, it has been used as a military bakery, hospital, and school. Completely renovated in 1964, it now contains a small museum whose historical exhibits include maps, photos, relics, and costumed mannequins. Open Mon. to Fri. 0900-1600; Sat. 0900-1200.

Danish West Indies and Guinea Company: Completed in 1749, it was used to house provisions, offices and personnel. After 1833 it became a military depot and then the telephone office. It is currently used as the post office and U.S. Customs.

Government House: Faces onto King St. at the corner of Queen Cross Street. Once housing both the governor and the administrative offices, it is the landmark public building on

Governnment House

the island. At its core is a two-story townhouse. Built in 1747, it was acquired in 1771 for use as the governor's residence. In 1828, the neighboring home of a merchant-planter was acquired by Governor-General Peter von Scholten. A link was built between the two dwellings a few years later. The flanking wings were added about 1800 and a third story in 1862. Walk through the iron gates to the reception hall. Although the departing Danes had left nothing in the ballroom save the pitch pine floor, in 1966 the Danish government donated the furniture found there now. The four antique chairs in the antechamber were donated by Queen Margarethe of Denmark during her 1976 visit. Although virtually nothing remains of the Crugar Hardware Store across the street where a youthful Alexander Hamilton once clerked, the present commercial structure is named for him anyway.

The Lutheran church: Built in the late 1740s as the Dutch Reformed church and acquired by the Lutherans after they vacated the Steeple Building. The tower over the front porch was added in the late 1830s.

PRACTICALITIES

practicalities: Uniformly expensive place to stay with no campsites on the island. Cheapest place in town is Club Comanche (tel. 773-0210), 1 Strand St., which charges $30-38 s, $40-65 d, and $8 per extra person, off season (tel. 773-0210). **food:** Not a cheap place to eat either. Hamilton Mews, which stays open until 0300, serves sandwiches and drinks, as do Heart of Palm and The Pig's Ear. Brady's, King Cross St., serves West Indian food. Nightly happy hour. Ritz Cafe, Queen Cross St., also has a happy hour. Many restaurants and hotels have an assortment of tourist-oriented nightlife ranging from steel bands to country music to limbo dancing. Check *This Week in St. Croix* for details.

shopping: Not nearly as big a commercial venue as St. Thomas, St. Croix, nevertheless, has a wide selection of duty-free goods including famous Cruzan rum. King St. and Camagniets Gade (Company Street) are the main shopping locales. Produce is sold in the open air farmers' market. Bookstores include

Jeltrup's Books on King Cross St. and Tropicat Paperback Exchange at 15 Church Street.

services and information: A tourist information service is located inside the Scalehouse. The National Park Service gives out information inside the Old Danish Customs House. Emergency service (24 hours) is available at the Charles Harwood Hospital (tel. 773-1212). The Florence Williams Public Library is on King Street. The post office is located inside the Danish West Indies and Guinea Company Warehouse.

CHRISTIANSTED ACCOMMODATIONS

All rates given are lowest; a range of prices may be in effect. Room tax is 6% additional.
KEY: ★ = Continental Plan (CP) applies. ★ ★ = $3.00 pp pn energy charge.
★ ★ ★ = 10% service charge applies.

NAME / ADDRESS	TELEPHONE	HIGH S	HIGH D	ROOM RATES DATES	LOW S	LOW D
Anchor Inn 58A King St.	524-2030	71	84	16 Dec.- 15 April	50	63
Caravelle Queen Cross St.	773-0687	63	73	19 Dec.- 14 April	54	61
Charte House 2 Company St.	773-1377	35	45	15 Dec.- 14 April	30	35
Club Comanche ★ ★ 1 Strand St.	773-0210	35	50	15 Dec.- 14 April	30	40
King's Alley	773-0103	60	70	1 Dec.- 30 April	40	50
Lodge ★ 43A Queen Cross St.	773-1535	50	60	15 Dec.- 14 April	44	55
Pink Fancy ★ 27 Prince St.	773-8460	120		19 Dec.- 14 April	60	
Tropical Inn ★ ★ ★ 48 King St.	773-3403	40	50	14 Dec.- 15 April	35	45

FREDERIKSTED

Located on the W coast of the island, this town has great views and an impressive colonial legacy. Its tree-lined streets still harbor a wide variety of colonial architecture. Get here fast, though, because Colonel Sanders and his architectural tribe of concrete behemoths are moving in. Cruise ship passengers see this town only in their peripheral vision as they are being speedily bused to Christiansted.

history: Established on 19 Oct. 1751 and named for King Frederick V, the town grew slowly. There were exactly two houses in 1755 and still only 314 residents by 1766. Many of the original buildings in town were destroyed by the 1867 tidal wave or the fire (caused by labor riots) of 1-2 Oct. 1878, in which most of the town burned to a crisp. The majority of the remarkable restorations and reconstructions date from then.

SIGHTS

Fort Frederick: Originally built to discourage smuggling and completed in 1760, this quiet but imposing structure has played an important role in the island's history. From here, the flag of the new American republic was saluted for the first time in 1776. According to local legend, an American brigantine was in port here when independence was declared. When a homemade Stars and Stripes was hoisted, the fort, ignoring the rules of neutrality, returned the cannon fire. This was the first salute to an American ship. Here also, on 3 July 1848, Governor-General von Scholten read the proclamation emancipating the slaves. Restored in 1976, the fort houses a museum. The exterior leads to replicas of living quarters. **the Customs House:** Located to

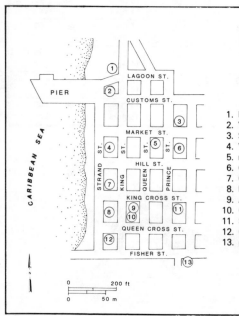

FREDERIKSTED

1. Fort Frederick
2. Visitors Bureau and Customs House
3. St. Patrick's Cathedral
4. Victoria House
5. market
6. Old Danish School
7. Christiansted Hotel
8. hospital
9. Apothecary Hall
10. Cumberland Castle
11. St. Paul's Episcopal Church
12. Old Library (Bell House)
13. post office/Old Danish Customs House

the S of the fort, this late 18th C. structure houses the tourist bureau.

Victoria House: Located a block or two S of the Customs House. This private home, most of which was consumed in the flames of 1878 and rebuilt thereafter, is a local landmark, an excellent example of Victorian architecture, with its elaborate gingerbread trim.

Bell House (Old Frederiksted Public Library): Two blocks farther at Queen Cross Street. Once owned by a man named Bell who, appropriately enough, decorated the stairs with those charming chiming objects. Presently used as an Arts and Crafts Center. The Dorsch Cultural Center, an open theater used for local cultural events, is attached to the main structure.

Cumberland Castle: A short walk uphill at the corner of King and Queen Cross streets. This former mansion is closed to the public. **Old Apothecary Hall:** Just beyond Barb Mc-

Connel's restaurant to the L on Queen St. stands this unusually designed late 19th C. building. **St. Paul's Episcopal Church:** Incorporating both classical and gothic elements in its design, this sturdy building, survivor of several hurricanes, was built in 1812.

old Danish school: About 1½ blocks away on Prince Street. Designed in 1835 by Hingelberg, a famous Danish architect in his time, it now houses government agencies. **St. Patrick's Cathedral:** Across Market Street. A mid-19th C. reconstruction of the original 18th C. cathedral. **Mt. Victory School:** Located outside of town on Creque Dam Road. One of eight schools built around 1840 in accordance with von Scholten's edict proclaiming compulsory education for all children.

events: New Year's Day features a children's parade. A special ceremony takes place in town on 3 July, Danish West Indies Emancipation Day.

ISLAND WIDE ACCOMMODATIONS

All rates given are lowest; a range of prices may be in effect. Room tax is 6% additional.
KEY: C'd = Christiansted vicinity. F'd = Frederiksted or vicinity. K'gs = Kingshill vicinity.
★ = Continental Plan (CP) applies. ★★ = $10% service charge. ★★★ = 15% service charge.
☆ = $2.00 pp, pn energy charge. ☆☆ =$2.75 pp, pn energy charge.
• = 2% energy tax. •• = 5% energy charge.

NAME / ADDRESS	TELEPHONE	HIGH		ROOM RATES	LOW	
		S	D	DATES	S	D
Cane Bay Reef Club Box 1407, K'gs	778-2966	65 420/wk		21 Dec.- 14 April	45	
King Christian Box 3619, C'd	773-2285	50	60	15 Dec.- 16 April	40	45
King Frederick Beach ★, ★★ Box 1906, F'd	771-2105	49	54	15 Dec.- 14 April	29	34
Royal Dane ★, ★★ 13 Strand St., F'd	772-2780	40	45	15 Dec.- 1 April	30	35
Sprat Hall ★★★, ☆ Box 695, F'd	772-0305	70	85	16 Dec.- 30 April	50	
Tamarind Reef ☆☆ Box 1112, C'd	773-0463	90		20 Dec.- 31 Mar.	65	
The Fredericksted 20 Strand St., F'd	772-0500	59	76	1 Dec.- 30 April	40	50

ISLAND WIDE ACCOMMODATIONS (CONT.)

The Inn Box 1307, K'gs	778-2121	35	45	15 Dec.- 15 April	32	38
Villa Morales Box 422, F'd	772-0556	22	24	n/a	22	24
Waves at Cane Garden Bay Box 1749, K'gs	778-1805	55	65	15 Dec.- 15 April	30	40
Bay Garden House Est. Orange Gr., C'd	773-2211	174/wk		15 Dec.- 15 April	130/wk	
Caribbean View ★ ★ ★ LaGrand, C'd	773-3335	65		16 Dec.- 14 April	40	
Coakley Bay Star Rte., C'd	773-1500	120/wk		15 Dec.- 15 April	80	
Colony Cove Golden Rock, C'd	773-1965	105/wk		2 Dec., 15 April	40	
Granada Del Mar LaGrande, C'd	773-7472	135/wk		20 Dec.- 15 April	65	
Mill Harbour ★ ★ ★ Est. Golden Rock, C'd	524-2008	105/wk		15 Dec.- 15 April	75	
Turquoise Bay • 53 Little Princess, C'd	773-0244	495/wk		15 Dec.- 14 April	40	50
Ackies Box 828, C'd	773-3759	25	30		25	30
Shakur's Box 2853, C'd	772-2724	20	35		25	30
Chenay Bay •• Box T, C'd	773-2918	392/wk		21 Nov.- 20 April	36	48
Cottages by the Sea Box 1697, F'd	772-0495	39	47	15 Dec.- 14 April	28	32
Northside Vly Villas Box 281, F'd	772-0558	200/wk			200/wk	
Sunset Beach Cottages Box 1395, F'd	772-0199	50	85	15 Dec.- 15 April	30	

above, clockwise: Ponce Art Museum, Puerto Rico (Roger LaBrucherie); colmada (general store), Bani, Dominican Republic (R. LaBrucherie); San Jose Church and Plaza, Puerto Rico (R. LaBrucherie); church at Coamo, Puerto Rico (R. LaBrucherie); Peace Monument *(El Monumento)*, Santiago, Dominican Republic (R. LaBrucherie);

above, clockwise: El Morro from the air, San Juan, Puerto Rico (Roger LaBrucherie); Annaberg ruins, St. John, USVI (USVI Division of Tourism); Altos de Chavon, Dominican Republic (DR Tourist Information Center); Fort San Cristobal, Old San Juan, Puerto Rico (R. LaBrucherie); Puerto Rican petroglyphs (Institute of Tropical Forestry)

AROUND THE ISLAND

There is a wealth of scenic beauty, including a small rainforest in the W end of the island. Fountain River, a 4,085-acre estate formerly owned by the Rockefellers, covers a tenth of the island's land area and includes Davis Bay Beach and tax-exempt Fountain Valley Golf Course. Covering another 1,600 acres on the S coast in the island's center, the locally unpopular Amerada Hess Corporation runs one of the world's largest oil refineries; it produces 700,000 barrels per day. Largest of the island's few remaining Senepol cattle ranches, Fritz Lawaetz's Annaly Farms spreads across 5,000 acres near the island's NW corner.

beaches: Facilities have recently been built near Christiansted at Altona Lagoon and near Frederiksted's Fort Frederick. Near Christiansted heading E are the Buccaneer Beach at Reef Bay, Shoys Beach, Tamarind Reef Beach, Reef Beach, and Cramer Park Beach. Nearer to town, Hotel on the Cay's beach is open to public use. Round the E point is Isaac Bay, a difficult-access nudist beach. Farther on are Grapetree Beach and Jack's Bay Beach. To the W of Christiansted are Judith's Fancy, Salt River, Canebay, and Northstar beaches. La Grange Beach and Tennis Club and St. Croix Country Club are just outside town. Both charge admission, but the latter is open to the public only on weekends. Sandy Point Beach is to the S of Frederiksted while Rainbow Beach, Spratt Hall Beach (and accompanying renovated greathouse-restaurant-hotel combination), and Monk's Nath Beach are to the north.

plantations and ruins: Judith's Fancy, NW of Christiansted and near St. Croix by the Sea, is the most picturesque ruin on the island. Prosperity Plantation, near Frederiksted on Mahogany Rd., still has its greathouse and manager's residence intact. Near Fredensfield are the ruins of Morning Star plantation. The Mt. Victory and Annaly ruins are near Creque Dam Road, Spratt Hall, a French plantation on the W coast above Frederiksted, has been transformed into an inn.

Point Udall: This nonsensical non-site is said to be the easternmost point in the United States. (It's not; that distinction belongs to Wake I. in the South Pacific.) Its true claim to fame is as the part of the Virgin Islands first sighted by Columbus on 14 Nov. 1493 during his second voyage.

West Indies Laboratory: At Teague Bay on the N shore. Established in 1971 as a branch of New Jersey's Farleigh Dickinson University. Scientists here study island flora, fauna, marinelife and ecology. The campus offers credit and non-credit courses, lectures, seminars and field trips. A Hydrolab is located at Salt River. For more information write West Indies Laboratory, Annex Box 4010, Christiansted, St. Croix USVI 00820 (tel. 773-3339).

St. Croix Marine Station: On the N coast at Estate Up Twist. This branch of the University of Texas Marine Science Institute and the Arkansas Marine Laboratory has continual courses and projects.

Island Center: Located, aptly, in the center of the island off Centerline Rd. near Sunny Isle Shopping Center. Its 10 acres contain a 1,200-seat amphitheater which showcases cultural events.

St. George Botanical Garden: Located off Centerline Rd. about four miles W of Frederiksted. Originally a 16-acre estate, it contains the ruins of a greathouse, rum factory, lime kiln, baker's and saddlemaker's shops, and a stone dam. Note the garden with its pre-Columbian crops (maize, cassava and sweet potatoes) and the old cemetery. Enter through the stone gates along a road flanked on either side by rows of royal palms, the trees grown by Hebraic kings in the Garden of Babylon. Concerts are occasionally held here on Sundays. Open daily 0730-1530; free admission.

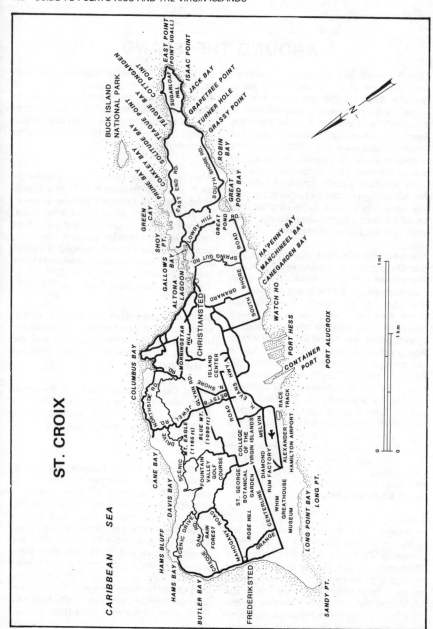

Whim Greathouse

Whim Greathouse: Located two miles off Centerline Rd. near Frederiksted, this large sugar estate complex was originally known as St. John's Rest. Restored by the St. Croix Landmarks Society, it was owned by an eccentric Dane named Christopher MacEvoy, Jr. Oval-shaped and roofed, this comparatively small one-story estate house has a large number of windows. Built around 1794, its yard-thick walls are made of cut stone and coral held together with lime-and-molasses mortar. A moat surrounds the building. Antiques (both Cruzan in origin and imports) fill the insides. To the rear, the cook house and attached museum contain displays of sugar production artifacts, a pot-still for making rum, engravings, weapons, and the tombstone of Anna Heegard, the famous mistress of Governor-General von Scholten. Reconstructed *in situ* from numbered blocks brought from Nevis, the windmill fairly represents the ones in use during the island's sugar heyday. The recreated Apothecary Shop (1832) has finishing touches right down to the rocking chair and the fine collection of original bottles and vials on the shelves. Other displays include the ruins of the sugar processing factory, the Scottish steam engine, and the watchhouse. Open daily 1000-1700; $2 admission with guided tour.

BUCK ISLAND REEF NATIONAL MONUMENT

The only underwater National Monument in the U.S., tiny Buck Island lies two miles off the N shore of St. Croix. An incredible 22,000 people visit this seductive nymphet of an island every year. Proclaimed a national monument in 1961, the island was inhabited from the 1750s when Dutch settlers called it Pocken-Ey Land because of the presence of Pokholdt *(Lignum vitae)* trees. Later, the name was changed to Buck which referred to the goats which replaced the *Lignum Vitae* trees. Introduced in the 1750s, these goats did their best to eat up the vegetation and turn the island into a desert before they were removed in the 1950s. Today, the visitors are permitted onshore only between 0800-1700 daily. Dramatically reforested since the goats' departure, the island today is as close to nature now as it's ever been. Even though the spectacular stuff is really underwater, it's worth a visit just for the island itself. More than 40 species of birds flutter around 62 species of trees. The island is a rookery for frigate birds and pelicans. A nature trail runs along the top of the mile-long island; follow the trail to the top of the island for a spectacular view of St. Croix. The beach here is superior to any on St. Croix.

downstairs: Originally a simple fringing reef, a magnificent barrier reef stretches 2,000 yards along the eastern half of the island. Its effect is one of sheer fantasy. Swim past the elkhorn coral that marks the entrance to the reef and follow the markers along the bottom to find your way along the 30-min. underwater trail. While underwater, check out the rainbow gathering of fish including the queen angelfish, the foureye butterflyfish, the smooth trunkfish, and the French and blue angelfishes. Others include the yellowtail, spadefish, red snapper, tilefish, trumpetfish, and several varieties of parrotfish. Fish here are so naive and trusting that they'll eat right out of your hand. While you're investigating

the downstairs branch of this living natural history museum, note the primitive multicellular animals. Most primitive of all are the sponges, which come in all shapes and sizes. A dinosaurian prototype of the starfish, the flexible, multi-armed crinoid anchors itself to crevices with its central, white, root-like pedestal. One of many reef organisms capable of producing sounds underwater, the spotted drum *(Equetus punctatus)* produces a continuous discordant and eerie symphony of snaps, pops, grunts and scraping noises.

getting there: Access is limited to private and chartered boats. Expect to pay at least $15 for the 5½-mile sail. A variety of all shapes and sizes of boats (including catamarans, yachts, native sloops, trimarans and glass-bottomed boats) leave from Christiansted's King's Wharf.

practicalities: If you plan on snorkeling, hiking, fishing or picnicking, pack appropriately. Although there is a well-equipped picnic area, no food is available on the island so bring your own. Beware of sunburn, cuts from coral,

spiny sea urchins, jellyfish, fire coral. Never reach into a dark hole lest you be savaged by a moray eel. Maneuver your boat slowly through park waters. For further information contact Superintendent, Christiansted National Historic Site, Box 160, Christiansted, St. Croix, USVI 00820 (tel. (809) 773-1460).

FROM ST. CROIX

for St. Thomas: Sunaire, Coral Air and Virgin Islands Seaplane Shuttle ($29 OW) fly daily. **for St. John:** Virgin Islands Seaplane Shuttle flies daily ($35 OW). **for Tortola:** Virgin Islands Seaplane Shuttle flies once daily. **for Vieques:** Vieques Air Link flies three times daily ($25 OW). **for San Juan:** Oceanair, Crownair, and Coral Air fly daily.

for the Southern Caribbean: LIAT flies to Antigua, Barbados, Dominica, and Point a Pitre (Guadeloupe). LIAT and Coastal Air Transport fly to Nevis. LIAT flies to St. Kitts and St. Maarten. LIAT and BWIA fly to St. Lucia.

THE BRITISH VIRGIN ISLANDS

INTRODUCTION

Quiet and peaceful, the British Virgin Islands offer solace to the traveler weary of the commercialism and despoiled atmosphere of the Caribbean's larger islands. Incredible scenery lies both above and below the water. These islands are the premier yachting destination in the Caribbean, and their beautiful beaches and hiking trails are attractive to landlubbers as well.

THE LAND

Comprising the eastern portion of the Virgin Islands archipelago, these islands, like their neighboring American cousins, are primarily volcanic in origin. (A notable exception is Anegada, which is a limestone and coral atoll.) Grouped for the most part around the Sir Francis Drake Channel, these 50 or so islands, cays, and rocks date from eruptions that took place 25 million years ago. Altogether, the islands comprise 59 sq miles of land area, with Tortola, the largest and most rugged, taking up 21 of these. Rivers are nonexistent, and owing to the aridity of the climate, water is in short supply. The only notable mineral deposit is the salt on Salt Island.

climate: Really fine! Set within the tradewind belt, temperature on these islands rarely drop more than 10 degrees F at night; daytime temperatures range between 80-90 degrees throughout the year. Rain, and water in general, is scarce.

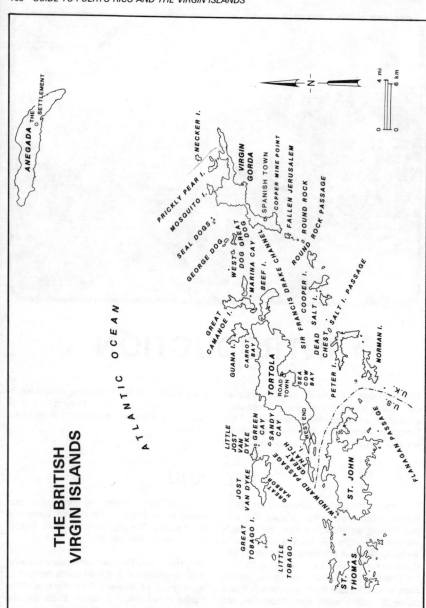

THE BRITISH
VIRGIN ISLANDS

ATLANTIC OCEAN

ANEGADA

THE SETTLEMENT

NECKER I.

PRICKLY PEAR I.

MOSQUITO I.

VIRGIN GORDA

SPANISH TOWN

COPPER MINE POINT

FALLEN JERUSALEM

SEAL DOGS

GEORGE DOG

WEST DOG

GREAT DOG

MARINA CAY

BEEF I.

ROUND ROCK

ROUND ROCK PASSAGE

GREAT CAMANOE I.

GUANA I.

CARROT BAY

SIR FRANCIS DRAKE CHANNEL

COOPER I.

DEAD SALT I.

CHEST

SALT I.

SALT I. PASSAGE

TORTOLA

ROAD TOWN

SEA COW BAY

WEST END

PETER I.

NORMAN I.

LITTLE JOST VAN DYKE

GREEN CAY

SANDY CAY

JOST VAN DYKE

GREAT HARBOR

THATCH

WINDWARD PASSAGE

U.K.

U.S.

ST. JOHN

FLANAGAN PASSAGE

GREAT TOBAGO I.

LITTLE TOBAGO I.

ST. THOMAS

4 mi

6 km

HISTORY

Columbus sailed by the British Virgin Islands on his second voyage in 1493. In the early 1500s the Spaniards settled for a while on Virgin Gorda to mine copper, and stopping in on Tortola, gave it its name (meaning "turtle dove"). At first, few migrants were attracted by Tortola's steep hills. Unsettled and unclaimed, it remained the province of buccaneers who utilized its hidden caves as hideouts. The first actual settlement on Tortola was by pirates at Soper's Hole, West End. The Dutch began the first permanent settlement on Tortola in 1648. A mixed band of pirates drove out the Dutch in 1666 and, in turn, invited the English to come in. Soon after, however, the French took the island, but the British recaptured it in 1672. A migration of Anguillans followed. With the exception of the islands already taken by Denmark, the British gradually began to occupy all of the unclaimed islands remaining in the Virgin

Islands group. Before the end of the 17th C., the planter class had achieved a degree of prosperity. (Planters here, however, never made the fortunes their counterparts did on the flatter, wetter islands such as St. Croix and Barbados.) Crisis followed crisis in the 18th C. as the European nations brought their chess game to the Caribbean. By 1720, the population was 1,122 whites and over 1,500 blacks. The Virgins (including Anguilla) were given their own lieutenant governor under the British-regulated Leeward Islands government. Along with Anguilla, St. Kitts and Nevis, the Virgins were incorporated into the separate Leeward Islands Colony in 1816. More than half the white residents fled in 1831 after discovery of a slave plot which, had it succeeded, would have resulted in the murder of them all. In 1853 a revolt began in Road Town and spread all over Tortola and nearby islands. Tortola was reclaimed by the bush

IMPORTANT DATES IN B.V.I. HISTORY

1493: Columbus sails by the British Virgins. Some of present-day Virgins included in grant to Earl of Carlyle.

1648: Dutch buccaneers settle Tortola.

1668: English buccaneers expel Dutch.

1680: Planters from Anguilla begin to settle Tortola and Virgin Gorda; deputy governor and council selected.

1685: English settlements on Tortola and Virgin Gorda raided by Spaniards.

1718: Spanish attack Tortola and attempt settlement.

1774: British House of Assembly commences meeting in Road Harbour, Tortola.

1802: Road Harbour (present-day Road Town) becomes a free port.

1803: Last public slave auction held on Tortola.

1808: Slave trade abolished by Britain.

1816: Along with Anguilla, St. Kitts, and Nevis, the Virgins are incorporated into the separate Leeward Islands Colony.

1834: Slavery abolished on British islands.

1853: Revolt begins in Road Town and spreads all over Tortola and nearby islands; cholera outbreak reduces population by 14 percent.

1872: Islands placed under Leewards Island Administration and admitted as a separate colony.

1905: Government Savings Bank established.

1922: First hospital opened.

1943: First secondary school opened.

1949: Demonstrations held throughout the islands demand representative government and closer association with the U.S. Virgin Islands.

1956: Leeward Islands Federation dissolved; commissioner of B.V.I. becomes administrator.

1959: First issue of first newspaper (*Tortola Times*) published.

1966: Queen Elizabeth II and Duke of Edinburgh visit.

1967: New constitution granted.

and remained largely wild for decades. In 1872, the islands were placed by Britain under the Leeward Islands Administration and admitted as a crown colony. Severe hurricanes in 1916 and 1924 caused extensive damage. The Legislative Council was abolished in 1902, and the governor-in-council became the sole legislative authority. A presidential legislature for the islands was established in 1950 with elected and appointed members.

The 1967 constitution granted the islands a ministerial government, and a few years later, after the de-federation of the Leewards Island Colony, the Virgins were set up as a separate colony. On 31 Dec. 1959, the Office of the Governor of the Leewards was abolished; the administrator on Tortola became the Queen's Representative. The British Virgin Islands had obtained their present territorial status.

GOVERNMENT

One of the most stable in the Caribbean, the B.V.I. are a self-governing territory (read: colony) with a governor appointed by the British queen. The current governor is David Robert Barwick, who was appointed in Jan. 1982. The island's chief minister is elected by the locals. Residents seem unconcerned with independence and at present content with the status quo. These islands were once seen as being the least important place in the British Empire. When asked where the British Virgin Islands were, Sir Winston Churchill is said to have replied that he had no idea, but he should think that they were as far as possible from the Isle of Man. As the British Empire continues to contract, the symbolic importance of these islands has grown. Her

distinguishedness Queen Elizabeth II has seen fit to arrive here by royal yacht twice in little over a decade.

ECONOMY

Until very recently the British Virgin Islands have known nothing but poverty. Tourism, however, responsible for more than half of the $20 million GNP, has brought a measure of prosperity. These islands have a standard of living second in the Caribbean to only the U.S. Virgin Islands. And they have gained the benefits of financial shoulder-rubbing with their wealthier neighbor, without contracting its serious problems. Since the 1940s, thousands have migrated to the U.S.V.I., relieving population pressures and transferring savings back home. After the collapse of

the plantation system in the 19th C., the planters returned and either sold the land cheaply or gave it to their former slaves. As a consequence—in contrast to other Caribbean islands where a small elite control the land—the common people of the B.V.I. own their own turf. In some cases, land rights are leaseless and hereditary. In general, they sensibly prefer to rent rather than deed land. Most goods are imported. There is no industry to speak of, and agriculture is largely confined to garden plots.

PRACTICALITIES

getting there: The easiest—but most expensive—way is to fly from San Juan or St. Thomas to Tortola or Virgin Gorda. British Caribbean's flights from Miami are the only direct flights from the continental U.S. Otherwise, you'll have to change planes in one of these two places. LIAT ($100 RT), Crownair and Air BVI fly from San Juan to Beef Island, Tortola, daily; Crownair flies from St. Thomas to Beef Island, Tortola, daily; Virgin Island Seaplane Shuttle flies from St. Croix and St. Thomas to West End, Tortola, on Mon., Wed., and Friday. Air BVIA and Crownair fly from San Juan to Virgin Gorda daily; Crownair flies from St Thomas to Virgin Gorda daily. No discount air fares are available. Virgin Island Seaplane Shuttle, whose flights land right in West End, leaves from St. Croix and St. Thomas for Tortola. From St Thomas ferries are available to Tortola, Virgin Gorda, and Jost Van Dyke. Boats from St. John leave for West End, Tortola, and occasional daytrips for Virgin Gorda are available.

getting around: No local transport save expensive shared taxi service (from Road Town to Brewer's Bay or Cane Garden Bay, for example, it costs $3 pp) available on Tortola and Virgin Gorda; rates are fixed by the local government. A beautiful but strenuous way to see the island is on foot. Slopes are incredibly steep, but views are magnificent. Other alternatives include renting a car or using your thumb. Hitching is easy: both locals and visitors are usually happy to get riders, but don't try it after dark. Cars rent for around $25 per day plus gas ($1.60/gal.) with unlimited mileage. International Car Rentals (tel. 49-42193/4) in Road Town has the lowest rates. Air BVI flies from Beef Island to Virgin Gorda daily. Bicycles are available from Hero's Bicycle Rental in Road Town at $2 per hour plus $30 deposit; Harrigan Rent-A-Cycle on Virgin Gorda rents Puch mopeds for $15 pd or $90 per week.

accommodations: Although these islands have intentionally geared themselves towards tourism for the super rich, some good values include campsites on Tortola and Jost Van Dyke. The only reasonably priced accommodations are on Tortola (see "accommodations" and chart under "Tortola").

food: High prices prevail. Locals get by with small vegetable gardens and food sent over from St. Thomas by boat from relatives. Small stores sell groceries on the islands. If camping, it's best to bring over everything you can, save the ridiculously cheap demon rum.

shopping: Other than the duty-free alcohol (one liter) allowed by U.S. customs, there's not much to buy here besides some souvenirs in shops; most are imported from the other Caribbean islands. Some alternative souvenirs include the postage stamps and sets of mint coins offered by the post office in Road Town on Tortola, and the British Virgin Islands Caribbean seasoning marketed in Road Town.

money: The US dollar reigns supreme here. Because of the physical proximity and economic ties with the U.S.V.I., the dollar was made the official currency back in 1962. Measurements are the same as in the United States. Time here is permanently Eastern Daylight Time (EDT).

B.V.I. PUBLIC HOLIDAYS

1 Jan.: New Year's Day
March: Commonwealth Day (movable)
April: Easter Monday (movable)
May-June: Whit Monday
June: Sovereign's Birthday (movable)
1 July: Territory Day (movable)
Aug.: Festival Monday, Festival Tuesday, Festival Wednesday (movable)
21 Oct.: St. Ursula's Day (movable)
14 Nov.: Birthday of Heir to the Throne
25 Dec.: Christmas Day
26 Dec.: Boxing Day

broadcasting and media: Cable TV brings over a number of stations from the U.S.V.I. and Puerto Rico. The only AM station is 10,000-watt ZBVI which broadcasts weather reports every half-hour from 0730-1830. Only newspaper is the weekly *Island Sun.*

visas: Visitors may stay for up to six months, provided they have return or onward tickets, sufficient funds (as judged by the customs official), and pre-arranged accommodations. (In practice, the last two are seldom required for shorter stays.) Although a passport is required for entry, birth certificates or voter registration cards are sufficient for U.S. or Canadian citizens. Cruising permits are required for all charter boats.

health: In Road Town is a hospital, eight doctors, two dentists, and two visiting eye specialists. There is only one doctor on Virgin Gorda. **conduct:** People here are among the most friendly and hospitable in the whole Caribbean. Keep in mind, however, that the local culture is still highly conservative, so be sure to dress conservatively (e.g., confine your bathing suit to beach areas) and adopt a suitable demeanor. There's remarkably little theft here; however, reasonable caution is advised.

services and information: Good telephone service (25 cents for local calls) is available. For information about the area, Cyril Woodfield's superbly informative and free bimonthly *The Welcome* is a must.

BRITISH VIRGIN ISLANDS TOURIST BOARDS OFFICES

British Virgin Islands
Box 134, Road Town, BVI
(809) 49-43134

UNITED STATES
B.V.I. Tourist Board
370 Lexington Avenue
New York, NY 10017
(212) 696-0400

UNITED KINGDOM
B.V.I. Tourist Board
48 Albemarle Street
London W1X 4AR, England
(01) 629-6353/4

CANADA
Mr. (Bill) William Draper
801 York Mills Road, Ste. 201
Don Mills, Ontario, Canada M3B 1X7
(416) 283-2239

WEST GERMANY
Capt. H.G. Friedrichs MM
West India Committee Representative
Lomerstrasse 28
Hamburg 70, West Germany
(4940) 695-8846

TORTOLA

Ferries from St. John to St. Thomas ply along beautiful coasts and past romantic, deserted islets to reach this very attractive island. Although development has made an impact here (most of the British Virgin Islands' 10,000 population reside on Tortola), there is none of the sprawling concrete architecture that has spoiled the majesty of St. Thomas. Protected from heavy traffic by a bypass, the administrative capital Road Town (pop. about 1,500) still retains its small-town flavor. The rest of the island has only been touched by a well-disguised and harmoniously built hotel here and there. Split lengthwise by a ridge of sharply ascending hills, the island is studded with islets, coves, sandy beaches, and bays. Sugarcane cultivation having ceased long ago, much of the land has been reclaimed by nature. If you look carefully, however, you can still see the outlines of what once were fields.

ROAD TOWN

Road Town was originally known as Road Harbour. Small but charming, this is the administrative capital of the B.V.I. and the only settlement truly worthy of the description "town." Not much happens here except a bake sale on Saturdays. Roosters and hens, a goat or two, and an occasional herd of cattle supplement the pedestrian population. **getting around:** It's easy and comfortable to walk everywhere in town.

SIGHTS

Best place to begin a walking tour is Road Town's small but excellent museum on the main street. Inside are old glass bottles retrieved from the RMS *Rhone* and other items from the HMS *Nymph,* finds from the plantation era, Indian relics including *zemis,* furniture, pictures of various buildings, etc. Ex-

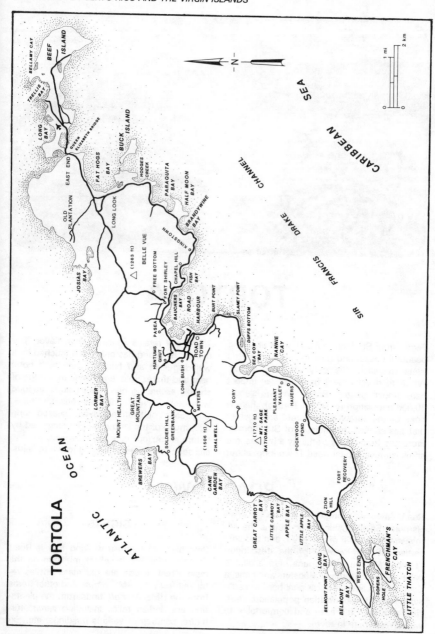

tensive exhibits planned for the backyard include boat and sail making, rope and net making, a cooper, basketmaker, blacksmith, tinsmith, stone mason, and more. Responsible for the museum is the British Virgin Islands Historical Society (Box 116, Road Town, Tortola, BVI), an ambitious group of individuals striving to preserve what remains of the B.V.I.'s cultural heritage. Because influences from outside the islands are so pervasive, many old structures have been pulled down in a misguided attempt to modernize the islands. At the museum, be sure to talk to Sandra Phillips, the friendly and informative assistant curator. The Administration Building, facing Sir Oliva Georges Plaza, was constructed in 1866 from local stone. The century-old De Castro Building is a bit farther on; it contains an unusual brick circular staircase. The wooden columns and stone walls inside Cell 5 Restaurant, once a private residence, are also of note. Down the street to the L stands Britannic Hall, built by a surgeon in 1910. A bit farther and also on the L is the early 19th C. St. Georges School Room. The Anglican and Methodist churches are nearby. The prison (still in use) is the oldest building in town. Just past the corner of Fleming St. and Joe's Hill Rd. lies the Sunday Morning Well, where the Emancipation Act was reportedly read on 1 Aug. 1834. The Legislative Council sits in session and court hearings are held in the Court house or Legislative Council Chamber nearby. The Survey and Planning Building, near the Police Headquarters, was originally a cotton factory. At the other end of town near Peeble's Hospital stands Government House, the governor's residence and the most representative example of colonial architecture in Road Town. Four forts surround Road Town: George, Shirley, Charlotte, and Burt. Although the latter three are in ruins, Fort Burt has been converted into a hotel. The Old Methodist Church is probably Road Town's finest timber-framed building. Other landmarks include H.R. Penn's shop, Niles rum shop, and the unique Grocery and Meat Market. The pickup truck parked out in front is the oldest vehicle on the island. The so-called Purple Palace is the most unusual and conspicuous architectual landmark on the island.

the place not to stay...

accommodations: Best deal in town is Way Side Inn Guest House, which has all-year rates of $20 s or d. Vanita Parsons has slightly cheaper rooms but is not recommended. Nearby accommodations include Maya Cove (Box 399, Road Town) which charges $9 pp (summer) and $12.50 pp (winter); all rooms have kitchenettes and attached bathrooms. All rates are based on double occupancy with 50 percent extra charge for single rooms and reductions for stays of a month or longer. Sea View Hotel (tel. 49-42483, Box 59, Road Town) charges $28 s, $29 d, $32 studio s, $38 d, $60 t (summer) and $32 s, $33 d, and $35 studio s, $45 studio d $45, $68 studio t (winter). Facilities include swimming pool, bar, and restaurant. The Castle Hotel (tel. 49-42553/2515, Box 206, Road Town) charges $30 s, $40 d, $55 t (summer), and $42 s, $55 d, $75 t (winter) with special weekly rates available. Suites $10 extra per day. Rooms are a/c and a swimming pool is available.

TORTOLA ACCOMMODATIONS

All rates listed are lowest; a range of prices may be in effect. Service charges vary and 7% government tax applies. High season runs from 16 Dec. through 15 April unless otherwise specified by key legend.
KEY: S = single; D = double; PW = per week; St = studio; W1 = Winter season 1 Nov. to 30 April; W2 = Winter season 1 Dec. to 30 May.

NAME	ADDRESS	TELEPHONE	HIGH		LOW	
			S	D	S	D
Long Bay Hotel	Box 433 Road Town	49-54252	88	66	30	40
Treasure Isle Hotel	Box 139 Road Town	49-42501	94	98	60	68
Moorings—Mariner Inn	Box 139 Road Town	49-42332	75	95	45	54
Sugar Mill Hotel	Box 425 Road Town	49-54355	88	93	45	55
Fort Burt Hotel	Box 187 Road Town	49-42587	80	90	45	55
The Castle	Box 206 Road Town	49-42553	50	65	30	40
Sebastians on the Beach	Box 441 Road Town	49-54212	40	50	20	30
Sea View Hotel	Box 59 Road Town	49-42483	32	33	28	29
Village Cay Marina W1	Box 145 Road Town	49-42771	45	55	36	40
CSY Yacht Club	Box 157 Road Town	49-42741	50	50	50	50
Smugglers Cove Hotel	Box 4 West End	49-54234	58	73	48	58
BVI Aquatic Hotel W2	Box 605 West End	49-54541	25	40		
Cane Garden Beach Hotel	Box 570 Cane Garden Bay	49-54639	45	50	25	30
Tamarind Country Club	Box 509 Road Town	49-52477	28	40	23	28
Marias by the Bay	Box 206 Road Town	49-42595	60	80	35	48
Way Side Inn Guest House	Box 259 Road Town		20	20	20	20
Buccaneer Inn	Sopers Hole West End	49-54559	25	30	15	20
Belmont Grove Villas ST	Long Bay Beach		55	55	30	30
Harbour View Guest House	Box 547 Cane Garden Bay	49-54549	120 wk	240 wk	100 wk	200 wk
Jennie's Housekeeping Unit	Box 116 Road Town	49-43300	200 wk		175 wk	
Mountain Valley Estates	Box 402 Road Town	49-52233	30	50	20	35

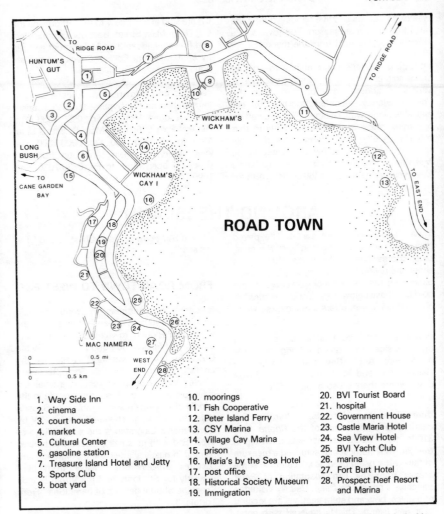

1. Way Side Inn
2. cinema
3. court house
4. market
5. Cultural Center
6. gasoline station
7. Treasure Island Hotel and Jetty
8. Sports Club
9. boat yard
10. moorings
11. Fish Cooperative
12. Peter Island Ferry
13. CSY Marina
14. Village Cay Marina
15. prison
16. Maria's by the Sea Hotel
17. post office
18. Historical Society Museum
19. Immigration
20. BVI Tourist Board
21. hospital
22. Government House
23. Castle Maria Hotel
24. Sea View Hotel
25. BVI Yacht Club
26. marina
27. Fort Burt Hotel
28. Prospect Reef Resort and Marina

food: There's a variety of small restaurants, a bakery, and two supermarkets. Breakfasts—as at the New Happy Lion Bar & Restaurant on Main Street—start at $3.50, sandwiches run from $1.75 each, and fish and chips from $3.50. Most famous restaurant is Cell 5 on Main Street. Local dishes can be found at Maria's Restaurant on the waterfront at Wickham Cay I, Scatcliffe's Tavern near the cinema, and at the Mid Town Restaurant on Main Street. The Ample Hamper, located inside Village Cay Marina, has every kind of imported delicacy for the more gourmet minded.

entertainment: Not exactly downtown Manhattan, to say the least. Most of the entertainment happens out of town at Cane Garden Bay. Stanley's has a steel band nightly (except Sun.) from 2030 until whenever. Rhymer's has an electric band most Sundays. Bananas, out at West End, occasionally has a live band. Much more happens at these places—in the way of barbecues and live bands—during the height of the winter season. The town's sole cinema is up the road from the market.

shopping: Shops cater mainly to arriving cruise ship passengers and visiting yachties. A variety of goods (many of them from the "down islands"—located to the S) are available along with T-shirts ("Get Hooked on a Virgin," etc.) and other such items that tourists usually buy. Stamps are available from the new philatelic bureau located in the Mill Mall behind Barclay's Bank on Wickham's Cay, while authentic coins (80 cents' worth for

$1) are sold at a window to the left outside the G.P.O. on Main Street. Best bookstore is Past and Presents, located on Main Street and run by affable Madge Collins. Check out her antique sets of sterling silver.

services and information: Located next to Immigration on the bypass, the BVI Tourism Board is open Mon. to Fri. 0900-1630. The General Post Office, on Main Street, is open Mon. to Fri. 0800-1600, Sat. 0900-1300. The local library, on Main Street up from the prison, is open Mon. to Fri. 0830-2030, Sat. 1000-1400.

AROUND THE ISLAND

Travel here is steep but sweet. The paved concrete roads are embossed with the criss-cross impressions of rake heads. These roads shoot sharply up hills—giving way to majestic panoramas before descending in curves to the bold blue bays below. Sky World, a restaurant above Road Town, offers a 360-degree view.

beaches: The finest beaches are all located on the N side of the island at Long Bay, Little Apple Bay, Apple Bay, Carrot Bay, Cane Garden Bay, and at difficult-to-reach Josias Bay—where there's also good surfing.

dive sites near Tortola: Premier dive destination is the wreck of the *Rhone*. This 310-ft., two-masted steamer was drowned in the Oct. 1867 hurricane. It achieved a measure of fame after being used as a location in some scenes from the film adaptation of Peter Benchley's novel *The Deep*. Usually visited in two dives, bow and stern sections are located near Salt Island. Thickly covered with coral, the bow section lies 80 ft. down while the stern is at 30 feet. "Blond Rock," resembling a natural amphitheater, lies in 12 ft. of water, covered with fire coral. Less than 100 yards from Ginger I., SE of Tortola, is "Alice in Wonderland," with its profuse cornucopia of corals. Other sites include the *Rhone's* anchor (with its coral-encrusted chamber pot and anchor), "Painted Walls"

(off the SW point of Dead Chest I.) and "The Indians."

FROM ROAD TOWN TO WEST END

Bordering the Caribbean, this road was built only in the 1960s. A red-and-white sign to the R a few miles out of town marks the site of the dungeon of Pockwood Pond Fort. Built by the Dutch in 1648, it was later rebuilt by the English Royal Engineers. Fort Recovery, erected by the Dutch in 1660, is a small circular fort which now faces the seaside in the middle of a private resort complex. At Soper's Hole, an anchorage sheltered on the SW by Frenchman's Cay, stands the small village of West End with its small collection of houses painted in pastel shades and immigration and customs offices. Boats leave from here regularly for St. John, and the Virgin Islands Seaplane Shuttle fies out of here. (See "From Tortola.")

accommodations: Ellie Foot's Turtle Dove Lodge (tel. 49-54430, Box 11, West End) has cabins for $15 s, $25-35 d. Weekly and monthly rates and a 20 percent summer discount are available. Buccaneer Inn (tel. 49-54559) at Soper's Hole, West End has rooms from $15 s and $20 d summer. BVI Aquatic Hotel (tel. 49-54541, Box 605, West End) has rooms from $25 s and $40 d summer.

beach at Cane Garden Bay

CANE GARDEN BAY

One of the most beautiful beaches on the island is located here. Pink Rhymer's Beach Bar and Restaurant has beach chairs and a tire swing. Stanley's is a hop, skip, and jump away. Callwood's Distillery, run by surly Mr. Callwood, has some of the most potent rum in the Caribbean. He charges $3 for a fifth, $4 for a quart, and $5.50 for a half gallon. His is one of the three functioning distilleries left on the island. (The others are at Baughers Bay and at Meyers.) For the sunset, ascend to Soldier's Hill above. Between Cane Garden Bay and Carrot Bay to the SW, the overgrown ruins of St. Michael's Church lie atop Windy Hill. **stay:** Cane Garden Bay Beach Hotel, Box 570 (tel. 49-54639); $25 s, $30 d summer.

BREWERS BAY

A steep and winding road from Road Town leads over the hills and down to this secluded campground. From the top of the road leading down, there's a majestic view of Jost Van Dyke with Little Jost and Sandy Cay in the background. Dark reefs shine through the crystal-clear water. The road leads down into a rustic campsite after passing by the ruins of an old sugar oven.

accommodations: Run by Noel Callwood together with his partner Styles, this campground only starts to fill around mid-Dec,; between April and then you'll have the place virtually to yourself. As close to the life of Robinson Crusoe as you can imagine. Good snorkeling out on the reefs, and a good place to base yourself for island walks. Bare sites below the coconut trees rent out for $5 per night for two (extra persons $1.) Already erected tents rent out for $14 for two (extra persons $2.50.) Showers are available; a terrace near the office has chairs and tables.

food: Expensive food is sold at the commissary. Bring your own from town or St.

Thomas. There's a sandwich and refreshment bar, but it's closed off season. Coconuts drop at your feet; bring along your own machete to hack them open. You'll probably spot Lanah by the side of the road shelling cashews; she bakes delicious bread, coconut and guava tarts, sugarcakes with almonds, and other goodies. Her sea grape wine ($8 a bottle) is legendary.

Sage Mountain: It's a three- or four-hour hike from Brewers Bay (or a half-hour drive) to the trailhead which leads to the top of Mt. Sage (1,710 feet). A very attractive area with the remains of old houses and orchids peeking out from the primeval forest. Highest mountain in the entire Virgin Islands, it has been declared a protected area under the administration of the National Park Trust.

FROM ROAD TOWN TO THE EAST

St. Phillip's Church, or the "African Church," is at Kingstown. This church was built for the use of Africans who had been removed from the bowels of a slave ship around 1815 (after the abolition of the slave trade, but before emancipation). Known as the Kingstown Experiment, these slaves were placed in a freed reservation after serving an apprenticeship with the planters. Hub of Quaker activities and seat of government for a while after it had been transferred from Spanish Town on Virgin Gorda. Fat Hogs Bay still contains a ruined Quaker cemetery. The Long Look-Look East area is second in terms of population.

Beef Island: Some maintain that this island's name stems from the period when it provided beef for buccaneers; others claim it comes from the cows a solitary old lady used to bring to pasture here. Whatever the true explanation, this must be one of the smallest islands ever to boast an international airport. A 300-ft. channel, which separates the island from Tortola, is spanned by the Queen Elizabeth Bridge which her Imperial Majesty herself dedicated in 1966. (Although a tollkeeper collects a 25-cent toll during the day, it's scot-free at night.) Crossing the bridge, the road to the L leads to the remains of a cattle estate house. Near the 3,600-ft. runway is Long Beach — suitable for a dip before departure or after arrival. Marina Cay, a small, six-acre island nearby, was once the home of Rob White, author of *Our Virgin Isle.*

FROM TORTOLA

for Virgin Gorda: *Speedy's Fantasy* (ferry) departs from Road Town Mon., Wed., Fri., and Sat. at 0900, 1330, and 1630. Air BVI flies to Virgin Gorda from Beef Island seven times a day. **for Jost Van Dyke:** No direct route. *Bomba Charger* (ferry) departs Mon. and Sat. at 0830 from St. Thomas. **for Anegada:** Air BVI flies three times a week from Beef Island. **for Peter Island:** Ferries leave Caribbean Sailing Yachts (CSY) Dock daily at 0700, 0830, 1000, 1200, 1330, 1530, 1730, 1830, and 2230.

for St. Thomas: *Bomba Charger* departs from Road Town ($11 OW) Mon. to Fri. at 0615, with an additional departure Wed. at 1515, and Sat. at 0615 and 1500. *Speedy's Fantasy* departs Road Town Tues. and Thurs. at 0715 and 1525; Sat. at 0915. *Native Son* leaves Road Town for St. Thomas (via West End) Mon. to Fri. at 0615 with an additional departure Wed. at 1415; Sat. at 0615 and 1400, and Sun. at 1530. *Bomba Charger* departs West End Mon. to Fri. at 0700, 1030, and 1500; Sat. at 0700, 1030, 1530, and 1815, and Sun. at 1630. *Native Son* leaves West End Mon. to Fri. at 0700, 1030, and 1500; Sat. at 0700, 1030, 1430, and 1745.

by air: Virgin Islands Seaplane Shuttle flies twice on Mon., Wed., and Friday. AIR BVI and Crownair fly daily from Beef Island Airport.

for St John: *Sundance II* leaves West End Mon. to Sat. at 0915 and 1615 and Sun. at 1730. *Native Son* departs Sun. at 0930 for St. John and Red Hook. **for St. Croix:** Virgin Islands Seaplane Shuttle flies Mon., Wed., and Friday.

for the southern Caribbean: Air BVI flies to Anguilla, St. Kitts, and St. Maarten. LIAT flies to Antigua, St. Lucia, and Dominica.

OTHER ISLANDS

JOST VAN DYKE

Less than four miles N of St. John, Jost Van Dyke seems to be more American than British in character. Named after a Dutch pirate, this long, narrow island has hills running like a camel's humps from head to tail. Main town is Great Harbour (pop. 150) where customs, facilities, school, and a church are located. No cars, trucks, motorbikes, or airlines. Get around by foot or water taxi. To the W of Great Harbour is White Bay, which contains a long white sand beach. **getting there:** Can only be reached by private sailboat or by *Bomba Charger* ($25 RT), which leaves St Thomas Mon. and Sat. at 0830; returns Mon. at 1500 and Sat. at 1800.

accommodations and food: Best deal is to camp. Tula's N & N Campground, Little Harbour, has both bare and tent sites available. Bare sites go for $15 for three people. Tents are $25-35 per couple. For more information

write Box 8364, St. Thomas, USVI 00801; tel. (809) 774-0774, 775-3073. Eat at Foxy's, Little Harbour Coral Inn, Abe's By the Sea, or Rudy's Bar and Restaurant. The latter has a barbecue pig roast every Tues. night.

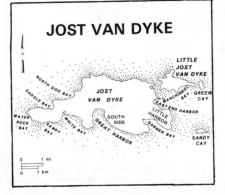

VIRGIN GORDA

Third largest but second most important of the group is Virgin Gorda (named the "fat virgin" by the Spanish because its mountainous profile is reminiscent of a woman lying on her back). Eight square miles in area, its 10-mile length naturally divides itself into two parts. While the NE is mountainous, the SE is flat. All lands above 1,000 ft. are part of the National Park; the highest point, Gorda Peak, is 1,370 feet. At the top, accessible by road, is an observation tower. Spanish Town, more a settlement than a town, is a pretty but otherwise totally unremarkable place. Modern amenities (roads, phones, electricity) have come here only recently.

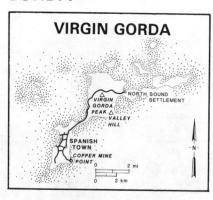

VIRGIN GORDA

SPANISH TOWN AND THE VALLEY

1. ferry dock
2. Plaza Supermarket
3. Telephone Exchange
4. Vanterpool's Store and Luncheonette
5. Nurse Iris O'Neil Clinic
6. yacht harbour and shopping centre
7. Fischer's Cove Hotel
8. Vanterpool's Rosy Bar and Grocery

history: During the late 1600s, while ownership of Tortola was disputed between the English and Dutch, Puerto Rican Spaniards occasionally raided settlements here. The original seat of the colonial government was located at Spanish Town around 1710. Although population exceeded 7,500 in the early 17th C., currently only 1,443 people reside on Virgin Gorda. Population declined after the introduction of the sugar beet to Europe and the emancipation of slaves in 1834.

getting there: *Speedy's Fantasy* leaves from Road Town Mon., Wed., Fri., and Sat. at 0900, 1330, and 1630; it returns at 0800, 1130, and 1530. On Tues. and Thurs., the ferry operates between St. Thomas and Virgin Gorda. Leaves Charlotte Amalie, St. Thomas, at 0845 and 1700, and returns (to Road Town, *not* St. Thomas) at 0630, 1130, and 1445. On Sat. it leaves St. Thomas at 1530 and departs from Virgin Gordon for Road Town at 1445. Leaving across from the Windward Hotel in Charlotte Amalie, *Bomba Charger* also runs between St. Thomas and Virgin Gorda ($28 RT): Sun. at 0800, return 1330; Wed. 0830, return 1430; Thurs. 1700, return 0515; and Fri. 1700, no return. Another ferry runs from Red Hook, St. Thomas, to Virgin Gorda via Cruz Bay, St. John, Thurs. at 0800; returns at 1500.

beaches: Sixteen of them—enough for a week's exploring. Although Little Dix and Biras Creek have been developed, Savana and Pond are excellent for shell hunting. The Baths, premier tourist site in the British Virgin Islands, is located at the S tip of the island. At this magnificent beach area, huge granite boulders the size of houses topple over one another above underlying grottos of clear turquoise water. Enter the dim caverns to bathe. Light enters between the cracks, giving each grotto a different atmosphere which changes continually as the tide pounds in and out. Nearby at Copper Mine Point are the rather undistinguished ruins of a copper mine which was first mined by Spaniards from Puerto Rico during the 16th century.

dive sites near Virgin Gorda: Nearest and most accessible is "The Blinders." Located near The Baths, it is a mirror image of them—30 ft. underwater. Virgin Gorda shares some of the same dive sites as Tortola, such as "Alice in Wonderland" and the *Rhone.* Other Virgin Gorda sites include Wall to Wall, the Chimney, Oil Nut Bay, Van Ryan's Rock, Two Ray Bay, Tiger Mountain, Tow Rock.

accommodations: Cheapest place to stay is Olde Yarde Inn near the yacht harbor, but even off season ($35 d), it's far from cheap. It may be better to visit on a daytrip from St. Thomas, Tortola, or (available occasionally) from St. John. One place you most probably can't afford to stay in (at $210-$760 per day!) but probably wouldn't want to miss checking out is the Rockresort Little Dix Bay. Constructed in 1964 at a cost of $9 million, this resort—at $136,000 per room—is the most expensive of its size ever built.

ANEGADA

Most atypical and northernmost of all the Virgin Islands, Anegada ("drowned land") received its name because the surf pounding its reefs rises so high that it threatens to engulf the entire island. Every rule that applies to other Virgin Islands are excepted here: it's neither steep nor craggy; there are no mongooses, Anglican churches, or water shortages. The Settlement, a collection of unremarkable frame buildings, is home for most of the island's 250-strong population. Besides fishing, most people make a living by working on other islands. Several major tourist development schemes have been proposed, but happily for the sake of the natural environment, have never materialized.

the land: Nine miles long and a mile wide, the island's highest point is a mere 28 ft. above sea level. Consisting of limestone grating, it is completely flat in the S, and central portions feature scattered lagoons, salt ponds, and marshes, as well as glorious beaches. A 15-sq-mile Pacific atoll in the Caribbean, its surrounding reefs are its most spectacular feature. It is the only British Virgin Island with freshwater springs of any size.

flora and fauna: A great variety of animal and plant life thrives here, some of which cannot be found elsewhere in this island group. The monotony of the bracken and mangrove vegetation is punctuated by spreads of lilac-colored wild orchids *(Petramicra elegans)* which grow in profusion along Red Pond's salt flats. Birds include roseate spoonbills, snowy and reddish egrets, the northern water thrush and the more commonplace frigates, plovers, and pelicans. Iguanas, one local delicacy, have been hunted to near extinction, while flamingos have been caught and roasted to the extent that Flamingo Pond—once a habitat for great flocks of the birds—has been entirely depopulated of them. In former times, huge swarms of enormous mosquitos, known as "giant nippers," roamed the island, appearing and disappearing in 10-year intervals. Their bites, in large concentration, have proved fatal to sheep and sent wild goats fleeing into villages for human protection. These goats, as well as small wild horses and cattle, still roam freely.

history: Used first by the Indians who left heaps of conch shells behind them on the E end, the island's maze of reefs afforded protection for pirates like Kirke, Bone, and Norman. Although the first settlers did grow some food and cotton, they came here expecting to profit from the spoils of the frequent shipwrecks. No sooner was the cry of "vessel on the reef!" heard than the residents, sidearms in hand, would be off and running and competing to be first aboard. The shipwrecks, which occurred with alarming frequency, were occasionally helped along by unscrupulous residents who would set out lamps to lure unsuspecting ships onto the treacherous reef. Even though the reefs were well marked on charts, shipwrecks still occurred because of a powerful and unknown NW current which prevails from March to June. More than 300 ships met their doom here, and today, 138 wrecks are charted. These include the *Paramatta*, a British steamship which hit Horseshoe Reef in 1853 in the dead of night; the HMS *Astraea*, a 32-gun British frigate which sank in 1808; and the *Rocus*, a Greek freighter carrying the unusual cargo of animal bones, which went down off the E coast.

getting there: No regular ferry service. Fly from Tortola's Beef Island on Air BVI. Don't plan on sailing here unless you're very experienced; more than 13 miles of barely penetrable reef surround this island.

accommodations and food: Only one small, expensive hotel, The Reefs. Its rooms go for $65 s, $110 d, off season. Camp at Cow Wreck or one of the other bays.

dive sites around Anegada: With an estimated 17 wrecks per sq mile—some lying *atop* one another—the area should be a diver's paradise. However, many are disintegrated and lie buried in silt—thus limiting their visibility. Settled 35 ft. down, the *Paramatta* lies broken into two parts and overgrown with elkhorn coral. Animal bones litter the deck of the *Rocus* which lies 40 ft. down. There's also a noose which marks the spot where her captain, unable to face Greek authorities, hung himself. Although nothing is left of the *Astraea* itself, cannonballs, cannons, iron ballasts, and anchors remain. Humpback whales migrating from S. America to Greenland are commonly sighted in the Anegada Passage from mid-Feb. to mid-April.

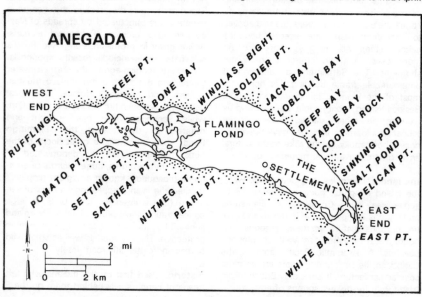

SMALLER ISLANDS

Besides the larger and better-known islands, there are numerous small islands and cays. Many are imaginatively named: Cockroach, Asbestos Point, Great Dog, The Indians, Dead Chest, King Rock, Lizard Point, The Invisibles. Some of the more interesting and anecdotal are described below.

Norman Island: Some claim this is Stevenson's Treasure Island. Reportedly, treasure from the *Nuestra Senora* was recovered here in 1750. Adventurous mariners can anchor S of Treasure Point, where there are four caves. Row into the southernmost cave with a dinghy and see where Stevenson's Mr. Fleming supposedly took his treasure — eerie and dark except for phosphorescent patches on the ceilings. Bats fly overhead and the only sound is the whoosh of the sea being sucked in and out. Watch out for tides and the wild cattle which roam on the land above.

Peter Island: Accessible by sailboat or by private ferry from Tortola. Dominated by Peter Island Hotel ($155-475 pd) and Yacht Harbour. Amway Corporation, which administers the resort, owns the entire island save the 15 acres owned by fisherwoman Estelle La Fontaine. She has steadfastly refused to sell out despite substantial pressure. The beach at Deadman's Cay, just five min. downhill from the units, has been acclaimed as the best in the British Virgins. According to local lore, the shining pink shells on the graves in the nearby cemetery serve to stave off evil spirits. While the beach at Little Deadman's is near its parent, Spring Bay is a stiff half hour-hike away.

Salt Island: Off the NW point of this island is a small settlement where the entire population (of nine) resides. Islanders collect salt from the three salt ponds as they have been doing for the past 150 years. Formerly, these ponds supplied salt for the Royal Navy. They're still owned by the illustrious British queen whose

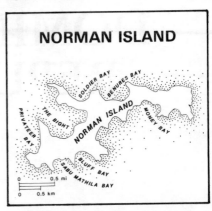

NORMAN ISLAND

representative comes over once a year to collect a bag of salt for the rent! Salt I. is the number-one diving destination in the B.V.I. because of the *Rhone,* a British mail packet ship which went down in the hurricane of 1867, crashing on the sharp rocks at Black Rock Point. Viewed in the crystal-clear water, it's a veritable underwater museum.

Cooper Island: Home of the Cooper Island Beach Club which is run by Tortola's Treasure Isle Hotel whose clientele is ferried over here for free; moorings in the marina are free to beach club patrons. Good swimming and snorkeling on the beach. Follow a trail to the top of the hill for a panoramic view of the surroundings.

Fallen Jerusalem: When viewed from the sea, this island resembles the ruins of an ancient city. It excites the imagination of all who see it.

Bellamy Cay: Off the coast from Beef Island, this popular yacht-in rendezvous spot serves a buffer dinner with live entertainment nightly. Great Camananoe, nearby, has the ruins of a greathouse on it.

THE DOMINICAN REPUBLIC

INTRODUCTION

In addition to being the second largest nation (after Cuba) in the Caribbean, the Dominican Republic also has the longest recorded European presence of any location in the Americas, dating back to that resplendent year 1492. Only slightly larger than Vermont and New Hampshire combined, and with a population of 6.3 million, the Dominican Republic is small enough that nearly every point is readily accessible by vehicle.

Although parts of the country have been developed (overdeveloped in some cases) for the mass tourist market, much remains untouched, unspoiled, and virtually unvisited. The Dominican Republic offers the highest mountain in the Caribbean, the authentic Spanish atmosphere of Old Santo Domingo, the vast plains of sugarcane surrounding La Romana, deserted coasts and white sand beaches, and a very Latin lifestyle.

THE LAND

Covering the eastern two-thirds of Hispaniola, the island it shares with Haiti, the Dominican Republic lies 1,000 km (600 miles) SE of Florida, and is separated from Puerto Rico to the E by the 110-km-wide (68-mile) Mona Passage. One of the world's most geographically diverse countries, its 50,210 sq km (19,386 sq miles) comprise more than 20 distinct geographic regions with a remarkable variety of scenery: everything from lush tropical jungle to semi-arid deserts to some of the most agriculturally productive land in the entire Caribbean. Agriculture and animal husbandry flourish in the fertile alluvial soils of the county's lowlands, most fertile and extensive of which is the 5,180-sq-km (2,000-sq-mile) Valle de Cibao. The 1,800-sq-km (650-sq-mile) Valle de San Juan lies to the south. The other major valley, the Neiba or Hoya de Enriquillo comprises 1,839 sq km (710 sq miles) of semi-arid to arid land below sea level. Largest of the other lowland regions is the Llanura Costera del Caribe (Caribbean Coastal Plain) to the N, which covers more than 2,900 sq km (1,100 sq miles). There are also a number of other small valleys and basins.

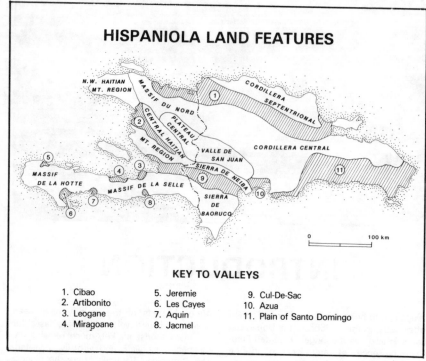

HISPANIOLA LAND FEATURES

KEY TO VALLEYS

1. Cibao
2. Artibonito
3. Leogane
4. Miragoane

5. Jeremie
6. Les Cayes
7. Aquin
8. Jacmel

9. Cul-De-Sac
10. Azua
11. Plain of Santo Domingo

rivers and lakes: For the most part, the rivers are shallow. The Valle de Cibao contains the Yaque del Norte, the longest river, as well as the Yuna. The Valle de San Juan, S of the Cordillera Central, is drained by a tributary of the Artibonito and, to the SE, by the Yaque del Sur. Among the numerous rivers to the E are the Ozama, which cuts through Santo Domingo, as well as the Macoris. Lago Enriquillo, in Valle de Neiba, is the largest natural lake; the only other lies in the same valley near Neiba Bay. Artificial lakes have been created by the construction of dams on the Yaque del Norte at Tavera and on the Nizao at Valdesia. Of the many islands located off the coast, only three are inhabited: Isla Saona, the largest, off the SE tip; Ilsa Beata, off Peninsula de Perdenales near the Haitian border; and tiny Isla Catalina, a few miles SW of La Romana.

mountains: Dominating its rough terrain are four parallel mountain ranges that traverse the country from the NW to the E, where they are crossed by a single range of low mountains. These largely unpopulated ranges divide the country and separate the capital city of Santo Domingo from the rich agricultural Valle del Cibao and the N coast. The main range is the Cordillera Central, extending from Santo Domingo NW into Haiti, where it becomes the Massif du Nord. Its ridges crest between 1,500-2,500 m (4,921-8,202 ft.) and contain Pico Duarte (3,175 m, 10,417 ft.) the Caribbean's highest peak. Flanked along the N coast by the Cordillera Septentrional, the Cordillera Central is bordered on the S by the Sierra de Neiba. The E portion of the latter is separated from a similar range, the Sierra de Martin Garcia on Samana Peninsula, by swamps surrounding the mouth of the Yuna River. Still farther S, the Sierra de Baorucu extends from Haiti while the Cordillera Oriental, a narrow band of hills, forms a minor chain to the east.

climate: Although the Dominican Republic has a tropical maritime climate, trade winds and ocean currents prevent the temperatures from rising above 32.2 degrees centigrade. Even though temperatures rarely fall below 15.6 degrees C, frost commonly gilds the mountains. The rainy season is from May to Nov. with maximum precipitation in late spring and fall. While areas like Barahona and Montecristi are extremely arid, others like may receive 2,500 mm (100 inches) or more annually; average temperature is about 139.7 cm (55 inches). Hurricanes hit the Caribbean coast from June through November.

flora and fauna: Few of either are indigenous. Among those native are the *caiman* (alligators) which are found near the mouths of the Yaque del Norte and Yaque del Sur rivers and in Lake Enriquillo. The only rodents, aside from the imported rat, are the *agouti* and the *solenodon*. Iguanas are among the few lizards; the snake population has declined owing to the presence of the mongoose. The pink flamingo population is on the wane as well. Other birds include the nightingale and the *jilguero* or musician bird. Native trees include tall stands of pine which flourish in the remote central highlands; imported trees include eucalyptus, almond, and the breadfruit.

DOMINICAN REPUBLIC CLIMATE CHART

	Daily Average Air Temp. °F	Rainfall Days	Rainfall Inches
January	84	7	2.4
February	85	6	1.4
March	84	5	1.9
April	85	7	3.9
May	86	11	6.8
June	87	12	6.2
July	88	11	6.4
August	88	11	6.3
September	88	11	7.3
October	87	11	6.0
November	86	10	4.8
December	85	8	2.4

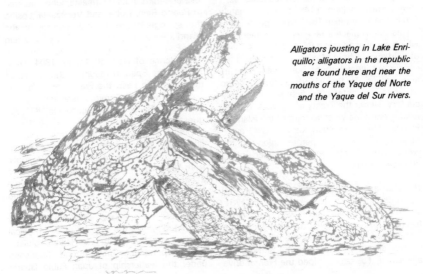

Alligators jousting in Lake Enriquillo; alligators in the republic are found here and near the mouths of the Yaque del Norte and the Yaque del Sur rivers.

HISTORY

the Spanish era: Modern Dominican history began in 1492 with the arrival of Columbus and the Spanish. Spain, the first great colonial power in the Americas, established Santo Domingo as its New World headquarters, and exterminated the native Indian population through forced labor and imported diseases; it shrank from a million in 1492 to approximately 500 in 1548. Begun in 1503, the importation of slaves put in place a race-regulated hierarchy which survives to this day. With the discovery of gold and silver in Mexico and Peru, and the concurrent depletion of both gold deposits and Indians on the island, Santo Domingo began to lose luster in the first part of the 16th century. Under the Treaty of Ryswick in 1697, Spain ceded the western third of the island to France. This area, then known as "Hayti," became the most prosperous colony in the world, while Santo Domingo slipped into a 250-year slump.

the Haitian occupation: Haitian slaves, led by Toussaint L'Ouverture, revolted in 1791, sparking a confused civil war. Toussaint's forces fought with the Spanish against the French, until they heard of the emancipation of the slaves by the French. Shifting his allegiance, Toussaint helped the French drive the Spanish from Saint-Dominique, the French name for Haiti. Appointed governor of the French colony of Saint-Dominique by the French Convention, Toussaint marched into Santo Domingo in 1801. His new constitution freed slaves, causing the Spanish colony to lose one-third of its white elite, who migrated to Puerto Rico, Cuba, and Venezuela. Losing the struggle to re-establish control of the island's eastern sector, Dessalines (who had replaced Toussaint) proclaimed the independence of Haiti on 1 Jan. 1804. From 1804-09 the Spanish fought (with the help of the British) to keep the French and Haitians out, but the *criollo* Dominicans eventually succeeded in driving out the Spanish in 1821. Requesting admission to Simon Bolivar's Republic of Gran Colombia, the Haitians, under the leadership of Jean Pierre Boyer, overran and occupied the Dominican Republic from 1822-42. The Haitian occupation remains a bitter memory. Although the slaves were emancipated, emigration increased, sugar and tobacco production were paralyzed, all church properties were seized, and the economy stagnated under the weight of a tyrannical bureaucracy and plundering Haitian soldiers. An independence underground flourished under the leadership of Juan Pablo Duarte and his secret society *La Trinitaria,* and on 27 Feb. 1844, the Dominican rebels seized Ozama fortress in Santo Domingo. Caught by surprise, the Haitians hastily exited, and a provisional government took control.

independence: Duarte, however, was reluctant to take control of the presidency, and he soon found himself usurped and exiled by two self-appointed generals, Buenaventura Baez and Pedro Santana. Alternating as president over the next 45 years, these two dictators helped fill their own pockets more than they helped anyone else. By 1861 the country was bankrupt. In his third term as president, Santana announced that the Republica Dominicana would again become a Spanish colony. By midsummer, Santo Domingo was once more swarming with Spaniards, and by mid-fall, the Dominicans were revolting again. Independence was not re-established until 1865 when Baez took his third crack at the presidency. He was, however, forced to leave the country after five months because of a

One of two usurpers of liberator Duarte, Buenaventura Baez's presidencies were hardly "good adventures" for the nation. He nearly succeeded in having the U.S. annex the country and fled with US$300,000 during his fifth term.

revolt led by Gen. Gregorio Luperon. Soon called back from exile, Baez convinced the Grant administration to sign a treaty annexing the country, but the treaty failed to pass the U.S. Senate by only one vote! Falling from power for the fourth time, Baez was replaced from 1874-79 by reformist Ulises Espillat. Unable to control the situation, he fell and Baez returned for his final fling at the presidency. But after only two months, he took $300,000 and fled to Puerto Rico—leaving his country in shambles behind him. General Luperon took another turn as president, only to be replaced in 1882 by his lieutenant, Ulises Heureaux. Although he incurred a large foreign debt, Heureaux succeeded in achieving political stability and modernizing the economy during his 17 dictatorial years at the helm. However, as he became more ruthless and authoritarian, his unpopularity increased, and he was shot and killed at a public gathering by Ramon Caceres, an opposition leader. Defaulting on numerous international loans and failing either to sell the Samana Peninsula to the U.S. or make the country a U.S. dependency, Heureaux's legacy was a D$32 million foreign debt—10 times the amount outstanding when he assumed the presidency!

political factionalism: Between 1899-1906, the country polarized into two competing factions: "Horacistas," followers of Horacio Vasquez, and the "Jimenistas," followers of Juan Isidro Jimenez. The ensuing conflict further reduced the economy. In 1907, the entire country was placed under receivership by Theodore Roosevelt who, sensing an opportunity to expand U.S. influence, negotiated an agreement whereby the U.S. would administer the now $40 million Dominican debt by collecting and distributing customs duties. Under its terms, the U.S. would collect the export customs duties (principal source of government revenue), and deliver 45 percent of them to the Dominican government while using the remainder to pay off the external debt. At the time of the agreement (1905), Heureux's assassin, Ramon Caceres, had become president. Following tradition, he too was assassinated in 1911. During the course of the ensuing civil war, Jimenez became president. Given the continued degeneration of the Dominican political system, coupled with the spread of German influence in Haiti, the Wilson administration was watching events carefully. On 16 May 1916, President Jimenez was impeached by the Dominican Congress, and a rebellion followed. American troops landed and began an eight-year occupation. Although bands of patriots rebelled and were forcibly put down, many Dominicans welcomed the enforced political stability brought about by the occupation. In 1924, after elections which left newly elected but aging Horacista General Vasquez in charge, the Marines exited.

the Trujillo era: For six years everything went relatively smoothly. Vasquez prolonged his term from four to six years, then repealed the ban on re-election. But, in 1930, a revolt was spearheaded from Santiago. With the tacit support of the head of the national guard—a young but ruthlessly clever fellow named Rafael Trujillo—the rebels toppled Vasquez. Trujillo first encouraged rebel leader Rafael Estrella Urena to run for president and then "convinced" him to run for vice-president. Winning the 1930 election with more votes than there were eligible voters,

Trujillo went on to establish a reputation that has made his name synonymous with totalitarianism. In the history of the Western Hemisphere, there has never been a dictator more ruthless or bloodthirsty than Trujillo: it is estimated that half a million people were executed during his rule. One night in 1937, under Trujillo's orders, his troops massacred 12,000-25,000 Haitians whom he had invited in to work on the sugar plantations. More than any other leader in the history of the Dominican Republic, Trujillo shaped and, through his lasting legacy, continues to shape the nation's political, economic, and social fabric. Dominating the nation between 1930-61 and turning it into his personal fiefdom, Trujillo amassed an empire estimated at between 300 million and one billion dollars. Together with his family and friends, he came to control nearly 60 percent of the country's assets, including the majority of the sugar industry, the best lands, airlines, and dozens of other concerns. Approximately 60 percent of the labor force worked for Trujillo—either directly or indirectly, and an incredible cult of adulation grew around the man. Santo Domingo was renamed Ciudad Trujillo, the highest mountain was named Pico Trujillo, and he became the godfather of scores of children brought to mass baptisms. But nothing

REPUBLICA DOMINICANA
FERIA
DE LA
PAZ Y CONFRATERNIDAD
DEL MUNDO LIBRE
1955   1956
CORREOS   CORREOS
7¢   ¢7
GENERALISIMO DOCTOR
RAFAEL LEONIDAS TRUJILLO MOLINA
BENEFACTOR DE LA PATRIA
PADRE DE LA PATRIA NUEVA

Friends with the likes of Nicaragua's Anastasio "Tacho" Somoza, Generalisimo Doctor Rafael Leonidas Trujillo Molina, Benefactor de la Patria y Padre de la Patria Nueva, was born in the little village of San Cristobal in 1891. Before entering the National Police in 1918, Trujillo worked as a telegraph operator with a gang of hoods nicknamed "the 44," and as a weigher at sugar estates. Promoted to lieutenant colonel and Chief of Staff by then-President Vasquez in 1924, he was further elevated to Brigadier General and Chief of the National Army—the successor of the National Police—in 1927. Running for president in 1930, he won with more votes than there were eligible voters. The rest, as they say, is history.

above, clockwise: cobblestones, Old San Juan, Puerto Rico (H. Pariser); Fort San Cristobal, Old San Juan, Puerto Rico (Roger LaBrucherie); *bateye* at Tibes Ceremonial Center, Puerto Rico (H. Pariser); statue of Ponce de Leon, Plaza de San Jose (church behind), Puerto Rico (R. LaBrucherie); El Morro, Old San Juan, Puerto Rico (H. Pariser); sugar factory site, Cinnamon Bay, St. John, USVI (H. Pariser)

above, clockwise: woman waiting at bus stop, Old San Juan, Puerto Rico (H. Pariser); sailing, USVI (H. Pariser); Carnival participants, St. Thomas, USVI (USVI Dept. of Commerce); scuba diving, USVI (USVI Division of Tourism); board sailing, Dominican Republic, (DR Tourist Information Center); *bomba y plena,* Puerto Rico (H. Pariser)

resting under God's heaven lasts forever—not even dictators—and Trujillo's regime began to sag during the late 1950s. Plummeting sugar prices and his unsuccessful plot to assassinate President Betancourt of Venezuela (which resulted in a trade and arms embargo by the members of the OAS) increased the opposition's clout. On 30 May 1961, Trujillo was assassinated by a seven-man hit team allegedly coached by the CIA. The middle-class assassins missed their opportunity to seize power, and Trujillo's iron fist was inherited by son Ramfis, along with puppet president Joaquin Balaguer.

the second American intervention: Under American pressure, Balaguer allowed exiles to return and permitted the growth of opposition parties. Taking US$90 million, Ramfis and the rest of the family fled the country in November 1961. A seven-man Council of State, which included Balaguer as well as two of Trujillo's assassins, was formed on 1 Jan. 1962 but was overturned by a military coup. Two days later, a counter-coup restored the Council but forced Balaguer into exile. Victor in the Dec. elections was Juan Bosch, charismatic and fiery head of the social democratic Dominican Revolutionary Party (PRD). First democratically elected president in the nation's history, his two-to-one victory over Viriato Fiallo's National Civic Union represented a victory of the people over the traditional ruling elites. Promising democratic, economic, and social reforms, his administration quickly ran into difficulties trying to fulfill its pledge. The Catholic Church and the Army felt threatened by the regime—in particular by its promise to extend participation in the political process to Marxist groups—and in Sept. 1963, after only seven months in office, Bosch was overthrown in a bloodless military coup led by Col. Elias Wessin y Wessin. The military replaced Bosch with a three-man civilian junta dominated by Donald Reid Cabral, a local CIA agent nicknamed *El Americanito* ("the little American"). Bosch's PRD, however, wasn't idle, and on 24 April 1965, the party staged a rebellion. With U.S. encouragement, the military, led by Gen. Wessin, counter-attacked, but on 28 April

they were driven back and defeated in a decisive battle. In addition, following the precedent set by Wilson 50 years before him, President Johnson, concerned with prevention—at all costs—of another Cuba, and with sending a message to the North Vietnamese, ordered troops in that same day. Altogether, 23,000 American troops occupied the nation. Although the U.S. attempted a token internationalization of the occupying forces and claimed that the invasion was to protect and evacuate U.S. citizens, the real intent was to prevent the return of Juan Bosch and the constitutionalists. On 31 August 1965, the war was halted when the U.S. pressed constitutionalist and conservative forces to sign an Institutional Act and an Act of Reconciliation, which led to the appointment of Hector Garcia-Godoy as interim president.

Balaguer and beyond: Given the prevailing repressive atmosphere, and the attacks and recriminations launched by his supporters, Bosch lost the 1966 elections to Balaguer by a landslide. Balaguer won 57 percent of the vote to Bosch's 39 percent, but he also spent US$13 million on the campaign. Ruling from 1966-78, the former Trujillo puppet president, often seen as a civilian *caudillo* (general), proved himself a shrewd administrator. His administration was characterized by graft and abuse; he turned a blind eye to the mysterious right-wing death squad, known as *La Banda,* whose 2,000 victims included three newsmen. Re-elected twice in farcical elections, he presented a hyperbolic image of prosperity which in no way accorded with the underlying realities of a socially and economcally devastated nation. In the 1978 elections, when millionaire rancher Antonio Guzman, head of the PRD, took an early lead, the military seized the ballot boxes. Captain America, personified this time by the Carter administration, came to the rescue. Secretary of State Cyrus Vance, together with the head of the Canal Zone-based U.S. Southern Military Command, flew to Santa Domingo. Under U.S. pressure and with the threat of a general strike hanging over his head, Balaguer had no choice but to compel the military to return the ballot boxes. After granting considerable concessions to the Balaguer camp, Guzman became president. The Guzman years were undistinguished; Salvador Jorge Blanco, also of the PRD, replaced him in an election held in May 1982.

GOVERNMENT

Historically, as just described, the Dominican Republic has been plagued by self-serving megalomaniacal dictators who have provided the role models for political leadership up to the present. Although he has been dead for nearly a quarter century, the shadow of Trujillo still looms large over the Dominican political scene. This *caudillo* on horseback, though despicable, was nonetheless a brilliant showman who brought a degree of order and organization to the country. Like a woman who cannot decide between two suitors, the nation is still continually torn between authoritarianism and democracy.

political structure: The country is currently on its 25th constitution! As in many other Latin American nations, the system of checks and balances and citizens' rights associated with democracies have been guaranteed by each constitution and cast aside as soon as the ink has dried. Elected to a four-year term by direct vote, the president heads the executive branch of government. Because the people have come to expect a personal and paternalistic approach from their leader, an extraordinary amount of power is couched in the executive branch. Head of the public administration and supreme chief of the armed forces, the president also appoints cabinet members. The bicameral legislature is divided into the Senate and the Chamber of Deputies. One senator from each of the 26 provinces (and from the National District of Santo Domingo) is elected by direct vote to four-year terms. The 91 members of the Chamber of Deputies are apportioned with regard to the population of each province. The Congress has broad legislative powers, including the ability to approve treaties, regulate the national debt, levy taxes, and to proclaim a state of national emergency. The judicial branch is headed by the Supreme Court of Justice; its members are elected by the Senate.

political parties: A grand total of 13. The current ruling party is the Dominican Revolutionary Party (PRD). Rejecting both Reaganomics and Castronomics, this left-of-center party prefers instead to steer an independent course. Second most powerful is the Reformist Party (PR) which dominated the political scene between 1965-78. Its power base rests in the church, the middle class, and the peasantry. Juan Bosch's Dominican Liberation Party (PL), which frequently takes an orthodox Marxist and pro-People's Republic of China line, was founded after he broke with the PRD in 1974. Dating from 1978, the Democratic Union is a breakaway from the PL. Founded by 1963 coup coordinator Gen. Elias Wessin y Wessin, the Quisqueyan Democratic Party is ultra-right. More middle line parties include the Revolutionary

official coat of arms of the Dominican Republic

Social Christian Party, the National Civic Union, and the Movement of National Reconciliation. Two other small parties are the Movimiento Municipal del Pueblo and the Movimiento de Integracion Democratica. Banned in 1964, the Dominican Communist Party was again given official status in 1977 and nominated its first presidential candidate the next year. Underground terrorist organizations include the Communist front Dominican Popular Movement (DMP) and the Cuban-inspired Fragua (Forge).

ECONOMY

The Dominican Republic's economy has historically revolved around a single crop, sugarcane, and one foreign nation, the United States. Although attempts have been made to diversify the economy, the country is so dependent upon sugar that price fluctuations, imposed from abroad, have managed to topple many administrations. Second only to Puerto Rico as a market for U.S. goods in the Caribbean, the U.S. also buys two-thirds of the country's exports.

foreign investment: A growth in U.S. investments has often followed U.S. political/military intervention in the Dominican Republic. As the major source of investment capital, U.S. firms operate 125 subsidiaries in the country. Companies with substantial investments include Esso, Alcoa, 3M, Xerox, Gillette, Colgate, Palmolive, and Phillip Morris. Many fear that these multinationals are striving to take over the government. In an attempt to cope with this problem by taking matters into their own hands, the government purchased the Rosario Dominicana, the largest open-pit gold mine in the Western Hemisphere. Until it sold its holdings in 1984 to the Franjul family of Palm Beach, Florida, the name of Gulf and Western was synonymous with the evils associated with foreign control. Gulf and Western, through such activities as union-busting and bribery, managed to antagonize both the left and the right, and many, including the Dominican Liberation Party, had called for its nationalization. Elements of its $200 million stake in the country ranged from sugar refineries to real estate and top hotels. Sometimes referred to as a "state within a state," its annual sales exceed the nation's GNP! Acquiring the sugar plantations and refinery of the South Puerto Rico Sugar Company in 1966, Gulf and Western moved to destroy the independent sugarcane workers' union; a company-controlled union was substituted. In a nation in which only 14 percent of the land is arable and 75 percent of the population is either landless or cultivating subsistence plots, Gulf and Western owned a full two percent of that land area. Less than half of this was used for sugar; the rest was devoted to ranching and other export crops. The company also held a major share of the tourist industry, with its own multimillion-dollar resort complex (Casa del Campo) in La Romana, as well as control of luxury hotels in Santo Domingo. In 1969, Gulf and Western set up an industrial free zone (in which goods are manufactured utilizing cheap Dominican labor) near La Romana—the first company to do so. Unions are prohibited, and wages are uniformly low. Workers here receive 45 cents per hour, or US$18 per week—in a country where it takes US$31 per week to feed a family of six. Under the current wage levels, an hour's work will fetch one can of Campbell's soup or buy two pounds of rice.

other sectors: Nearly 75 percent of the nation's export revenues derive from agriculture, half of which come from sugarcane, which also provides for a third of national employment. The other major export crops include tobacco, cocoa, and coffee. Now accounting for 25 percent of the nation's exports, mining is the second major sector. Ores include gold, silver, bauxite, ferronickel and *dore* (a gold-silver alloy). A remaining 12-25 percent of export earnings come from light industries: clothing, electronics, leather goods, textiles, and industrial staples. Tourism realizes US$100 million in revenues yearly.

current economic situation: In return for an IMF loan, the government agreed to moves which had severe repercussions. The peso was devalued 200 percent and import subsidies were ended. The cost of imports rose dramatically—basic foodstuffs by up to 100 percent, pharmaceutical products by 300 percent. Public reaction was swift. In April 1984 the country was rocked by three days of food-price rioting which left 55 dead and 150 wounded. Today, the Dominican Republic is in a severe economic crisis: sugar prices have dropped 20 percent in the past five years, the economy is still feeling the long-term effects of the 1979 hurricanes, which cost over US$1 billion in damages, and owing to decreasing demand, ferronickel sales continue to decline. Unemployment and underemployment are estimated at 40 percent; the nation's balance of payments deficit has skyrocketed to US$300 million.

THE PEOPLE

ethnic composition: Mulattos, considered a separate race in official censuses, comprise 73 percent of the nation's 6.3 million population and have dominated the political structure since Trujillo—another middle-class mulatto. Whites, making up 16 percent, are descendants of Spaniards (including Canary Islanders and Sefardic Jews, other Europeans, Lebanese, and German Jews. Blacks, who make up another 11 percent, descend from African slaves, Haitians, and former American slaves who fled here in the 19th century. Other ethnic communities include Japanese, Chinese, and other East Asians. American expatriates number around 13,000. Although there is little overt racism, there is considerable prejudice and discrimination levelled against resident Haitians.

language: Spanish, as it is spoken in the Dominican Republic, is among the purest in Latin America, and there are only three minor dialects. A smattering of African and Indian names and terms remain, and, as in neighboring Puerto Rico, American English terminology has made inroads into colloquial speech.

RELIGION

Catholicism: The history of the Catholic Church in the Americas began here, and more than 90 percent of all Dominicans consider themselves very Catholic. The first Mass was celebrated here in 1493, the first Catholic see established in 1511, the first archbishopric in 1511, and the first cathedral was built in 1541.

Columbus' bones are allegedly holed up in the tomb of this, the first cathedral in the Americas, which stands in Old Santo Domingo. Catholicism came to the Dominican Republic with the Spanish. Here the first Mass was celebrated, the first Catholic see established, and the first cathedral built. Yet, although 90 percent of all Dominicans consider themselves to be Catholic, the church's impact is less than in many other Latin nations.

Yet, the impact of the Catholic Church is not as great as in other Latin nations. Only Cuba and Haiti have fewer priests per inhabitant than Dominicana, and the Church here is poor in property compared with its extensive holdings elsewhere in Central America. During the Trujillo years the Church gained influence and helped lend an aura of legitimacy to Trujillo's regime. In 1936, Trujillo was decorated with the Order of St. Gregory the Great by the Vatican. Not only did the Vatican support Trujillo's 1955-56 "Year of the Benefactor," but the pope sent Francis Cardinal Spellman to represent him at Trujillo's 1956 Congress of Catholic Culture. Upon the occasion of Trujillo's daughter Angelita's marriage, Pope Pius XII dispensed a special blessing upon the entire family. The Church turned against Trujillo only during the last two of his regime. Today, however, the Church has regained its voice of conscience, and accordingly, its status with the people.

others: Of the two percent non-Catholic population in the nation, the majority are Protestants or *evangelicos,* living mostly in the eastern coastal provinces. The Protestant community has grown tremendously since the first missionary landed in 1899. Other religions include Judaism, centered in Santo Domingo and Sosua, and a number of cults. Besides the Liberista Cult and the Brotherhood of the Congo, the most prevalent cult is Voodoo. Most adherents are Haitian immigrants or their descendants. Reviled by the Catholic hierarchy and many Dominicans, Voodoo is usually practiced in secret.

FESTIVALS AND EVENTS

Dominicana has fewer patron saint festivals *(fiestas patronales)* than other Latin American nations. The most famous of these is held at Higuey on 21 January. The *Carnival* is celebrated the three days preceding Lent. Independence Day features carnival-like festivities, while Holy Week features a display of numerous effigies and the burning of Judas Iscariot. Although Christmas is the most joyous holiday of the year, street dancing, music, and fireworks help usher in the New Year.

DOMINICAN REPUBLIC FESTIVALS AND EVENTS

1 Jan.: New Year's Day
21 Jan.: Our Lady of Altagracia's Day
26 Jan.: Duarte's birthday
27 Feb.: Independence Day
Mar.-April: Good Friday (movable)
1 May: Labor Day
16 Aug.: Restoration Day
24 Sept.: Feast of Our Lady of Mercy
25 Dec.: Christmas Day

PRACTICALITIES

getting there: Dominicana, Pan Am, and American Airlines fly nonstop from New York City. Lowest price for the 3½-hour flight is with Pan Am who offers a 21-day excursion fare for $299 RT; restrictions apply. Dominicana flies OW for $169; they also fly from New York and Miami to Puerto Plata. Excursion fares of 21 days are $230 RT to Santo Domingo and Puerto Plata; Pan Am and Eastern's prices are comparable. Dominicana also flies from San Juan ($65 OW, $110 RT). Note, however, that Dominacana is notorious for delays, lost luggage, and overbooking. Santo Domingo may also be reached by air from Port-au-Prince (the land border with Haiti is closed) and from Mayaguez (with Dominicana, $45 OW); however, there are no direct flights from Jamaica—you must come via Port-au-Prince.

getting around: Excellent bus service runs along a network of good roads. *Publicos* or *conchos* are cars which travel certain routes in Santo Domingo and Santiago; *publicos* also travel between cities. In some areas where there is no public transport available, it may be necessary to hitch. Rental cars are available.

internal flights: Flights with Alas del Caribe leave from Santo Domingo's Herrera Airport for Santiago, Puerto Plata, Barahona, and La Romana. Unless you're in a hurry, however, there's no value in taking these, and even if you're in a hurry they won't necessarily save you a great deal of time.

accommodations: Plenty of reasonably priced accommodations are available. The larger hotels exact a five-percent accommodation tax and a 10-percent service charge. There are no campsites or youth hostels.

food: Although it may not be one of the world's great cuisines, you'll be able to fill your stomach amply. Plenty of pizza, fruit drinks of every conceivable variety, good beer (try *Presidente),* and innumerable streetside edibles. Standard dishes include *sancocho* (a thin potpourri of a stew), *sopa criolla dominicana* (made with meat, pasta, greens, onions, and spices), *mangu* (green plantain puree served with codfish), and the *pastelon de vegetables* (a deep-fried vegetable pastry). More exotic dishes include *pipian* (goats' offal stew) and *mondongo* (tripe soup). A good range of dairy products is found in supermarkets; small food stores are known as *pulperas* or *bodegas.*

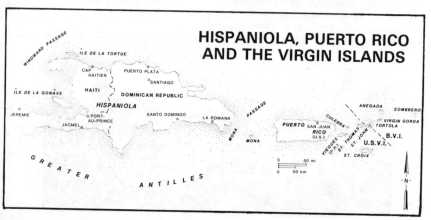

HISPANIOLA, PUERTO RICO AND THE VIRGIN ISLANDS

DOMINICAN REPUBLIC TOURIST OFFICES

SANTO DOMINGO
The Dominican Republic Ministry of Tourism
Cesar Nicolas Pension 9
Box 498
Santo Domingo, Dominican Republic
(809) 688-5537

SPAIN
Dominican Republic Information Center
Nunez de Balboa 37
4to. Izquierda (SIC)
Madrid, Spain
431-5354

PUERTO RICO
Dominican Republic Tourist Office
1300 Ashford Avenue
Santurce, PR
(809) 725-4774

ITALY
Dominican Republic Tourist Office
Via Serbelloni 7
Milano, Italy
793459

LUGANO, SWITZERLAND
Dominican Republic Information Center
Via Rochentto 5 Box 63
CH.-6904 Lugano, Switzerland
(091) 525-321/22

ZURICH, SWITZERLAND
Dominican Republic Tourist Office
Zollikerstrasse 141
8034 Zurich, Switzerland
(01) 550242

WEST GERMANY
Dominican Republic Tourist Office
Grosse Bockenheimer Strasse, 6
D-6000 Frankfurt AM, Main 1, West Germany

VENEZUELA
Dominican Republic Information Center
Final Av. Casanova, Centro Comercial 777
Local 18, Chacaito, Caracas, Venezuela
71320-713239

MIAMI
Dominican Republic Tourist Office
100 N. Biscayne Blvd. Ste. 1807
Miami, FL 33132
(305) 371-2813

NEW YORK
Dominican Tourist Information Center
485 Madison Avenue
New York, NY 10022
(212) 826-0750

money: Monetary unit is the Dominican peso (D$), which had been set on a par with the US dollar since 1947. However, the currency has been officially devalued several times since 1983, and the current exchange rate is approximately US$1 to D$3. Dominican currency may not be imported or exported. Banks are open 0800-1430.

measurements: A mixture of metric and U.S. systems is used. Distances and weights are in metric. Electricity is 115 V AC, 60 Hz—same as in the U.S. The nation operates on Atlantic Standard Time (AST), one hour ahead of Eastern Standard Time.

visas: Citizens of the U.S., Canada, Mexico, Jamaica, Venezuela, and Portugal are re-quired to have a passport, voter's registration card, or birth certificate. Europeans must have a valid passport. Everyone needs a tourist card—which is really a way of collecting a visa fee without issuing a visa; it costs US$5 and may be obtained beforehand at consulates and embassies abroad or at the airport.

health: It is recommended that you not get sick here. Although there are hospitals, clinics, and private practitioners in Santo Domingo, Santiago, and other urban centers, medical care is inadequate. Don't drink tap water unless it's been boiled—even at hotels.

conduct: Dominicans are renowned for their hospitality. Trying to speak or speaking Spanish will go a long way here. Although a mixture of N. American and Spanish customs prevail, dress and social customs are conservative. **theft:** Keep in mind the high level of poverty and take appropriate precautions.

services and information: Government offices are open Mon. to Fri. 0730-1330. Telephone service is available in the cities. *Santo Domingo News* is the free weekly tourist periodical written in English.

shopping: Shops are open Mon. to Fri. 0800-1200 and 1500-1800. Some are open Saturday. For the best buys, avoid the touristic shops and bargain hard.

broadcasting and media: Press is relatively free of controls. Daily newspapers in Santo Domingo include *El Caribe, Listin Diario, La Informacian,* and the afternoon *El Nacional* and *Ultima Hora. Ahora* is a weekly political and economic review. There are approximately 100 radio staions (AM, FM, shortwave) and four television stations—which largely rehash American programs.

SANTO DOMINGO

Set right on the edge of the Caribbean, Santo Domingo, capital and chief seaport of the Dominican Republic, is a sprawling, thriving metropolis of 1.3 million. With the largest concentration of people in the country, it also has the highest growth rate—the population has more than tripled in the past 30 years. This city is far more exciting than any other Caribbean capital. Divided into two sections, Old Santo Domingo still retains much of the flavor it had when it was the first Spanish capital of the Americas. The modern sector, with its broad boulevards, ultramodern museums, embassies, and libraries, is a world unto itself.

history: Founded in 1496 by Columbus' brother Bartholemew, this was the first outpost of the Spanish in the New World, where the first street, university, church, hospital, and mint were established. From here Ponce de Leon sailed to colonize Puerto Rico, Hernando Cortez set out on his invasion of Mexico, and Diego de Velasquez headed out to colonize Cuba. Originally known as Nuevo Isabella, the name of the town was changed either in honor of Columbus' father (whose name was Domingo) or for the day the town was founded (Sunday). During the Trujillo era, the city was renamed Ciudad Trujillo. Also at that time, the then newly erected bridge E of town spanning the Ozama River was named in honor of Rhadames, Trujillo's 12-year-old son, and avenues were named after his daughter "Queen Angelita I."

OLD SANTO DOMINGO

A real gem of a place to visit, most of the old buildings have been restored by the government (with a US$10 million investment) in cooperation with local residents. Walking is the best way to see the sights, and no place is too far to walk to. Almost eerie at night, the town makes an immediate and indelible impression.

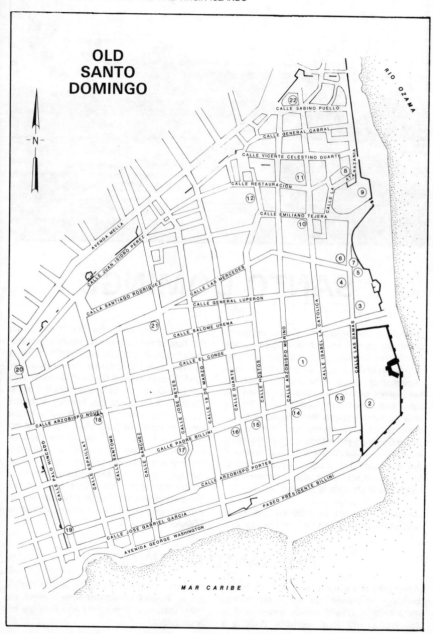

**OLD
SANTO
DOMINGO**

-N-

RIO OZAMA

CALLE GABINO PUELLO

CALLE GENERAL CABRAL

CALLE VICENTE CELESTINO DUARTE

CALLE RESTAURACIÓN

CALLE EMILIANO TEJERA

AVENDA MELLA

CALLE JUAN ISIDRO PEREZ

CALLA SANTIAGO RODRIGUEZ

CALLE LAS MERCEDES

CALLE GENERAL LUPERON

CALLE SALOME URENA

CALLE EL CONDE

CALLE 19 DE MARZO

CALLE JOSE REYES

CALLE SANCHEZ

CALLE DUARTE

CALLE HOSTOS

CALLE ARZOBISPO MERINO

CALLE ISABEL LA CATOLICA

CALLE LAS DAMAS

CALLE LA ATARAZANA

CALLE ARZOBISPO NOUEL

CALLE ESPAILLAT

CALLE SANTOME

CALLE PADRE BILLINI

CALLE ARZOBISPO PORTES

PASEO PRESIDENTE BILLINI

CALLE PALO HINCADO

CALLE JOSE GABRIEL GARCIA

AVENIDA GEORGE WASHINGTON

MAR CARIBE

SIGHTS

Catedral Primada de America (Catedral de Santa Maria la Menor): First and oldest in the Americas, this cathedral was constructed between 1523 and 1545. Pass through the 2½-ton main door to view the elaborate tomb of Christopher Columbus. No one knows if it actually contains the bones of the 15th C. navigator or not: another elaborate chapel in Seville, Spain, makes the same claim. The president, bishop, and mayor come here each year on 12 Oct. to open the three caskets and shed a little light on the situation. Friezes around the base depict important episodes in Columbus' life. In the first chapel to the R of the altar, see where Sir Francis Drake nodded out in his hammock during his 1586 stay. He chopped off the hands of the bishop's statue and chipped off the nose of another during a fit of anger. Exit via La Callejon de Los Curates, a small alleyway, to Calle

---

OLD SANTO DOMINGO

1. Catedral Primada del America (Catedral de Santa Maria la Menor)
2. Fortaleza Ozama/Torre del Homenaje
3. Hostel Nicolas de Ovando
4. Panteon National
5. Capilla de Nuestra Senora de los Remedios
6. Museo de las Casas Reales
7. Reloj de Sol
8. La Ataranza
9. Alcazar de Colon
10. Casa De Colon
11. Museo Duartino
12. Ruinas de Monasterio San Francisco
13. Iglesia Convento De Santa Clara
14. Casa de Tostado (Museum of the Dominican Family)
15. Convento de los Dominicanos
16. Capilla de la Tercera Order
17. Iglesia de la Regina Angelorum
18. Iglesia de Carmen
19. Puerta de la Misericordia
20. Puerta del Conde
21. Iglesia de las Mercedes
22. Iglesia de Santa Barbara

Isabela la Catolica where *Museo Duartino,* the former home of the independence leader, contains mementos of the revolution.

Alcazar de Colon: The home constructed in 1510 by order of Don Diego Columbus (Columbus' son) during his tenure as viceroy. Once a crumbling ruin, it has been magnificently reconstructed, at a cost of US$1 million, using stone of the same type as the original. It opened on Columbus Day 1957. Inside, an armored knight rides a wooden horse; antique pottery, furniture, and musical instruments abound. The authentic furnishings from Spain give you a real feeling for the Spanish colonial era. Note the three 17th C. tapestries depicting Columbus' story, the 16th C. tiled kitchen, and the ivory-encrusted desks. Also see the 16th C. Flemish carving of the death of the Virgin. (Admission D$0.75, open Mon. to Sat. 0900-1700.)

Fortaleza Ozama: On Calle Las Damas, oldest street in the New World, offices of the *Direccion Nacional de Parques,* a children's library, and *Planarte,* a small but superb crafts shop, are located within *Casa de Las Bastidas* inside. Crafts fairs are held seasonally in Gonzalo Fernandez Obevido Plaza here. Dominating all this is the grim and somber *Torre de Homenaje.* Oldest fortress in the Americas, constructed by Nicolas de Ovando in 1503, ships were hailed from the top. Prisoners were incarcerated here during the Trujillo era. Nearby Hostal Nicolas de Ovando is a 16th C. mansion transformed into a hotel; visitors are welcome. The National Pantheon, across the street, was originally a Jesuit convent (1714) and then a theater. Now heroes and public figures are buried here, honored with a small eternal flame and elaborate candelabra.

Capilla de Nuestra Senora de Los Remedios: Chapel of the Remedies, where the earliest residents attended Mass, has stark and simple interiors. Recently restored, it was built in the early 16th century.

Museo De Las Casas Reales: Also on Calle Las Damas, one of the finest small museums in the Caribbean. Enter below the heraldic

Statue of Columbus stands in his plaza opposite the cathedral.

shield of Emperor Charles V. See superb collections of handblown glass, armor and weapons, intricately decorated crossbows, even samurai armor. A major exhibit illustrates life on the *Concepcion,* a Spanish galleon which capsized off the Dominican coast. Finds displayed here are absolutely enthralling. (Open Tues. to Sun. 0900-1700. D$0.50 admission.) *Reloj de Sol,* a sundial built in 1753, is across the street. La Ataranza, first commercial center of the New World, is farther up next to the Alcazar. These eight 16th C. buildings have been turned into shops.

Casa del Cordon: Constructed in 1503, this was the first stone structure built in the New World. Its name stems from the belt of St.

Francis engraved over the door. In 1586 Sir Francis Drake besieged and looted the capital, and then demanded a ransom of 25,000 ducats to return it to the Spanish. The rich brought their jewels here to be weighed, but they were not quick enough for Drake: he systematically burned and tore down parts of the town as well as looting churches and—for good measure—hanging several friars before setting sail for greener pastures.

Ruinas de San Francisco: The carved white cord, symbol of St. Francis, also decorates this monumental 16th C. complex, first monastery in the Americas. Sacked by Drake, it was devastated again by the 1673 and 1751 earthquakes.

Calle Padre Billini: On this street, heading toward Palo Hincado, are a number of sights. Iglesia Convento de Santa Clara was built in 1522 and served as asylum and church for the Clarissa sisters. Casa de Tostada (early 16th C.) has a unique geminated (double) window. Inside is the Museum of the Dominican Family XIX (open Tues. to Fri. 0900-1730, Sat. and Sun. 0900-1600, free admission). The Convento de los Dominicanos, founded 1510, was granted the title of University by Pope Paul III in 1538, making it the first in the Americas. Its unique ceiling illustrates the medieval concept linking the elements of the universe, Christian icons, and classical gods in one unified system. The four evangelists represent Mars, Mercury, Jupiter, and Saturn, while the Sun personifies God. The 18th C. Chapel of the Third Order is located next to the *Iglesia de la Regina Angelorum* (1537) where the remains of philanthropist Father Billini are interred.

others: The Puerta de la Misericordia (Gateway of Mercy), corner of Palo Hincado and Calle Arzobispo Portes, gave protection to the masses in the face of natural disasters. Here, Mella fired the first shot of the revolt against Haiti on 27 Feb. 1844. The modern concrete and marble mausoleum inside Puerto del Conde Park was built in 1976 to house the remains of revolutionary heroes Duarte, Sanchez, and Mella. The ruins of the fortress nearby were originally part of the city walls,

the Dominican Convent, site of the first university in the Americas

and the main defense on the city's NW side. The Church and Convent of Our Lady of Mercy, corner of Calle Mercedes and Jose Reyes, was built in 1555 and sacked during Drake's 1586 attack. Far to the N, off Ave. Mella, are the unique uneven towers and accompanying fort of Iglesia de Santa Barbara. Built in 1562 to honor the patron saint of the military, it was sacked by Drake and, in the usual pattern, destroyed by the 1591 hurricane.

METROPOLITAN SANTO DOMINGO

Overlapping with Old Santo Domingo and sprawling seemingly endlessly, metropolitan Santo Domingo contains the new city with its museums, numerous parks, and the *cinturon de miseria* ("belt of misery"), the vast, squalid slums which are home to thousands of Santo Domingo's urban poor.

SIGHTS

Plaza de la Cultura: Turn R on Calle Bolivar at the Hot Pepper Disco and then L onto Cesar Nicolas Penson until you reach this complex of ultramodern buildings in a park-like setting. This area was once the personal property of Trujillo. You could easily spend the better part of a day here roaming about from place to place. And, what's more, you may have to share them only with the staff. Every building is of splendid architectural design, and Museo del Hombre Dominicano, corner of Pedro Henriquez Urena and Maximo Gomez, is the best of the lot (open Tues. to Sun. 1000-1700, D$0.50 admission; tel. 687-3622). It contains poignant photos of life in a sugarcane village, the unique throne car the pope rode during his 1979 visit, an extensive collection of Taino artifacts, carnival displays, etc. A good introduction to the pulse and tempo of the crazy

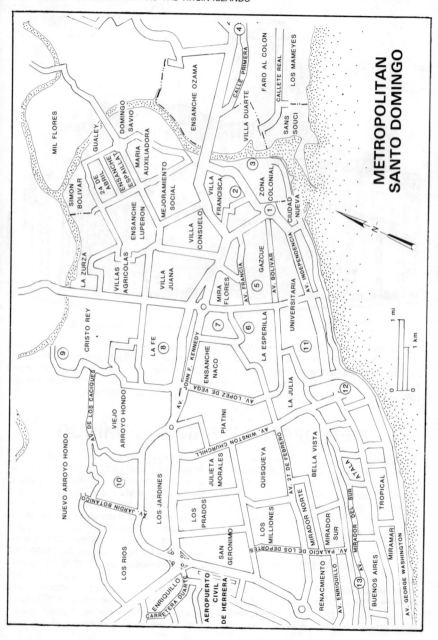

METROPOLITAN
SANTO DOMINGO

The National Theater is a center for opera and symphony performances.

pastiche of African, Spanish, and Taino cultures that make up Dominicana. **Galeria de Arte Moderno:** Located on Pedro Henriquez Urena, this gallery contains fantastic woodcarvings, stained glass, oils, and photographs. Excellent display and arrangement (open Tues. to Sun. 1000-1700. D$0.50 admission, free on Tues.; tel. 682-8280). Horrible piped-in music may be a distraction so bring your Walkman and some jazz or classical tapes. **Museo Nacional de Historia y Geografica:** On Cesar Nicolas Penson. Worthwhile chiefly for its comprehensive collection of Trujillo memorabilia on display in *sala* 3. One of the few places you'll see this despot's name mentioned directly (open Tues. to Sun. 1000-1700,

D$0.50 admission). **Museo de Historia Natural:** Has whale skeletons, stuffed animals, and displays of the cosmos. (Same times and price as above.) **Biblioteca Nacional:** Right on Cesar Nicolas Penson; operates Mon. to Fri. 0900-2100. Houses tons of books and a small art gallery. **Teatro Nacional:** A center for opera and symphony is on Ave. Maximo Gomez (tel. 682-7255).

Jardin Botanica Nacional: Bus 6A runs past this remarkable two-sq-km botanical garden, containing more than 200 species of palm trees, an ornate Japanese garden, largest floral clock in the world, plant, orchid, and aquatic plant exhibits, a museum, and cafeteria. The *Gran Canada,* a series of artificial ponds, is great for bird-watching. Train, boat and carriage rides are also available. Open Tues. to Sun. 0900-1200, 1400-1700.

METROPOLITAN SANTO DOMINGO

1. Puerto del Conde
2. Mercado Modelo
3. Alcazar Colon/post office
4. Los Tres Ojos
5. Plaza de la Cultura
6. Plaza Criolla
7. Centro Olimpico Juan Pablo Duarte
8. Hipodromo Perla Antillana
9. Zoologico
10. Jardin Botanica
11. Ciudad Universitaria
13. Paseo de los Indios

Parque Zoologico Nacional: Take a 6A or 6B bus. One of the largest and most majestic zoological parks in the Americas. Beautiful landscaped gardens. Extensive habitats permit animals to roam freely over a 10-sq-km area. Monkeys swing on poles on an artificial island across from dromedaries munching on grass. An authentic African feel to the place. Walk through the aviary, beautifully designed and covered with netting. There're pony rides and a special zoo for the children. A miniature train (D$0.75) covers the grounds. Open Mon. to Sat. 0900-1730; D$0.50 admission.

Parque de Atracciones Infantiles: Built on the site of the old zoo and botanical garden. Take buses 6A, 6B, or 7. Located between Avenida Bolivar and Cesar Nicolas Penson. There are a number of small animal exhibits, a string of caves, magic carpet ride, carousel, pony rides, and a cafeteria. Open Tues. to Thurs. 0900-2100, Fri. to Sun. 0900-2100, D$0.10 admission.

Parque Mirador del Sur/Paseo de Los Indios: Located on a narrow stretch of land between Ave. Anaconda and Ave. Mirador Del Sur. Built to commemorate the Indians, it's situated on top of a long limestone terrace, perfect for viewing the city and watching sunsets. Kite-flying contests take place here on occasion. There are also plant exhibits, an underground cave with a lake, train, restaurant, and refreshment stands. Free admission. Get here by no. 6A, 6B, or 5 bus.

snoozing in Santo Domingo

Parque Litoral Del Sur, La Caleta: Extends the entire length of Ave. 30 de Maya and Ave. George Washington along the shoreline, following the highway to *La Caleta,* next to the International Airport. *La Caleta,* site of an Indian burial ground, has a small museum with archaeological exhibits. Take a no. 10 bus.

Parque Los Tres Ojos (The Three Eyes): A series of four interconnected underwater ponds of volcanic origin. Stalactite and stalagmite formations. Pull yourself across from one to another by ferry. Outside, vendors sell sculptures carved from stalactites. Ask to see the obscene ones!

others: Avenida de Los Estados Unidos, nearby, is a Balaguer-planned highway bordered by park which collapsed when he was voted out of office. Slum dwelling squatters have moved in. Centro de Los Heroes, presently a collection of rundown government office buildings, was the setting for the 1955-56 "Fair of Peace and Fraternity of the Free World," on which Trujillo squandered an incredible US$40 million, a third of that year's national budget. At the opening of the fair, the dictator's 16-year-old daughter Maria was crowned Queen Angelita I. She wore a US$80,000 satin coat with a 75-ft. Russian ermine train. Fundacion Garcia Arevalo, at km 4½ on the Carretera Duarte, has a fine collection of pre-Hispanic art. The titanic sculpture along the *Malecon* (waterfront) is of Fray Anton de Montecrios who protested the Spanish exploitation of the Indians. It was a gift from Mexico in Oct. 1982. Nearest beach is Boca Chica, 20 km east.

PRACTICALITIES

accommodations: Best of the cheap hotels that aren't used for short-time prostitution is Hotel "La Fama," Ave. Mella 609 (tel. 689-1275). Many Haitian smugglers stay here. Clean and secure with fan and sink in rooms; D$5.50 s. Other *pensiones* and hotels in surrounding area. Hotel Anaconda, Palo Hincado 303 (tel. 688-6888), has rooms with a/c, private bath, and hot water; D$15 s, D$20 d, D$25 t.

Hotel Aida, off Calle El Conde, costs D$15 with fan, D$20 with a/c, s or d. Clean, airy rooms and pink hallways. Hotel Commercio, corner of Hostos and El Conde, charges D$18.40 s, D$23 d. Has a/c and private bath. Hotel Bolivar, Ave. Bolivar 62 (tel. 685-2200), charges D$20 s or D$23.60 d. All rooms equipped with bath, fan and TV. Hotel Antilla, Ave. Independencia, charges D$20 s, D$21.60 d, with bath and fan. Also try Hotel Victoria, Calle 19 de Marzo 33, Independencia, near Puerto del Conde, and Villy Guest House, Pasteur 4.

food: Many cafeterias clustered around the vicinity of El Conde are open late. Cafeteria Viego Roma, Ave. Bolivar, across from Puerto El Conde, serves great lunch and dinners. Daily specials are D$2.50 or select what you want. Maria Autore serves great pizza. For vegetarians, moderately priced Restaurante Vegetariano, Calle Casimiro de Maya 7, is walking distance from El Conde. Street vendors hawk peanut brittle, fruits, *dulce de leche* (a traditional sweet), and other goodies as cheap as D$0.25. Supermarkets are well stocked with milk, cheese, and other staples.

entertainment: Plenty of good nightlife. *Perico ripeao,* groups of three or four street musicians, serenade all up and down the *Malecon,* the waterfront boulevard. Many discotheques. Intimo 2, Calle Hostos, is great for couples. Sir Franics Drake, across from the Alcazar, and Raffles Pub, 352 Hostos, are the two bars frequented by expatriates and Dominican returnees from the States. Casa de Teatro, a drama workshop and experimental theater, is on Calle Arzobispo Merino (tel. 689-3430). The Palace of Fine Arts, Ave. Independencia (tel. 682-6384) and the National Theater at Culture Plaza (682-7255) have opera and symphony performances. Casa de Francia, corner of Las Damas and El Conde, has frequent cultural events and concerts. Movies in English are shown at the Independencia in the rear of Puerto del Conde and at theaters along the *Malecon.* Porno films (D$1) are shown across from the market on Calle Mella. Hookers hang out around and within Puerto del Conde, on Ave. Duarte and the *Malecon.*

shopping: Find most stores along Aves. Duarte, Mella, and Calle El Conde. Mercado Modelo, Ave. Mella, is chock full of stalls offering leatherwork, ceramics, *dulce* (sweets), boats made from cow's horn, and amber necklaces. Upstairs are huge sausages, whole barracudas, severed pig heads and feet; the thump and crack of cold steel hitting bone reverberates throughout. A *botanica* sells Fortune Teller, Gambler's, Amour, and other good luck aerosol sprays to believers in spiritualism. Another shop sells tarantulas framed in glass. Out back, the market overflows with tomatoes, peppers, eggplants, cucumbers, potatoes, carrots, pumpkins, and tropical fruits. La Sirena, Ave. Mella 258, is a large discount store selling toiletries and innumerable household items. Stock up here if traveling to other islands. Bilingual dictionaries for D$2 at Casa Cuello, Calle El Conde. For high-quality crafts check out *Planarte* inside Casa de Bastidas. Remember, if you go into a shop with a guide, you will pay more. Bargain hard.

art galleries: Institute Galerie de Arte Nouveau, corner of Aves. Independencia and Pasteur, is the best of the modern art galleries. Also try Arawak at El Conde 107, Auffant at El Conde 513, Candido Bido at Ave. Mella 9-B, Nader at La Ataranza 9, Rosa Maria at La Ataranza 7, Nouveau at Independencia 354, and Deniels at Independencia 1201.

services: Banks are open Mon. to Fri. from 0830-1430. Rates of exchange vary slightly. The General Post Office is at Calle Emiliano Tejera, opposite Alcazar de Colon. Open Mon. to Fri. 0700-1200, 1400-1800. You can mail letters only here and at major hotels. Postage is extremely cheap—just D$0.10 to mail a letter within the country! The sole tourist office is located at 59 Cesar Penson (tel. 688-5521). Get reliable but expensive medical care at Ave. Independencia 22. Apply for permits to visit the national parks in *Casa de Bastidas* (open Mon. to Fri. 0730-1430; tel. 682-7628, 685-1316). Tours of Parque de Haitises leave at 0600 and return at 2100 every Sat. and Sun. from this same office. Haiti has a tourist office at 103 Calle Arzobispo Merina. Instituto

Dominicano Americano, Ave. Abraham Lincoln, has a fine library (open Mon. to Fri. 1000-1200, 1500-1900). The American Embassy (tel. 682-2171) is at corner of Calle Cesar Nicolas Penson and Calle Leopoldo Navarro. The British Embassy (tel. 682-3218) is at 506 Avenida Independencia, while W. Germany's (tel. 565-8811) has the exceptionally long address of Calle Lic. Juan Tomas Mejia y Cotes No. 37 esq. Eullides Morillo, Apartado 1235.

from Santo Domingo: Many bus companies are in the area around Puerto del Conde. Expresos Dominicano, next to the gas station behind Puerto del Conde, has buses to Santiago (D$4) 10 times per day, and an express bus (D$5.50) leaves three times a day. For Puerta Plata (D$5), five times a day; La Romana (D$2.25), four times per day. Also many other destinations. Other companies: La Experiencia, Calle Los Martires, and Metro Buses, Ave. Winston Churchill. **for the airport:** Expresos Dominicana buses leave direct for Las Americas (D$2.25) Mon. to Fri. 0700, 0930, 1230, 1530, 1425, and 1730. Internal flights leave from Herrera Airport; Alas del Caribe fly to Santiago, La Romana, Barahona, and Puerto Plata.

VICINITY OF SANTO DOMINGO

Haina, Santo Domingo's main port, which also contains the world's largest sugarcane mill, is located just outside the capital. Farther W, San Cristobal was Trujillo's birthplace, and the Casa de Caoba, Trujillo's former home, can be reached by Land Rover bus leaving from behind the market. Scenic La Toma pools nearby are great for swimming. Stay at Hotel Constitucion or Hotel San Cristobal. Fine beaches are found at Las Salinas, Azua, and Barahona, and other beaches, accessible only by car, line the S coast starting at Barahona. Camp on the beach at San Rafael. Smack in the middle of saltwater Lago Enriquillo, Isla Cabritos is a small island which has been turned into a national park. See alligators, iguanas, and flamingos. Stay at Hotel Jimani in Jimani to the W of the lake. San Juan de Maguana, to the N of the lake, features the Corral de Los Indios, an ancient Indian meeting place, a few km N of town. Famous but overrated Boca Chica beach lies 20 km to the east. Other beaches include Playas Guayacanes and Embassy which lie farther east.

The solenodon, *a relative of the* tenrec *of Madagascar, is found only in Cuba and Hispaniola. This brown, ratlike mammal has a rather strange way of walking called "unglitude"; it places only the edge of its foot on the ground. Asleep by day, it prowls* at night, preying on insects, worms, mollusks, and small vertebrates. Standing on hind legs and tail, it tears its quarry apart with its claws before dining. Despite its multimillion-year history, the destruction of its natural environment, combined with the advent of the mongoose, have greatly decreased its numbers, and many fear it is already extinct.

ONWARD TRAVEL

LA ROMANA

Located 112 km from Santo Domingo just under the E hook of the nation's S coast, this city—once noted only for its sugar production—is now better known as a vacation resort. Casa de Campo is a specially developed complex for upper-class tourists. Altos de Chavon, set up on a plateau above the Chavon River, is an artists' village (complete with museum) built in 16th C. Spanish style. This city of 100,000 also has the nation's largest sugar refinery. Isla Catalina is a few km offshore to the west. **accommodations:** Cheapest is Hotel Roma.

economic history: La Romana became a sugar town when the existing mill was built in 1917. The plant has grown over the years and now produces half a million tons per year—the bulk of the sugar exported annually. In the early 1960s, Gulf and Western entered the picture. Investment by this gigantic conglomerate has grown to US$200 million and includes sugar, cement, cattle, factories, and the tourist complex Casa del Campo. In an attempt to make La Romana into the "Showcase of the East," Gulf and Western has poured an estimated $20 million into the town. Although the corporation has changed the face of the city, it has employed administrators educated in the rough atmosphere of Batista's Cuba. Subsequently, the company has been charged with bribery and intimidation. The independent labor unions have been destroyed and a company union substituted. The nearby free trade zone has also been dominated by Gulf and Western.

HIGUEY

Forty km NE of La Romana, the most notable feature of Higuey is the Basilica de Nuestra Senora de la Merced. Located on the spot where Columbus' forces planted their cross while fending off an Indian attack, miracles are attributed to the soil here, which the Dominicans come to gather. Legend has it

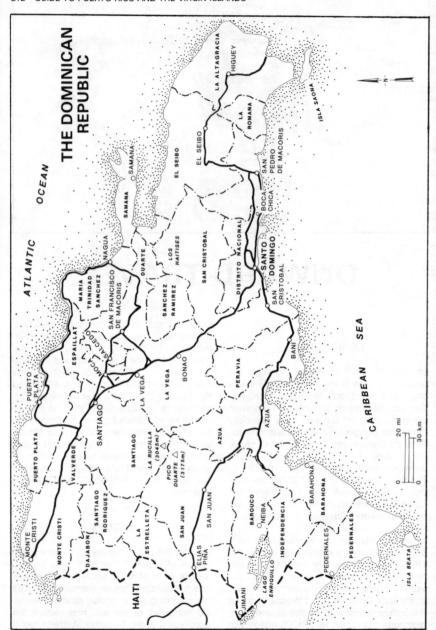

that a vision of the Virgin appeared on the cross and frightened the Indians away. Inside the shrine are kept two splinters of wood believed to have come from Columbus' original cross; it's said he cut wood for it from the *nispero* tree nearby. More modern but now more popular is the Basilica de Nuestra Senora de la Altagracia. This Dominican "Virgin of the Highest Grace" has eclipsed the Virgin Mary in popularity. Legend holds that an apostle, disguised as a pilgrim, came to Higuey and, asking the father of an ailing daughter for food and shelter, left a small picture of the Virgin behind. Gazing upon the picture, the child was healed, and the rest, as they say, is history. The modern church was constructed on the site where the picture was first admired, and an annual pilgrimage is made here on 21 January.

PENINSULA DE SAMANA

This beautiful peninsula, 120 km NE of Santo Domingo, is characterized by heavy rainfall and by a range of lush, forested mountains. The entire peninsula may be explored by boat, but the local boatmen charge an arm, leg, and a rudder. The main town of Samana is a popular honeymoon spot for rich Dominicans. It is a town of future passed: big things were planned for here, but they never developed. Once beautiful with narrow streets overhung by wrought-iron balconies, these were destroyed under Balaguer's rule and replaced with ugly concrete buildings and broad asphalt boulevards. Used primarily by pedestrians and horses, a four-lane highway borders the waterfront. The planned airport was never built, and the railroad, which once ran across the peninsula to Sanchez, has been shut down. A high bridge runs from a point near Samana to an offshore island, where a hotel was planned but never constructed.

history: Columbus fought with the native Arawaks at the Bay of Arrows in 1493. The remains of his fort still stand here. Samana was founded during the 1824 Haitian occupation, when a sloop carrying escaped American slaves wrecked in Samana Bay. Swimming ashore, they founded the town. Because of its isolated location, more than 50 years elapsed before the new settlement was discovered. Accordingly, the language and culture of America's Old South are still very much intact here, and Browns, Joneses, Kings, Smiths, and Greens abound.

vicinity of Peninsula de Samana: Located along the S shore of the Bahia de Sabana, Parque Nacional Los Haitises covers a 30-by-50-km area. Here, incredibly lush and verdant tropical islands appear like ships floating on the sea. (See "services" under "Metropolitan Santo Domingo" for visiting information.)

PUERTO PLATA

Most prominent town on the N coast, Puerto Plata is becoming the island's major tourist resort—the Ocho Rios of the Dominican Republic. Although some attractive 19th C. homes with overhanging balconies still stand, most have been torn down and replaced by specimens from the concrete box school of architecture. Second largest port in the nation, it handles 12 percent of exports and two percent of imports.

history: Discovered by Columbus on his first voyage. Seeing a high mountain capped by a snowlike mist resembling silver, he dubbed the spot "Silver Port." He commissioned Fray Nicholas de Ovando to establish the port here in 1502. By becoming a leading port on the Spanish Main, it came to live up to its name. In 1605, however, it had turned into a haven for smugglers and pirates and was destroyed by Spain. Re-established in 1750, it became a free port shortly afterwards.

getting there: Puerto Plata can be reached by bus or *publico* from Santo Domingo. Union

International Airport lies midway between Puerto Plata and Sosua. The approach from Santiago or Sosua, along the old road, has superior scenery.

sights: Surrounded by persistent hordes of salesmen, the premier sight in town is colonial fortress La Fortaleza San Felipe. Situated at the end of the *Malecon,* everything from coins to cannonballs are displayed inside its cramped interior. Depicted forever on horseback in the middle of the parking area, Gen. Gregorio Luperon fought to overthrow the Spanish from 1860-65. On Calle Duarte, the Amber Museum (also a salesroom) has exhibits of rare and unusual bits of amber of all sizes, shapes, and colors. A leaf, fly, and centipede are all entombed in pieces of amber here. Atop Isabel Torres (789 m; 2,565 ft.), Christ the Redeemer spreads his arms above a fort built by Trujillo. Take the *teleferico* cable car (D$1) to the top (not running on Tues. and Wednesday). Long Beach, crowded on weekends and not exactly the most spotless beach in the world, is at the end of town. Much better but farther W is undeveloped Punta Rucio.

accommodations and food: Cheapest are Ilra, Alpah, Luaronio, 12 de Julio, and the Palacio. Many cafeterias and small restaurants in town. Try cafeterias Los Bonilla, Madrid, La Javilla, and El Canario.

vicinity of Puerto Plata: Sosua lies to the E of Puerto Plata. Here are the only unassimilated whites on the island—a small group of German Jewish immigrants who migrated here in the 1930s and resettled on land donated by Trujillo. Tinned ham and sausage, butter, cheese, and bread are produced here. The homes of Santo Domingo's and Santiago's rich line the hills overlooking Sosua Bay.

SANTIAGO DE LOS TREINTA CABELLEROS

Once the island's largest city, "Santiago of the Thirty Noblemen" (pop. 400,000) has been relegated to a distant second place. Founded by 30 noblemen who named it after their patron saint, St. James, Santiago is often seen as the alter ego of Santo Domingo. Unlike the capital, with its urban sprawl and frenzied pace, this is a city of refinement where many of the most aristocratic and historic families live and where life takes a rather leisurely pace. Located in the N-central part of the country in the heart of the lush and fertile Cibao Valley, the economy runs on rum and tobacco. The beautiful town of San Jose de las Matas lies to the southwest. **getting there:** Can be reached by express and regular bus from Santo Domingo.

sights: These include the Museo de Artes Folklorios Tomas Morel, the Catedral de Santiago Apostol, and the Monumento a los Heroes de la Restauracion (originally constructed by Trujillo in his own honor). Negotiate for a carriage ride around the city. Markets are located at Del Sol and Espana. The Tourist Office is located on the second floor of the Ayuntamiento (Town Hall).

accommodations and food: Cheap *pensiones* include the Diris (tel. 582-4411), corner of Las Carreras and Juan Pablo Duarte, and the Alaska, at Benito Moncion and 16 de

Found in relative abundance in the Dominican Republic, amber, a lustrous resin, is one of the most mysterious and magical substances known to man. Warm to the touch, it burns like wood. When rubbed against wool or silk, it becomes charged with electricity, and this property caused the ancient Greeks to call it electron—the name from which electricity itself was derived. About one piece in 100 found in the Dominican Republic contains an inclusion like the ant to the left.

Augusto. Many sandwich and pizza places in town as well as Dominican-style restaurants.

VICINITY OF SANTIAGO

Parque Nacional Armando Bermudez y Parque Nacional Jose le Carmen Ramirez: Be sure to obtain permission to visit here at Park Headquarters in Santo Domingo. With an area of 153,994 ha, these parks contain the northern and southern slopes of the Cordillera Central, the country's principal mountain range. Here are the highest mountains in the Caribbean: Pico Duarte (3,175 m), Pico La Pelona (3,168 m), Pico La Rucilla (3,049 m), Pico de Yaque del Norte (2,995 m), and Poco del Gallo (2,650 m), among others. This area forms the gigantic watershed from which most of the rivers originate, including Yaque del Norte and a dozen or so others. Hydroelectric dams have been built at Taveras, Sabaneta, Sabana Yegu, and Bao. Dominated by pines, forests are found mostly in the regions surrounding Pico La Pelona up to Pico Duarte and from La Mediania hill to the south. Wild pigs are found in abundance in Totero Valley. Human life in this region scrapes by below subsistence level.

Pico Duarte: The brilliant Swedish botanist Erik Ekman ascertained that Pico Duarte was the highest mountain in the Antilles. Taking him at his word, Trujillo renamed the peak Pico Trujillo—replacing the former name of Pico La Pelona ("Baldy," for the treeless plain on its top). After Trujillo's fall, the mountain was renamed after the 19th C. revolutionary elder and founding father. **climbing Pico Duarte:** Be sure to obtain permission in advance from the park service in Santo Domingo. Begin at Jarabacoa and hitch to Monabao and then hitch or hike along the poor road to La Cienaga (no public transport)—stocking up on food along the way—and Casa Tabalone, at the entrance to the Parque Nacional J. Armanda Bermundez, where the trail begins. Follow the L bank of the Rio Yaque del Norte for a few km before turning up a steep mule track which winds its way around a series of ridges. Palms give way to coarse bracken ferns and *palo de cotorra* ("parrot tree"), a thin-stemmed tree with feathery leaves. At 1,800 m (5,900 ft.), the vegetation changes to jungle congested with a variety of ferns, bromeliads, orchids, epiphytes, mosses, lichens, tree ferns, and conifers. Pine forest takes over near the crude bush shelter and spring at 2,650 m (7,900 feet). From here follow a trail to the incredibly desolate summit. Allow two days from Casa Tabalone for this hike.

La Vega: A quiet town in the center of Cibao Valley. Stay at Royal, America, or Guaricano hotels. The top of nearby Santo Cerro offers an overlook of the entire Valle de la Vega Real.

Jarabacoa: A popular mountain resort town set amidst pine forests. Stay at Nacional or La Montana hotels.

Bonao: Halfway between Santo Domingo and Santiago along Carr. Duarte, Bonao (pop. 25,000) has been transformed by the discovery of mineral wealth and the arrival of the mining industry. Rich deposits of nickel, bauxite, silver, and gold were discovered here in the early 1970s. Note the contrast between the shanties of the miners—who work long hours under dangerous conditions for low wages—and the transplanted suburban lifestyle of the American expatriate community in *Barrio Gringo.* Stay at Hotel El Viejo Madrid or Yaravi Rooms.

BOOKLIST

ART, ARCHITECTURE, AND ARCHAEOLOGY

Buissert, David. *Historic Architecture of the Caribbean.* London: Heinemann Educational Books, 1980.

Fernandez, Jose A. *Architecture in Puerto Rico.* New York: Hastings House, 1965.

Gosner, Pamela. *Caribbean Georgian* Washington, D.C.: Three Continents Press, 1982. A beautifully illustrated guide to the "Great and Small Houses of the West Indies."

Kaiden, Nina, Pedro John Soto, and Vladimir Andrews, eds. *Puerto Rico, The New Life.* New York: Renaissance Editions, 1966.

Lewisohm, Florence. *The Living Arts & Crafts of the West Indies.* Christiansted, St. Croix: The Virgin Islands Council on the Arts, 1973. Local crafts illustrated.

Rouse, Benjamin I. *Puerto Rican Prehistory.* New York: Academy of Sciences, 1952.

Willey, Gordon R. *An Introduction to American Archaeology, Vol. 2, South America.* Englewood Cliffs, New Jersey: Prentice-Hall, Inc., 1971.

FLORA AND FAUNA

Jadan, Doris. *A Guide to the Natural History of Saint John.* St. John: Environmental Studies Program, 1979.

Kaplan, Eugene. *A Field Guide to the Coral Reefs of the Caribbean and Florida.* Princeton, N.J.: Peterson's Guides, 1984.

Little, Elbert L., Jr., Frank J. Wadsworth, and Jose Marrero *Arboles Comunes De Puerto Rico y las Islas Virgenes.* Rio Piedras: University of Puerto Rico Press, 1967.

Riviera, Juan A. *The Amphibians of Puerto Rico.* Mayaguez: Universidad de Puerto Rico, 1978.

de Oviedo, Gonzalo Fernandez. (trans. and ed. S.A. Stroudemire. *Natural History of the West Indies.* Chapel Hill: University of North Carolina Press, 1959.

HISTORY

Bonnet, Benitez and Juan Amedee. *Vieques En La Historia de Puerto Rico.* Puerto Rico: F. Nortiz Nieves, 1976. Traces the history of Vieques over the centuries.

Boyer, William W. *America's Virgin Islands.* Durham, North Carolina: Carolina Academic Press, 1983. A superb overview of the political and social history of the islands.

Crassweller, Robert D. *Trujillo: The Life and Times of a Caribbean Dictator.* New York: Macmillan, 1966.

Cripps, L.L. *The Spanish Caribbean: From Columbus to Castro.* Cambridge: Schenkman, 1979. Concise history from the point of view of a radical historian.

Deer, Noel. *The History of Sugar.* London: Chapman, 1950.

Dookhan, Issac. *A History of the Virgin Islands of the United States.* St. Thomas: College of the Virgin Islands, Caribbean Universities Press, 1974.

Flagg, John. *Cuba, Haiti, and the Dominican Republic* New York: Prentice Hall, 1965. History of Hispaniola from Columbus to Castro.

Golding, Morton J. *A Short History of Puerto Rico.* New York: New American Library, 1973.

Hicks, Albert C. *Blood in the Streets: The Life and Rule of Trujillo.* New York: Creative Age Press, Inc., 1946.

Hill, Valdemar A., Sr. *Rise to Recognition, An Account of Virgin Islanders from Slavery to Self-Government.* St. Thomas: St Thomas Graphics, 1971.

Hovey, Graham and Gene Brown, eds. *Central America and the Caribbean.* New York: Arno Press, 1980. This volume of clippings from the *New York Times,* one of a series in its "Great Contemporary Issues" books, graphically displays American activities and attitudes toward the area. A goldmine of information.

Hunte, George. *The West Indian Islands.* New York: Viking Press, 1972. Historical overview from the Western viewpoint with information added for tourists.

Jarvis, J. Antonio. *The Virgin Islands and Their People.* Philadelphia: Dorrance & Co., 1944. Fascinating account of the U.S.V.I. during the '40s.

Knight, Franklin W. *The Caribbean.* Oxford: Oxford University Press, 1978. Thematic, anti-imperialist view of Caribbean history.

Lewis, Gordon K. *Puerto Rico: Freedom and Power in the Caribbean.* New York: Monthly Review Press, 1963. Dated but still the most comprehensive general work in existence on Puerto Rican history and economics.

Lewis, Gordon K. *The Virgin Islands: A Caribbean Lilliput.* Evanston, Ill.: Northwestern University Press, 1972.

Lewisohn, Florence. *St. Croix under Seven Flags.* Hollywood, Fla.: Inernational Graphics, Inc., 1966. An absorbing account · of the history of the island.

———. *"What So Proudly We Hail,"* The Danish West Indies and the American Revolution. St. Croix: Prestige Press, 1976.

———. *The Romantic History of St. Croix.* St. Croix: St. Croix Landmarks Society, 1964.

Mannix, Daniel P. and Malcolm Cooley. *Black Cargoes.* New York: Viking Press, 1982. Details the saga of the slave trade.

Mendez, Eugenio Fernandez. *Historia Cultural de Puerto Rico 1493-1968.* Rio Piedras: University of Puerto Rico Press, 1980.

Rodman, Selden. *Quisqueya.* Seattle: University of Washington Press, 1964.

Silen, Juan Angel. *We, the Puerto Rican People.* New York: Monthly Review Press, 1971. Analysis of Puerto Rican history from the viewpoint of a militant Puerto Rican nationalist.

Wagenheim, Kal., ed. *Puerto Rico: A Documentary History.* New York: Praeger, 1973. History from the point of view of eyewitnesses.

Welles, Sumner. *Naboth's Vineyard. The Dominican Republic, 1844-1924.* New York: Payson and Clarke, Ltd., 1928.

Williams, Eric. *From Columbus to Castro: The History of the Caribbean.* New York: Random House, 1983. Definitive history of the Caribbean by the late prime minister of Trinidad and Tobago.

LANGUAGE

Highfield, Arnold R. *The French Dialect of St. Thomas, Virgin Islands: A Descriptive Grammar with Text and Glossary.* Ann Arbor: Karoma Publishers, Inc., 1979.

Rosario, Ruben del. *Vocabulario Puertorriqueno.* Sharon, Mass.: Troutman Press, 1965. Contains exclusively Puerto Rican vocabulary.

LITERATURE

Anderson, John L. *Night of the Silent Drums.* New York: Scribner, 1976. Fictional narrative of a Virgin Islands slave rebellion.

Babin, Maria Theresa. *Borinquen: An Anthology of Puerto Rican Literature.* New York: Vintage, 1974.

Baldwin, James. *If Beale Street Could Talk.* New York: Dial, 1974. Novel set in NYC and Puerto Rico.

Howes, Barbara, ed. *From the Green Antilles.* New York: Crowell, Collier, & Macmillan, 1966. Includes four stories from Puerto Rico.

Levine, Barry. *Benjy Lopez: A Picaresque Tale of Emigration and Return.* New York: Basic Books, 1980.

Sanchez, Luiz R. *Macho Camacho's Beat.* New York: Pantheon, 1981. Novel set in Puerto Rico.

Whitney, Phyllis A. *Columbella.* New York: Doubleday, 1966. Mystery-romance set in St. Thomas.

Wouk, Herman. *Don't Stop the Carnival.* Glasgow: Fontana Books, 1979. The classic novel of expatriate life in the Virgin Islands.

MUSIC

Bergman, Billy. *Hot Sauces: Latin and Caribbean Pop.* New York: Quill, 1984.

POLITICS AND ECONOMICS

Anderson, Robert W. *Party Politics in Puerto Rico.* Stanford: Stanford University Press, 1965.

Barry, Tom, Beth Wood, and Deb Freusch. *The Other Side of Paradise: Foreign Control in the Caribbean.* New York: Grove Press, 1984. A brilliant, thoughtfully written analysis of Caribbean economics.

Bayo, Armando. *Puerto Rico.* Havana: Casa de las Americas, 1966.

Blanshard, Paul. *Democracy and Empire in the Caribbean.* New York: The Macmillan Co., 1947.

Cripps, L.L. *Human Rights in a United States Colony.* Cambridge: Schenkmann Publishing Co., 1982. Once one gets past the ludicrous paeans to life in socialist countries, this book contains valuable information concening matters one never hears about stateside: Cerro Maravilla, the Vieques and Culebra takeovers, police brutality, etc.

Diffie, Bailey W. and Justine Whitfield. *Porto Rico: A Broken Pledge.* The Vanguard Press: New York, 1931. An early study of American exploitation in Puerto Rico.

Gooding, Bailey W. and Justine Whitfield. *The West Indies at the Crossroads.* Cambridge: Schenkmann Publishing Co., Inc., 1981. A political history of the British Caribbean during the 1970s.

Johnson, Roberta. *Puerto Rico, Commonwealth or Colony?* New York: Praeger, 1980.

Lewis, Gordon K. *Notes on the Puerto Rican Revolution.* New York: Monthly Review Press, 1974. A Marxist analysis of the past, present, and future of Puerto Rico.

Matthews, Thomas G. and F.M. Andic, eds. *Politics and Economics in the Caribbean.* Rio Piedras: Institute of Caribbean Studies, University of Puerto Rico, 1971.

Matthews, Thomas G. *Puerto Rican Politics and the New Deal.* Miami: University of Florida Press, 1960.

Mitchell, Sir Harold. *Caribbean Patterns.* New York: John Wiley and Sons., 1972. Dated but still a masterpiece. The best reference guide for gaining an understanding of the history and current political status of nearly every island group in the Caribbean.

O'Neill, Edward A. *Rape of the American Virgins.* New York: Praeger, 1972. Scathing history and revealing account of trouble in American Paradise.

Petrullo, Vincenzo. *Puerto Rican Paradox.* Philadelphia: University of Pennsylvania Press, 1947.

Roosevelt, Theodore. *Colonial Policies of the United States.* Garden City: Doubleday, Doran, and Co., 1937. The chapter on Puerto Rico by this former governor of the island is particularly fascinating.

Tugwell, Rexford Guy. *The Stricken Land.* Garden City, New York: Doubleday & Co., 1947.

Wells, Henry. *The Modernization of Puerto Rico: A Political Study of Changing Values and Institutions.* Cambridge: Harvard University Press, 1969.

SOCIOLOGY AND ANTHROPOLOGY

Abrahams, Roger D. *After Africa.* New Haven: Yale University Press, 1983. Fascinating accounts of slave life in the West Indies.

Acosta-Belen, Edna and Elia Hidalgo Christensen, eds. *The Puerto Rican Woman.* New York: Praeger, 1979.

Brameld, Theodore A., *Remaking of a Culture: Life and Education in Puerto Rico.* New York: Harper & Brothers, 1959.

Horowitz, Michael H., ed. *People and Cultures of the Caribbean.* Garden City, New York: National History Press for the Museum of Natural History, 1971. Sweeping compilation of social anthropological essays.

Kerr, Madeline. *Personality and Conflict in Jamaica.* Liverpool: Universities Press, 1952.

Mintz, Sidney W. *Caribbean Transformation.* Chicago: Aldine Publishing Co., 1974. Includes an essay on Puerto Rico.

Mintz, Sidney W. *Worker in the Cane: A Puerto Rican Life History.* New Haven: Yale University Press, 1960.

Price, Richard, ed. *Maroon Societies—Rebel Slave Communities in the Americas.* Garden City, New Jersey: Anchor Press, 1973.

Rand, Christopher. *The Puerto Ricans.* New York: Oxford University Press, 1958.

Steward, Julian W. *The People of Puerto Rico.* Urbana: University of Illinois Press, 1956. An early and thorough social anthropological study of Puerto Rico.

TRAVEL AND DESCRIPTION

Arciniegas, German. *Caribbean: Sea of the New World.* New York: Alfred A. Knopf, 1946.

Babin, Theresa Maria. *The Puerto Rican's Spirit.* New York: Collier Books, 1971. Excellent information regarding Puerto Rican history, people, literature, and fine arts.

Blume, Helmut. (trans. Johannes Maczewski and Ann Norton) *The Caribbean Islands.* London: Longman, 1976.

Bonsal, Stephen. *The American Mediterranean.* New York: Moffat, Yard and Co., 1912.

Caabro, J.A. Suarez. *El Mar de Puerto Rico.* Rio Piedras: University of Puerto Rico Press, 1979.

Caimite. *Don't Get Hit by a Coconut.* Hicksville, New York: Exposition Press, 1979. The memoirs of an Ohio painter who escaped to the Caribbean.

Creque, Darwin D. *The U.S. Virgins and the Eastern Caribbean.* Philadelphia: Whitmore Publishing Co., 1968.

Doucet, Louis. *The Caribbean Today.* Paris: editions j.a., 1977.

Eggleston, George T. *Virgin Islands.* Melbourne, Florida: Krieger, 1973. A somewhat dated (1959) travelogue of special interest to the cruise set.

Fillingham, Paul. *Pilot's Guide to the Lesser Antilles.* New York: McGraw-Hill, 1979. Invaluable for pilots.

Hanberg, Clifford A. *Puerto Rico and the Puerto Ricans.* New York: Hippocrene, 1975. Survey of the Puerto Rican historical experience.

Hansen, Knud. *From Denmark to the Virgin Islands.* New York: Dorrance and Co., 1947.

Hart, Jeremy C. and William T. Stone. *A Cruising Guide to the Caribbean and the Bahamas.* New York: Dodd, Mead and Company, 1982. Description of planning and plying for yachties. Includes nautical maps.
Hartman, Jeanne Perkins. *The Virgins: Magic Islands.* New York: Appleton-Century, 1961.

Hayward, Du Bose. *Star Spangled Virgin* New York: Farrar and Rhinehart, 1939.

Hazard, Samuel. *Santo Domingo, Past and Present; with a Glance at Haiti.* New York: Harper and Brothers, 1873.

Holbrook, Sabra. *The American West Indies, Puerto Rico and the Virgin Islands.* New York: Meredith Press, 1969.

Lewis, Oscar. *La Vida.* New York: Irvington, 1982. The famous chronicle of Puerto Rican life in 1966.

Lopez, Adalberto and James Petras. *Puerto Rico and the Puerto Ricans.* Cambridge: Schenkmann-Halstead Press, 1974.

Morrison, Samuel E. *The Caribbean as Columbus Saw It.* Boston: Little and Co.: 1964. Photographs and text by a leading American historian.

Naipaul, V.S. *The Middle Passage: The Caribbean Revisited.* New York: Macmillan, 1963. Another view of the West Indies by a Trinidad native.

Perl, Lila. *Puerto Rico, Island Between Two Worlds.* New York: William Morrow and Co., 1979.

Radcliffe, Virginia. *The Caribbean Heritage.* New York: Walker & Co., 1976.

Robertson, Alan H. and Fritz Henle. *Virgin Islands National Park: The Story Behind the Scenery.* Las Vegas: KC Publications, 1974.

Rodman, Selden. *The Caribbean.* New York: Hawthorn, 1968. Traveler's description of the Caribbean by a leading art critic.

Robinson, Kathryn. *The Other Puerto Rico.* Santurce, Puerto Rico: Permanent Press, Inc., 1984. Guide to the natural wonders of the islands.

Samoiloff, Louise C. *Portrait of Puerto Rico.* San Diego: A.S. Barnes, 1979. Descriptive and comprehensive profile.

Steiner, Stan. *The Islands.* New York: Harper & Row, 1974. An in-depth living journalistic portrait of the Puerto Ricans—on their island and on the mainland *barrios.*

Van Ost, John R. and Harry Kline. *Yachtsman's Guide to the Virgin Islands and Puerto Rico.* North Miami, Florida: Tropic Isle Publishers, Inc., 1984. Where to anchor in the area.

Waggenheim, Kal. *Puerto Rico: A Profile.* New York: Praeger, 1970. A revealing if dated survey of Puerto Rico's economy, geography, and culture.

Ward, Fred. *Golden Islands of the Caribbean*. New York: Crown Publishers, 1967. A picture book for your coffee table. Beautiful historical plates.

Wiarda, Howard J. *The Dominican Republic, A Caribbean Crucible*. Boulder, Colo.: Westview, 1982. Concise survey of the nation.

Wood, Peter. *Caribbean Isles*. New York: Time-Life Books, 1975. Includes descriptions of such places as Pico Duarte in the Dominican Republic and the Blue Mountain region of Jamaica.

GLOSSARY

agregado — refers to the sugarcane workers who, up until the late 1940s, labored under the feudal system wherein wages were paid partially in goods and services received.

anatto — a small tree whose seeds, coated with orange-red dye, are used to color cooking oil commonly used in the preparation of Puerto Rican and other Caribbean cuisines.

areytos — epic songs danced to by the Tainos.

asapao — a soupy rice dish containing beef, chicken, fish, or other seafood.

bacalao — dried salt cod, once served to slaves.

barrio — a city district.

bohio — Taino Indian name for thatched houses; now applied to the houses of country dwellers in Puerto Rico.

bola, bolita — the numbers racket.

bomba — Puerto Rican musical dialogue between dancer and drummer.

botanica — stores on the Spanish-speaking islands which sell spiritualist literature and paraphernalia.

calabash *(calabaza)* — small tree native to the Caribbean whose fruit, a gourd, has multiple uses when dried.

callaloo — Caribbean soup made with *callaloo* greens.

callejon — narrow side street; path through the cane fields.

campesino — peasant; lower class-rural dweller.

canita — "the little cane," bootleg rum (also called *pitorro*).

carambola — see "star apple."

Caribs — original people who colonized the islands of the Caribbean, giving the region its name.

caudillo — Spanish for military general.

cassava — staple crop indigenous to the Americas. Bitter and sweet are the two varieties. Bitter must be washed, grated, and baked in order to remove the poisonous prussic acid. A spongy cake is made from the bitter variety, as is *cassareep,* a preservative which is the foundation of West Indian pepperpot stew.

cays — Indian-originated name which refers to islets in the Caribbean.

century plant — also known as *karato, coratoe,* and maypole. Flowers only once in its lifetime before it dies.

cerro — hill or mountain.

chorizo — Spanish sausage.

compadrazgo — the system of "co-parentage" which is used to strengthen social bonds in Puerto Rico.

conch — large edible mollusk usually pounded into salads or chowders.

cuerda — unit of land measure comprising 97/100ths of an acre.

cutlass — the Caribbean equivalent of the machete; originally used by pirates.

duppy — ghost or spirit of the dead which is feared throughout the Caribbean. Derives from the African religious belief that a man has two souls. One ascends to heaven while the other stays around for a while or permanently. May be harnessed by good or evil through *obeah.* Some plants and birds are also associated with *duppies.*

escabeche — Spanish and Portuguese method of preparing seafood.

espiritismo—spiritualism.

estadistas—Puerto Rican advocates of statehood.

Estado Libre Asociado—"Free Associated State"; the Puerto Rican translation of the word "commonwealth."

fiesta patronales—patron saint festivals which take place on Catholic islands.

guava—indigenous Caribbean fruit, extremely rich in vitamin C, which is eaten raw or used in making jelly.

guayacan—the lignum vitae tree and its wood.

guiro—rasp-like musical instrument of Taino Indian origin which is scratched with a stick to produce a sound.

independentistas—advocates of Puerto Rican independence.

jibaro—the vanishing breed of impoverished but self-sufficient Puerto Rican peasant.

Jonkonnu—festivities dating from the plantation era in which bands of masqueraders, dressed with horse or cow heads or as kings, queens or devils. Now a dying practice throughout the Caribbean, it is preserved largely for tourists.

langosta—spiny lobster (really a crayfish) native to the region.

lechon asado—roast pig.

love bush—orange-colored parasitic vine, found on Jamaica, St. John, and other islands. Resembles nothing so much as the contents of a can of spaghetti.

rnanchineel—small toxic tree native to the Caribbean. Its fruit, which resembles an apple, and milky sap are lethal. See clearly marked specimens near Annaberg ruins on St. John.

mundillo—Spanish lacemaking found on Puerto Rico.

naranja—Puerto Rican sour orange; its leaves are used as medicine in rural areas.

Neoricans—term used to describe Puerto Ricans who have returned to the island from the States.

obeah—Caribbean black magic imported from Africa.

padrinos—godparents.

pasteles—steamed banana leaves stuffed with meat and other ingredients.

pastelitos—small meat-filled turnovers.

personalismo—used to describe the charisma of a Latin politician who appears and acts as a father figure.

pinonos—deep-fried plantain rings stuffed with spiced ground beef; found on Puerto Rico.

plena—form of Puerto Rican dance.

poinciana—beautiful tropical tree which blooms with clusters of red blossoms in the summer months; originates in Madagascar.

publico—shared taxi found on the Spanish-speaking islands.

sancocho (sancoche)—stew made with a variety of meats and vegetables; found in the Spanish-speaking islands.

santos—carved representations of Catholic saints.

sea grape—West Indian tree, commonly found along beaches, which produces green, fleshy inedible grapes.

senorita—young unmmarried female, usually used in rural Puerto Rico to refer to virgins.

sensitive plant—also known as mimosa, shame lady, and other names. Its leaves fold shut at the slightest touch.

star apple—large tree producing segmented pods, brown in color and sour in taste, which are a popular fresh fruit.

surrillitos—fried cornmeal-and-cheese sticks.

tachuelo—a variety of tropical hardwood.

taro—edible tuber also known as sasheen, tannia, malanga, elephant's ear, and *yautia*.

trigueno—literally "wheat colored," it denotes a mulatto or is used to differentiate brunettes from blondes.

velorio—Catholic wake.

woman's tongue—Asian plant whose name comes from its long seed pods, brown when dry, which flutter and rattle in the breeze, constantly making noise.

zemi (cemi)—idol in which the personal spirit of each Arawak or Taino Indian lived. Usually carved from stone.

SPANISH VOCABULARY

DAYS OF THE WEEK

domingo	Sunday
lunes	Monday
martes	Tuesday
miercoles	Wednesday
jueves	Thursday
viernes	Friday
sabado	Saturday

MONTHS OF THE YEAR

enero	January
febrero	February
marzo	March
abril	April
mayo	May
junio	June
julio	July
agosto	August
septiembre	September
octubre	October
noviembre	November
diciembre	December

NUMBERS

uno	one
dos	two
tres	three
cuatro	four
cinco	five
seis	six
siete	seven
ocho	eight
nueve	nine
diez	ten
once	eleven
doce	twelve
trece	thirteen
catorce	fourteen
quince	fifteen
dieciseis	sixteen
diecisiete	seventeen
dieceiocho	eighteen
diecinueve	nineteen
veinte	twenty
veintiuno	twenty-one
veintidos	twenty-two
treinta	thirty
cuarenta	forty
cincuenta	fifty
sesenta	sixty
setenta	seventy
ochenta	eighty
noventa	ninety
cien	one hundred
ciento uno	one hundred one
doscientos	two hundred
quinientos	five hundred
mil	one thousand
mil uno	one thousand one
dos mil	two thousand
un million	one million
mil milliones	one billion

primero	first
segundo	second
tercero	third
cuarto	fourth
quinto	fifth
sexto	sixth
septimo	seventh
octavo	eighth
noveno	ninth
decimo	tenth
undecimo	eleventh
duodecimo	twelfth
ultimo	last

CONVERSATION

¿ Como esta usted?	How are you?
Bien, gracias, y usted?	Well, thanks, and you?
Buenos dias.	Good morning.
Buenas tardes.	Good afternoon.
Buenas noches.	Good (evening) night.
Hasta la vista.	See you again.
Hasta luego.	So long.
¡ Buena suerte!	Good luck!
Adios.	Goodbye.
Mucho gusto de conocerle.	Glad to meet you.
Felicidades.	Congratulations.
Muchas felicidades.	Happy birthday.
Feliz Navidad.	Merry Christmas.
Feliz Ano Nuevo.	Happy New Year.
Gracias.	Thank you.
Por favor.	Please.
De nada.	You're welcome.
Perdoneme.	Pardon me.
¿ Como se llama esto ?	What do you call this?
Lo siento.	I'm sorry.
Permitame.	Permit me.
Quisiera...	I would like...
Adelante.	Come in.
Permitame presentarle...	May I introduce...
¿ Como se llamo usted?	What is your name?
Me llamo...	My name is...
No se.	I don't know.
Tengo sed.	I'm thirsty.
Tengo hambre.	I'm hungry.
Soy norteamericano (-na).	I'm an American.
¿ Donde puedo encontrar...?	Where can I find...?
¿ Que es esto?	What is this?
¿ Habla usted ingles?	Do you speak English?
Hablo (entiendo) un poco espanol.	I speak (understand) a little Spanish.
¿ Hay alguien aqui que hable ingles?	Is there someone here who can speak English?
Le entiendo.	I understand you.
No entiendo.	I don't understand.

Hable mas despacio, por favor	Please speak more slowly.
Repita, por favor.	Please repeat.

TELLING TIME

¿ Que hora es?	What time is it?
Son las...	It's
...cinco	five o'clock
...ocho y diez	ten past eight
...seis y cuarto	a quarter past six
...cinco y media	half past five
...siete menos cinco	five to seven
antes de ayer	the day before yesterday
anoche	yesterday evening
esta manana	this morning
a mediodia	at noon
en la noche	in the evening
de noche	at night
a medianoche	at midnight
manana en la manana	tomorrow morning
manana en la noche	tomorrow evening
pasado manana	the day after tomorrow

DIRECTIONS

¿ En que direccion queda...?	In which direction is....?
Lleveme a..., por favor.	Please take me to...
Lleveme alla, por favor.	Please take me there.
¿ Que lugar es este?	What place is this?
¿ Donde queda el pueblo?	Where is the town?
¿ Cual es el mejor camino para...?	Which is the best road for...?
De vuelta a la derecha.	Turn to the right.
De vuelta a la izquierda.	Turn to the left.
Siga derecho.	This way.
En esta direccion.	In this direction.
¿ A que distancia estamos de...?	How far is it to...?
¿ Es este el camino a...?	Is this the road to...?

¿Es...	Is it...	Hagame favor de decirme donde esta...	Please direct me to....
...cerca?	near?		
...lejos?	far?		
...norte	north	el telephono	the telephone
...sur	south	el excusado	the toilet
...este	east	el correo	the post office
...oeste	west	el banco	the bank
Indiqueme, por favor.	Please point.	la comisaria	the police station

> ¿*Habla Usted Espanol?*
> For more intensive language study,
> turn to page 242 for a selection of
> Spanish Language learning aids.

INDEX

Italicized page numbers indicate information in captions, call-outs, charts, illustrations, or maps.
"i" = illustration, "c" = chart, "m" = map

OTHER
MOON PUBLICATIONS
GUIDES

Finding Fiji
by David Stanley

Fiji, everyone's favorite South Pacific country, is now easily accessible either as a stopover or a whole Pacific experience in itself. No visas or vaccinations are required! Enjoy picture-window panoramas as you travel from exciting island resorts where Australians meet Americans halfway, to remote interior valleys where you can backpack from village to village. You'll fall immediately in love with Fiji's friendly, exuberant people. *Finding Fiji* covers it all—the amazing variety of land and seascapes, customs and climates, sightseeing attractions, hikes, beaches, and how to board a copra boat to the outer islands. *Finding Fiji* is packed with practical tips, everything you need to know in one portable volume. 20 color photos, 78 illustrations, 26 maps, 3 charts, vocabulary, subject and place name index, 127 pages.

Code **MN17**   **$6.95**

South Pacific Handbook 3rd. edition
by David Stanley

Here is paradise explored, photographed and mapped—the first original, comprehensive guide to the history, geography, climate, cultures, and customs of the 19 territories in the South Pacific. Experience awesome Bora Bora by rented bicycle; scale Tahiti's second highest peak; walk down a splendidly isolated, endless talcum beach in New Caledonia's Loyalty Islands; drink *kava* with villagers in Fiji's rugged·interior; backpack through jungles in Vanuatu to meet the "Hidden People"; marvel at the gaping limestone chasms of Niue; trek along Bloody Ridge in the Solomons where the Pacific War changed course; hitch rides on cruising yachts; live the life of a beachcomber in Tonga; witness the weaving of a "fine mat" under a Samoan *fale*; go swimming with free sea lions in the Galapagos; dive onto coral gardens thick with brilliant fish; see atoll life unchanged in Tokelau or Tuvalu; dance the exciting Polynesian dances of the Cooks. No other travel book covers such a phenomenal expanse of the earth's surface. 588 Smyth-sewn pages, 121 illustrations, 195 black and white photos, 12 color pages, 138 maps, 35 charts, booklist, glossary, index. 588 pages

Code **MN03**   **$13.95**

Japan Handbook
by J.D. Bisignani

Packed with practical money-saving tips on travel, food and accommodation, this book dispels the myth that Japan is "too expensive" for the budget-minded traveler. The theme throughout is "do it like the Japanese," to get the most for your time and money. From Okinawa through the entire island chain to Rishiri Island in the extreme north, *Japan Handbook* is essentially a cultural and anthropological manual on every facet of Japanese life. 35 color photos, 200 b/w photos, 92 illustrations, 29 charts, 112 maps and town plans, an appendix on the Japanese language, booklist, glossary, index. 504 pages.

Code   MN05   **$12.95**

Guide to Catalina Island
by Chicki Mallan

Whether they come by yacht, ferry, or airplane, visitors to Santa Catalina will find this the most complete guide to California's most unique island. *Guide to Catalina Island* provides essential travel information, including complete details on hotels, restaurants, camping facilities, bike and boat rentals; it covers as well boat moorings and skindiving locales, making it a must for marine enthusiasts. Everyone, however, will benefit from *Guide to Catalina's* other features—historical background, natural history, hiking trail guides, general travel and recreation tips. 4 color pages, photos and illustrations, index, 142 pages.

Code   MN09   **$5.95**

Backpacking: A Hedonist's Guide
by Rick Greenspan and Hal Kahn

This humorous, informative, handsomely illustrated how-to guide will convince even the most confirmed naturophobe that it's safe, easy, and enjoyable to leave the smoggy security of city life behind. *Backpacking: A Hedonist's Guide* covers all the backpacking basics—equipment, packing, maps, trails—but it places special emphasis on how to prepare such surprising culinary wonders as trout quiche, sourdough bread, chocolate cake, even pizza, over the fragrant coals of a wilderness campfire. This book won't catch trout or bake cake but it will, however, provide the initial inspiration, practical instruction, and cut the time, cost, and hard-knocks of learning. 90 illustrations, annotated booklist, index, 199 pages.

Code   MN23   **$7.95**

Alaska-Yukon Handbook
A Gypsy Guide to the Inside Passage and Beyond
by David Stanley

Embark from exciting cities such as Seattle, Vancouver, and Victoria, and sail to Alaska on the legendary Inside Passage. Tour the great wilderness ranges and wildlife parks of the North. Backpack across tundra to snowcapped peaks; stand high above the largest glaciers on earth; run mighty rivers. See nature as it once was everywhere. Travel by regular passenger ferry, bus, and train, or just stick out your thumb and go. Sleep in campgrounds, youth hostels, and small hotels tourists usually miss. Dine in unpretentious local eating places or just toss out your line and pull in a salmon. In addition to thousands of specific tips on Alaska and Yukon, this handbook includes detailed coverage of Washington and British Columbia. *Alaska-Yukon Handbook* is the only travel guide which brings this whole spectacular region within reach of everyone. 37 color photos, 76 b/w photos, 86 illustrations, 70 maps, booklist, glossary, index, 230 pages.

Code MN07 $7.95

Micronesia Handbook
by David Stanley

Apart from atomic blasts at Bikini and Enewetak in the late 40s and early 50s, the vast Pacific area between Hawaii and the Philippines has received little attention. For the first time, *Micronesia Handbook* cuts across the plastic path of packaged tourism and guides you on a real Pacific adventure uniquely your own. Its 210 packed pages cover the seven North Pacific territories in detail. All this, plus 35 maps, charts, color pages, photos, drawings, index. 210 pages.

Code MN19 $7.95

Indonesia Handbook 3rd. edition
by Bill Dalton

Not only is *Indonesia Handbook* the most complete and contemporary guide to Indonesia yet prepared, it is a sensitive analysis and description of one of the world's most fascinating human and geographical environments. It is a travel encyclopedia which scans, island by island, Indonesia's history, ethnology, art forms, geography, flora and fauna—while making clear how the traveler can move around, eat, sleep and generally enjoy an utterly unique travel experience in this loveliest of archipeligos. The London Times called *Indonesia Handbook* "one of the best practical guides ever written about any country." 137 illustrations and b/w photos, 123 maps, appendicies, booklist, glossary, index. 602 pages.

Code MN01 $12.95

Arizona Handbook
by Bill Weir

Giant cacti and mountain pines, ancient pueblos and sophis-ticated cities, deep canyons and soaring peaks—all these and more await you in Arizona, sunniest state in the country. From the Grand Canyon, whose walls contain two billion years of Earth's history, to Lake Havasu, new home of London Bridge, Arizona is also famous for unparalleled year-round outdoor recreation. Millions of visitors a year can't be wrong, and *Arizona Handbook* covers it all. Available Fall 1986.

Code   MN31

$10.95

Maui Handbook
by J.D. Bisignani

No "fool-'round" advice is offered on Maui's full range of ac-commodations, eateries, rental cars, tours, charters, shopping, and inter-island transport. With practical money-saving tips, plus a comprehensive introduction to island ways, geography, and history, *Maui Handbook* will pilot you through one of the most enchanting and popular islands in all of Oceania. Available Spring 1986.

Code   MN29

$7.95

Guide to Jamaica
by Harry S. Pariser

Jamaica is one of the most scenically beautiful islands in the Caribbean, and arguably the world. With an abundance of beach resorts and blue seas, the lush backdrop of 7,000-foot mountains completes the classical tropical paradise. Jamaica also has a highly distinctive national, contemporary, culture: Rasta adherents and the Maroon people; home of the lively reg-gae music; a rich folklore; coffee, rum, and ganja. No other guide treats Jamaica with more depth, historical detail, or prac-tical travel information than *Guide to Jamaica.* 4 color pages, 51 b/w photos, 39 illus., 18 maps, 10 charts, booklist, glossary, in-dex. 196 pages.

Code   MN25

$6.95

CARIBBEAN MAPS

Rand McNally Map: Puerto Rico
This full-color map includes street maps of San Juan, Aguadilla, Arecibo, Caguas, Mayaguez, and Ponce. Its special features include indices of Puerto Rico and San Juan, and a mileage chart. Scale: 1 inch = 2100 feet. Folded size: 4″ x 9″, unfolded size: 36¾″ x 25½″.

Code RM55   **$1.50**

West Indies and the Caribbean by Bartholomew
Bartholomew World Travel Maps are an internationally acclaimed series of detailed topographic maps, ideal for travel use. Using layer coloring to show relief, this fine, large format, easy-to-read map of the Caribbean clearly portrays all major and well-traveled sideroads, railways, and airports. Cities are graded by population where possible and items of special interest such as major antiquities and local landscape types are emphasized. The map is both political and physical in style and all detail is kept up-to-date. Size: 30″ X 40″. Folded size: 6″ X 10″.

Code BA40   **$6.95**

Jamaica by Hildebrand Maps
Hildebrand Maps produces a new line of sturdily-packaged maps designed especially for the traveler. This beautiful full-color map clearly presents Jamaica's topography, roads, towns and cities. The map is entirely up-to-date and thoroughly researched. Included on the map are facts and information of special interest to the traveler—climate, points-of-interest, currency, transportation, postal and telephone information, as well as detailed street maps of important areas. Scale: 1:400,000. Folded.

Code HD06   **$5.95**

OF RELATED INTEREST

The Tropical Traveller
by John Hatt
Compiled in this completely revised and updated new edition are over a thousand tips, covering every aspect of tropical travel—from travellers' cheques to salt tablets, from bribery to mugging, from mosquito bites to shark attack. Whether you are a sunbather, tourist, backpacker or explorer, you'll be sure to benefit from this amusing and reassuring reference book. "Helpful, accurate and funny" wrote the *International Herald Tribune*. Highly readable too. 16 illus., 6 tables, appendix, booklist, index. Size: 5 x 7½. 278 pages.
Code   HI43   **$8.95**

The Caribbean Bed and Breakfast Book
by Kathy Strong
Introductory chapters cover getting there, getting around, how to plan and reserve lodging, and what to know before you leave: climate, topography, transportation, customs, sights and money are all covered. The important details about the inns are described: addresses and phone numbers, architecture, history, grounds, services, and meals. A handy reference section lists rates, number of units, which credit cards are accepted, and whether children are allowed. 46 b/w photos, 11 drawings, 16 maps, appendix, index. Size: 5" x 8". 192 pages.
Code   EW02   **$9.95**

Exploring Tropical Isles and Seas: An Introduction for the Traveler and Amateur Naturalist
by Frederic Martini
With this entertaining and engrossing book , you'll learn about life on and around tropical isles—the climate, precipitation, and ocean currents—plus find handy information on the population, language, currency, and size of the islands. You'll also discover how natural forces like volcanos and erosion are constantly creating, shaping. and destroying islands and entire island groups. *Exploring Tropical Isles and Seas* even comes complete with detailed coverage of potential medical problems and precautions, including advice on how to treat coral cuts, stings, rashes, infections, and sunburn. This factbook will enhance your traveling experience a thousandfold. Covers the Hawaiian Is., Samoa, Galapagos, Tonga, Fiji, Guam, Palau, Barbados, Martinique, Jamaica, Puerto Rico, the Bahamas, and the Virgin Islands.
Code   PH70   **$15.95**

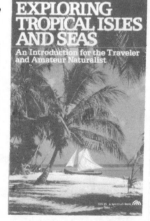

Images Of Puerto Rico
by Roger A. LaBrucherie
This is the finest photo-essay book on the island published to date. As is true of most books of the "coffee-table" genre, it is the book's spectacular color photographs which first command attention, but *Images* provides a well-researched, highly readable supporting text as well. This is not a travel guide, but rather a presentation of the history, culture, society and landscape of the island, in the *National Geographic* style. 177 color photos, hardcover. Size: 11" x 8½". 144 pages.

Code IM01 **$21.95**

Guide to the Alternative Bermuda
by Nelson E. Hay

This guide helps the traveler enjoy the beauties of Bermuda while avoiding the crowds and high prices. The author says, "I want you to know that you can vacation in Bermuda for less than half the cost quoted in most tourist literature, and you can experience a better Bermuda at that." Instead of the noise, crowds, and standing in line that most tourists have to deal with, spend your vacation away from the tourist traps, enjoying the hospitality of the locals, in the alternative Bermuda. 15 maps, 28 charts, booklist, index. Size: 5½" x 8½". 148 pages.

Code BS01 **$8.95**

Pelican Guide to the Bahamas
by James E. Moore

This in-depth look at the Bahamas provides complete, firsthand information that will greatly assist the visitor, no matter what his budget. Covering over 700 islands stretching from Florida to Haiti, it includes what to pack, how to get there, current prices, accommodations, restaurants, water sports, nightlife, shopping, guided tours, and island transportation. 12 maps, index. Size: 5½" x 8". 336 pages.

Code PU04 **$9.95**

Just Enough Spanish

This phrasebook is filled with the words and phrases that the traveler, student, or businessperson will want to use while in Spanish-speaking areas. Concentrating on the simplest but most effective phrases, *Just Enough Spanish* is an invaluable pocket-sized companion for everyday situations requiring the *right* phrase. Being able to use even a bit of the local language opens the doors to a rich realm of travel experience that would otherwise be missed, and this phrasebook has *Just Enough* of what you need. Size: 4" x 6½".

Code   PP14   **$3.95**

Spanish-English English-Spanish Dictionary

by Carlos Castillo and Otto F. Bond

This handy pocket-sized dictionary from the University of Chicago includes Latin American Spanish words, phrases, and slang, making it invaluable to the traveler in these regions. A special section deals with idioms and proverbs. Notes on Spanish usage in Latin America are especially helpful. Size: 4¼" x 6¾". 488 pages.

Code   UC10   **$3.95**

Language/30 Spanish

Language/30 is based on the famous accelerated language learning method developed for U.S. government personnel preparing for overseas duty. Stressing conversationally useful words and phrases, this course offers:

• 2 cassettes and a phrase dictionary in a long-lasting vinyl album.

• approximately 1½ hours of guided practice in greetings, introductions, requests and general conversation at hotels, restaurants and places of business and entertainment.

• native voices speaking with perfect pronunciation.

• all phrases spoken in Spanish and English so tapes can be used in your car.

• a special section by the famous linguist Charles Berlitz which introduces the course and gives helpful tips on its use.

Code   LG35   **$14.95**

MOONBOOKS TRAVEL CATALOG
The Portable Store for Independent Travelers

For the traveler, travel agent, librarian, businessperson, or aspriring globetrotter — here is the complete, *portable* travel bookstore comprising the best and latest sources available. Moon Publications, a leader in adventure guidebooks, has gathered within these pages the most comprehensive selection of travel guides, maps, atlases, language tapes, literature, and related accessories yet published. From unique guidebooks and hard-to-find maps to the acknowledged classics of the genre, here is your guide to virtually every destination on Earth — from Paris to Patagonia, from Alberta to Zanzibar. By means of popular credit cards, personal check, or money order, all are easily available direct from our warehouse. Whether your idea of adventure is snorkeling in the Red Sea, bushwacking in New Guinea, or sipping espresso in a Venetian cafe...let your journey begin with

Moonbooks Travel Catalog

MN27 $2.95

IMPORTANT ORDERING INFORMATION

1. codes: Please enter book and/or map codes on your order form, as this will assure accurate and speedy delivery of your order.

2. prices: Due to foreign exchange fluctuations and the changing terms of our distributers, all prices for books on these ad pages are subject to change without notice.

3. domestic orders: For bookrate (3-4 weeks delivery), send $1.25 for first item and $.50 for each additional item. For UPS or USPS 1st class (3-7 days delivery), send $3.00 for first book and $.50 for each additional book. For UPS 2nd Day Air, call for a quote.

4. foreign orders: All orders which originate outside the U.S.A. **must** be paid for with either an International Money Order or a check in U.S. currency drawn on a major U.S. bank based in the U.S.A. For International Surface Bookrate (3-12 weeks delivery), send U.S.$2.00 for the first item and U.S.$1.00 for each additional item. If you'd like your item(s) sent Printed Matter Airmail, write us for a quote before sending money. Moon Publications cannot guarantee delivery of foreign orders unless sent via International Air Express. Call for a quote.

5. Visa or Mastercharge payments: Minimum order U.S.$15.00. Telephone orders are accepted. Call (916) 345-5473 or 345-5413

6. noncompliance: Any orders received which do not comply with any of the above conditions may result in the return of your order and/or payment intact.

Moon Belts

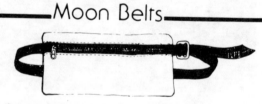

A new concept in money belts. Made from highly durable, water repellent polyester cotton blend fabric for maximum all-weather comfort. The 3.75x8 inch pouch is worn around the waist concealed inside your clothes. Many thoughtful features: One inch wide nylon webbing, heavy duty zipper, and 1 inch wide high test plastic slide for easy adjustability. The field-tested Moon Belt comes with extra long webbing; cut to your size, then simply seal end with lighted match. Accommodates Travelers Checks, passport, cash. Essential for the traveler. Only $5.95.

ORDER FORM
(See important ordering information opposite page)

Name _____

Address _____

City _____

State or Country _____ Zip _____

Quantity	Full Book or Map Title	Code	Price

California Residents please add 6 percent sales tax	
Domestic Shipping Charges for 1st item: $1.25	
($.50 for each additional item)	
Additional charges for International or UPS postage	
TOTAL ENCLOSED	

Make checks payable to:

MOON PUBLICATIONS   P.O. BOX 1696   CHICO   CALIFORNIA   95927-1696   USA

WE ACCEPT VISA AND MASTERCHARGE!

Please send written order with your Visa or Mastercharge number and expiry date clearly written

CHECK/MONEYORDER ENCLOSED FOR $ _____

CARD NO.   ☐ VISA   ☐ MASTERCHARGE   BANK NO.

☐☐☐☐☐☐☐☐☐☐☐☐☐☐☐☐☐☐☐   ☐☐☐☐

SIGNATURE _____   EXPIRATION DATE _____

MN21   THANK YOU FOR YOUR ORDER

ABOUT THE AUTHOR

Harry S. Pariser was born in Pittsburgh and grew up in a small town in Pennsylvania. After graduating from Boston University with a B.S. in Public Communications in 1975, Harry hitched and camped his way through Europe, traveled down the Nile by steamer, and by train through Sudan. After visiting Uganda, Rwanda, and Tanzania, he traveled by passenger ship from Mombasa to Bombay, and then on through South and Southeast Asia before settling down in Kyoto, Japan, where he studied Japanese and ceramics while supporting himself by teaching English to everyone from tiny tots to Buddhist priests. Using Japan as a base, he returned to other parts of Asia: trekking to the vicinity of Mt. Everest in Nepal, taking tramp steamers to remote Indonesian islands like Adonara, Timor, Sulawesi, and Ternate, and visiting rural areas in China. Returning to the United States in 1984 via the Caribbean (where he researched this book), he now lives in the Haight area of San Francisco where he reviews music concerts, cooks his own version of Asian food, draws etchings, and listens to jazz music.

Harry slides down the upper slopes of the summit of Gunung Lokon in Minahasa Province, North Sulawesi, Indonesia.